THE ALADDIN FACTOR

Also by
Jack Canfield and Mark Victor Hansen

◆

THE
ALADDIN
FACTOR

JACK CANFIELD
and
MARK VICTOR HANSEN

BERKLEY BOOKS, NEW YORK

A continuation of copyright credits appears on page 279.

THE ALADDIN FACTOR

A Berkley Book/
published by arrangement with the authors

PRINTING HISTORY
Berkley trade paperback edition / October 1995

Copyright © 1995 by Jack Canfield and Mark Victor Hansen.
Book design by Stanley S. Drate/Folio Graphics Co., Inc.

ISBN: 0-425-15075-5

BERKLEY®
Berkley Books are published by The Berkley Publishing Group,
a division of Penguin Putnam Inc.
375 Hudson Street, New York, New York 10014.
BERKLEY and the "B" design
are trademarks belonging to Penguin Putnam Inc.

PRINTED IN THE UNITED STATES OF AMERICA

*If there is something to gain and nothing
to lose by asking, by all means ask!*
—W. Clement Stone

◆

*We dedicate this book to
Patty Hansen, who helped
us bring the magic of Aladdin to
this book and to our lives,
and to our children,
Christopher, Kyle, Oran, Elisabeth and Melanie,
who never seem to have trouble asking
for what they want.
Thanks for being such perfect models!*

*We also dedicate this book to the natural
child in you, who still has grand visions,
big dreams, high hopes and a willingness
to do whatever it takes to make his or
her dreams a reality.*

Acknowledgments

◆

We would like to acknowledge the following people without whom we would never have been able to write this book:

Patty Mitchell Aubery, who orchestrated the entire "magical" team effort required to produce this book. She transcribed interviews, wrote stories, edited stories and retyped the final manuscript of this book several times. Her commitment to this project as well as to managing the Canfield Group included working many weekdays until 2:00 A.M. and lots of weekends. Thanks again, Patty!

Nancy Mitchell, our research assistant, who checked facts, located books and newspaper articles, verified quotes, typed many of the stories and orchestrated the entire permissions process for this book while staying on top of compiling and editing hundreds of stories for our ongoing *Chicken Soup for the Soul* book series.

Kim Wiele, who contributed very helpful information editing and typing many of the stories while successfully filling the biggest training of the year. Thanks, Kim!

Heather McNamara, who helped in every area of this book: typing, editing, retyping and researching stories, not to mention staying very late into the evenings to do whatever was necessary to complete this project.

Angie Hoover, Lisa and John Williams, Lynda McInturf, Julie and Judy Barnes and Michele Adams, who contributed in countless ways while keeping our offices running for the entire two months of April and May 1995, so that we could concentrate solely on this book.

Larry Price and La Verne Lee, who in addition to keeping Jack's Foundation for Self-Esteem and the Soup Kitchens for the Soul Project operating smoothly, supported our efforts in writing this book.

Wanda Pate, who transcribed over fifty hours of interviews for us. We could never have done this book without you!

Trudy Klefstad, President of Office Works, who transcribed numerous interviews and was there whenever we needed her.

Jeff Herman, our literary agent, who brought us and the book to the wonderful people at Berkley. Thanks for always being on the case!

The following people at The Berkley Publishing Group: David Shanks, President of Berkley; Hillary Cige, our editor, who believed in us from the beginning; Donna Gould and Liz Perl, our two genius publicists; Leslie Gelbman, Louise Burke and Lou Aronica, all of whom believed in this project and threw their entire organization behind it.

Arielle Ford and Kim Weiss, our publicists, who have worked diligently and effectively to make the world more aware of the work we are doing. Thanks for sharing the vision with such passion and professionalism!

Peter Vegso and Gary Seidler for always believing in us and taking us to the top.

Book Star in Culver City, California. We must have called them once a day for three months with endless questions, which they always quickly and cheerfully answered.

The hundreds of people who filled out questionnaires and granted us extensive interviews. There are too many people to list them all here, but the following people stand out for going way beyond the call of duty and the demands of friendship: Jay Abraham, Linda Albert, Thea Alexander, Kelle Apone, Dr. Gary Arthur, John Assaraf, Jeff Aubery, Dr. Harold Bloomfield, Jane Bluestein, Judith Briles, Jim Britt, Catherine Castle, Jim Cathcart, Stan Dale, Barbara De Angelis (who spent countless hours talking with and encouraging us), Vin Di Bona, Bernhard Dohrmann, T. Harv Eker, Rabbi Dov Peretz Elkins, Rick Gelinas (who is one of the all time great askers— and getters!—on the planet), David Gershenson (who helped us ask for and get a television deal with Vin Di Bona Productions for our *Chicken Soup for the Soul* books), Patricia Fripp, Mark Goulston, Kay Grace, Betty Mazzetti Hatch, Michael Hesse, Aimée Hoover, Norman Howe, Ron and Mary Hulnick, Claudette Hunter, Michael Jeffreys, Tom Justin, Danielle Kennedy, Ken Kerr, Brian Klemmer, Marilyn Kriegel, Marianne Larned, Marcia Martin, Hanoch McCarty (who has asked millions of people to join the kindness revolution), Russ

McGee, Jackie Miller, W Mitchell, Carla Morganstern, Jane Nelsen, Donna Nelson, Tim Peiring, Mary Phillips, Ken Pontius, John Prieskorn, Larry Price, Linda Price, Bob Proctor, Nido Qubein, Robert Reasoner, Maria Salomao, John Wayne "Jack" Schlatter, Mark A. Schnurman, Ron Scolastico, Frank Siccone, Bruce "Bear Man" Smith, Dr. Louis A. Tartaglia, Peter Vegso, Kay Walburger, Dottie Walters, Lilly Walters, Lloyd Weintraub, Diana von Welanetz Wentworth, Ted Wentworth, Brad Winch, Jack Wolf and David Yoho, Jr.

And especially Georgia Noble and Patty Hansen, our wives, who loved and supported us while we were not equally there for them during the final months of this project. Thanks for understanding one more time!

Jack wishes to acknowledge Anne Hyman, who opened it all up; Jack Gibb, who taught me to trust myself and the universe; W. Clement Stone, who taught me to ask for it all; Dr. Robert Resnick, who taught me to ask for it straight; and Martha Crampton, who taught me to ask my higher self. Thank you for teaching and inspiring me to not settle for anything less than the best and the truest in life.

When I was a beggarly boy,
And lived in a cellar damp,
I had not a friend nor a toy,
But I had Aladdin's lamp ...
—James Russel Lowel

Contents

◆

PART I

THE ALADDIN FACTOR

PART II

RELEASING THE GENIE

PART III

HOW TO ASK, WHO TO ASK AND WHAT TO ASK FOR

THE ALADDIN FACTOR

Introduction

◆

Once in a faraway land, a grubby child sat in the dust and gazed at the battered lamp he held between his knees. Dirty, old and dented, yet somehow still beautiful, the lamp warmed to his touch. Aladdin ran his fingers across an inscription on the side, barely legible because of the dirt. He spit on his shirtsleeve and rubbed the lamp so he could read the words:

Ask And It Shall Be Given.

No sooner had he finished reading, than the lamp seemed to shake and turn in his hands. His skin crawled and the hairs on the back of his neck stood up. Aladdin heard a booming voice that seemed to come from every corner of the marketplace.

◆

"Who are you and why have you called me?"

◆

The dust around Aladdin's ankles swirled and rose, enveloping his small frame. The colors of the rainbow swirled before his eyes and he felt as if he were being lifted into the sky above.

"Where am I, and what is happening to me?" Aladdin shouted.

◆

"You are with me, the Genie, for you have called for me," said the voice. "I am here to answer all of your questions and help you obtain all that you desire."

◆

"I desire only to be recognized for who I truly am. I appear to be a poor beggar, yet what I know to be true is that I am the Prince. If only people could see this, then

all the riches of the kingdom would be mine," replied
Aladdin.

◆

"Do you truly wish others to recognize your royalty?" asked the
Genie.

◆

"Yes, and more."

◆

"Then your wishes are my command. Sit at my feet, child, while I
weave a tale of wonder and success about learning how to ask for
what you want in life. I have brought many friends with me who will
share their stories. Gaze into the lamp, my son, and watch our tale
of transformation unfold."

◆

Until I knew I could ask for what I wanted, I had lived my life
in an unacknowledged state of resignation. I had silently
agreed not to be a nuisance or a bother, to never intrude on
anyone, to never take up anyone's time and certainly not to be
a "pest"!

Early in my marriage, my wife, Georgia, and I had a vacation cottage on a nearby lake in western Massachusetts. Since
the house was located on a hillside, we would park in the driveway above it and walk down a set of stairs into the kitchen
door. We were located many miles from town and whenever
we went shopping we would stock up with food and supplies
resulting in ten or more bags of groceries per trip. When we
would arrive home, I would bring in the bags and Georgia
would start unpacking the groceries and placing them on the
appropriate shelves.

Subconsciously I always resented the situation. I would be
going up and down what seemed like an endless set of stairs
while Georgia would have the easy job of simply taking things
out of the bags and stockpiling them. I especially resented it
when it was raining or snowing. This pattern, and my resentment, continued for many years.

One day, while attending a marriage enrichment seminar,
we were asked to list and share any resentments we had. I

shared my long-standing irritation at having always been the "pack mule" in our relationship when it came to the groceries and the long flight of stairs. *My wife's response changed my life forever.* She said, "Wow, I never had any idea you were unhappy with the arrangement. Why didn't you say something? I would have been glad to help you carry in the bags. All you had to do was ask."

All I had to do was ask? It was that simple? Why had I never thought of it? It simply hadn't occurred to me. But why? All of a sudden I had a stream of flashbacks to times when I had wanted help in my life and had been afraid to ask.

I wanted to ask my teachers in school to slow down and go over things again, but I was afraid they would think I was stupid.

I wanted to ask the guys at my summer job during high school to help me lift a big bale of peat moss I was moving, but I was afraid they would call me a wimp for needing help.

I wanted to ask a guy at school to show me how he made certain guitar chords, but I was afraid I might not learn them fast enough and he would resent me for taking up his time.

I had settled for less than the best of everything—mediocre seats at plays and drafty seats at restaurants. Cold or badly prepared food was never sent back. I settled for substandard rooms in hotels and flew coach when I could have been upgraded to first class. I accepted shoddy workmanship and poor performance. I wore clothes that didn't fit perfectly and occasionally bought shoes that were too tight. ("Don't worry. They'll stretch.") I was afraid to return or exchange unwanted gifts and I rarely, if ever, asked a salesclerk to help me find something I was looking for.

On the day I left for college, my stepfather handed me a twenty dollar bill and said, "If you ever need a helping hand, look at the end of your own arm." The underlying message was "You are on your own. You are now supposed to be self-sufficient. Don't ask for anything else." The prior eighteen years had consisted of the following from my mother, father and stepfather:

"If you ever get into trouble, don't come running to me for help."

"What are you asking me for? I don't know!"

"Do you think money grows on trees?"

"Who do you think I am—Rockefeller?"

"Quit asking me; that's the last I want to hear about it!"

"Don't ask so many stupid questions!"

"The answer is no, so quit bothering me!"

"Leave your mother alone. She's had a hard day."

"I said no—and that's final!"

I made less money than I was worth, laughed at jokes I didn't understand and never raised my hand in class. I accepted too many things without questioning authority and I bit my tongue when I wanted to ask somebody out for a date. I stared longingly at all the things I wanted, but I rarely got them. That was my life—a life of settling for less than what I wanted, less than I deserved, less than the best and less than what was possible.

—**Jack Canfield**

◆

"Jack told this story, Aladdin, to illustrate the five major barriers to asking for what you want. First, *ignorance* kept him trapped. He didn't know he could ask, and that it would be so simple. Second, an *erroneous belief* misled him. He thought that if his wife loved him, she would automatically know what he wanted and offer it. Third, *fear* was in control, not Jack. He was afraid of receiving a negative answer and further humiliation. Fourth, his *pride* stood in his way and contributed to his building up resentment toward the people in his life. And fifth, because he had *low self-esteem*, he didn't feel worthy of asking for and receiving the help he needed and deserved.

"These five barriers are links in a chain that keep you from asking for what you want. Until you break these links and escape the bondage they create, you cannot be free to fulfill your dreams."

◆

PART I

THE ALADDIN FACTOR

◆

Ask, and it shall be given to you;
seek, and ye shall find;
knock and it shall be opened unto you.

For every one that asketh, receiveth;
and he that seeketh, findeth;
and to him that knocketh
it shall be opened.
—Matthew 7:7—8

THE FIVE BARRIERS TO ASKING:
The Main Reasons We Don't Ask
for What We Want

1. IGNORANCE

A story is told of a thief in ancient times who stole a magnificent coat. The coat was made of the finest materials including buttons of silver and gold. When he returned to his friends after selling the coat to a merchant in the marketplace, his closest friend asked him how much he had sold the coat for.

"A hundred pieces of silver," was his reply.

"You mean to tell me you only got a hundred pieces of silver for that magnificent coat?" asked his friend.

"Is there a number higher than a hundred?" asked the thief.

Many of us don't know what to ask for. Either we don't know what is available to us because we have never been exposed to it, or we are so out of touch with ourselves that we no longer are able to perceive our real needs and wants. Some of us have become so numbed out that we are simply unaware of our natural yearnings and desires. We no longer know what we really want.

Most of us don't know how to ask. We have never learned the technology of making an effective request. We have not seen these effective communication skills modeled in our homes and we were not taught them in our schools or at work.

Many of us don't know whom to ask and when to ask. We have not learned how to identify likely prospects who can deliver what we ask for whether it be a hug, sage advice or an order for something we are selling. And many of us have never learned to read the nonverbal cues that people send us that tell us "I'm with you" or "not now."

Fear always springs from ignorance.   —Ralph Waldo Emerson

We don't know what is available and possible.

Most of us never knew you could buy a house for no money down until we read Robert Allen's books. We didn't know you could request a lower interest rate on your credit cards and get it until we heard Charles Givens speak. We didn't know you could ask for a free upgrade on your rental car or for a less expensive rate on your hotel room until someone told us that we could.

If our parents didn't teach us, if we didn't learn it in school and we never saw it modeled by anyone else in our lives, how were we supposed to know?

When you're used to getting just a piece of bread for a meal, you don't realize that you can ask for a plate of pasta. You have never seen a plate of pasta. You don't even know it exists. So, to ask for it is totally out of your reality. Hopefully, at some point, either someone shows you a plate of pasta, you read about it, or you hear about it enough so that it becomes real, and it's not just a fantasy anymore, and then you start thinking "Hey, I want that pasta."

—**Barbara De Angelis, Ph.D., Creator of Making Love Work;
Author of *Real Moments***

We don't know what we really need and want.

Most of us are out of touch with our real needs and desires because we were continually ignored, rejected or shamed for expressing them as a child. We may have been criticized, put down and ridiculed for boldly and repeatedly asking for what we wanted, so it became safer and less painful not to. We simply buried our desires.

The expression of our desires may have threatened, embarrassed or in some other way made our parents feel uncomfortable. It may have challenged their belief systems, standards or values. It may have been that we were asking for things that they didn't get as children, and subconsciously they resented us for asking.

Our childhood requests may have restimulated the repressed pain of the unmet needs of their own childhoods. They may even have resented us just because we were a boy or girl. And they may have deprived us of certain things as a way of punishing someone from their past that they had projected on to us. Or they may simply have feared the criticism of their neighbors or relatives for "spoiling" their child, for being too lax or lenient, or for being such an "easy touch."

No matter what the cause, the final effect is that we stopped feeling what we wanted because it was too painful. It was easier to go into a state of numbness and apathy. Eventually, "What do you want to do tonight?" drew answers like "I don't know," or "I don't care."

When asked what we want, we are simply out of touch with it.

We don't know how to ask.

Most of us never received any modeling or instruction in clear and straightforward asking at home. Most schools don't offer courses in communication skills that teach us how to make effective requests. What most of us did see over and over was nagging, whining, bitching, moaning and complaining. We saw innuendoes, hints and vague requests, but very rarely the straightforward communication of needs, wants and desires. If we never saw these skills demonstrated, it is very hard to learn and integrate them into our lives.

It wasn't anything anyone ever said. It was just that my father never asked for anything his whole life. I never saw him ask for anything. It wasn't modeled in my home, so I grew up thinking that a man was supposed to be totally self-sufficient.

—**Ron Hulnick,**
Author, *Financial Freedom in 8 Minutes a Day*

As a child I didn't see any women asking for what they wanted. My mother never asked for what she wanted. I didn't have any strong female role models as a child. There weren't a lot of successful women around.

—**Barbara De Angelis, Creator of Making Love Work,**
Author of *Real Moments*

2. LIMITING AND INACCURATE BELIEFS

The second barrier to asking for what we want are the limiting and negative beliefs that have been programmed into our subconscious and which now silently control all of our actions.

All that we are is the result of what we have thought.
—Dhammapada

Man is what he believes.   —Anton Chekhov

Where do these beliefs come from?

We are born with an empty data bank that has to be programmed. Many of us are hindered in our asking for and getting what we want by the negative and limiting beliefs we have taken on from our parents, teachers, churches, peers and the media. We can become constricted and even paralyzed by this parental and cultural conditioning.

We are taught that it is better to give than to receive; that if he really loved me, I wouldn't have to ask; and that being needy is a weakness. We have learned from our failures and our traumatic experiences in life that if you don't want too much, then you won't be disappointed; don't expect too much from men like your father; and it is safer to keep your mouth shut and appear the fool, than to open it and remove all doubt.

We are programmed by our parents.

I was conditioned away from asking by my parents. I remember my grandmother used to give me money. When she gave me money, I was supposed to somehow resist it. It was part of this game. My parents would say, "Don't take money from your grandparents," and my grandparents would say, "No, no, take it." Outside you say "No, no," and inside you want it really bad. The grandparents would put it in your sleeve or down your back, and finally you would say, "Oh, okay." That was the game.

I remember one day, I went to my grandmother's house, and because she had always given it to me, I said, "Grandma, can I have some money?"

She looked at me and said, "Tim, don't ever ask for money!"

I was shocked. I was a little kid and it made sense that if they wanted to give me money and I wanted it that I could ask. But there was this ethic, this unspoken morality where kids were to be subservient—they were to be seen and not heard. We didn't count for much, I guess.   **—Tim Piering**

Many of us grew up in homes where what we wanted was ignored, discounted, made fun of or put down. Our wants and desires were not important. We were not given choices, asked about our preferences or granted our requests. We were second-class citizens who were to eat whatever was put in front of us, wear what we were told and speak when we were spoken to.

See if any of these phrases are reminiscent of your childhood—or, perhaps even more disturbing, your own parenting?

- Quit bothering me with your whining and your questions.
- Quit hounding your mother.
- Leave your grandmother alone.
- I don't want to hear about it!
- I don't have time for that right now.

- Oh, no, not you again! What do you want now?
- You're so selfish. All you ever think of is yourself.
- You never consider anyone's needs but your own.
- It's my way or the highway, young lady!
- As long as you live in my house, you'll live by my rules.
- If you don't like living here, you can leave anytime.
- If you can't say something nice, don't say anything at all.
- When I want your opinion, I will give it to you.
- Hurry up; we've got a lot to do today.
- I don't care what you want.
- Just shut up and do what you're told.
- If you just keep your mouth shut and follow directions, everything will turn out fine.
- Do as you are told!

We are programmed at school.

In school, if you ask the teacher for help, you are called a "brown noser" or a "teacher's pet." In many urban schools, if you act like you care and you ask the teacher to explain something to you, you are accused of "acting white."

You are told to do your own work, and that getting help from or collaborating with others is cheating.

We learn very quickly that it is not okay to ask a stupid question. The teacher will give us one of those withering looks. Other kids will laugh or look irritated. So many of us just struggle along or tune out altogether.

It was funny about school.

He sat in a square, brown desk like all the other square, brown desks and he thought it should be red.

And his room was a square, brown room. Like all the other rooms. And it was tight and close. And stiff.

He hated to hold the pencil and the chalk, with his arm stiff and his feet flat on the floor, with the teacher watching and watching.

And then he had to write numbers. And they weren't anything. They were worse than the letters that could be something if you put them together . . .

And the numbers were tight and square and he hated the whole thing.

The teacher came and spoke to him. She told him to wear a tie like all the other boys. He said he didn't like them and she said it didn't matter.

After that they drew. And he drew all yellow and it was the way he felt about morning. And it was beautiful.

The teacher came and looked at his picture. "What's this?" she said. "Why don't you draw something like Ken's drawing? Isn't that beautiful?"

It was all questions.

After that his mother bought him a tie and he always drew airplanes and rocket ships like everyone else.

> —Excerpted from "About School," a poem that was handed to a Grade 12 English teacher in Regina, Saskatchewan. Although it is not known if the student actually wrote it himself, it is known that he committed suicide two weeks later.

We are programmed by the major media.

After years of television, men have learned that to be a real man means to suffer in silence, be macho, tough it out and never express vulnerability or deeper needs. Men learn to deflect the emotional discomfort of dealing with their real pain, needs or desires with a wisecrack or a put-down. This tough man image that men buy into gets in the way of asking others for help and assistance.

We are conditioned by our religious training.

Church doctrine, individual preachers and pastors, television evangelists and religious literature condition our beliefs about asking for what we want.

> *It is more blessed to give than to receive.*   —Acts 20:35

I was raised to be a saint. My mother was originally going to join the convent, but instead she got married and gave her first child—me—to the Virgin Mary and her mother. I was consecrated and offered up as a sacrificial lamb. My whole life was about offering it up. So I was never able to ask for myself, I was supposed to help the poor souls in purgatory or the starving children in Vietnam or whoever was hurting, hungry or homeless at the time. We were supposed to help them and not ask anything for ourselves.

I was taught that to want for yourself was being selfish. There's not enough for everybody else. Don't expect too much. I would always make sure everybody else had some before I had any.

When I was young, my hope was that I would die young and be a child martyr. Then, at least, my parents would love me. I was taught that you get your rewards in the next life; you don't get it in this life. That was my experience of the whole focus of the church—you can't ask for yourself; you have to devote yourself to helping others.

I nearly died of asthma from not asking for what I wanted.

—Marianne R.

We are programmed by our doctors.

Very early on we learn that the doctor is God. We are to do what the doctor says. The doctor does not have time for your foolish questions. Just follow the regime that has been laid out, please. Do not question the prescription, diagnosis or treatment program. We wait in their offices for hours without ever questioning why they don't learn to schedule their patients better. We put up with poor customer service and often arrogant attitudes. We are ignorant. They know. Just do as your told, and don't ask.

Recently a young mother brought her two-and-a-half-year-old into the emergency room with a high temperature of 106. The emergency staff calmed the mother and told her that many children run fevers and not to get too concerned. They told her that if the child wasn't better in the morning, she should consult her doctor then. The woman went home distressed but felt that these were medical experts and she shouldn't ask more questions about her baby's well-being.

She stayed awake the majority of the night with her baby, and at 6:00 in the morning, she noticed something that resembled a bruise under her baby's arm. She then looked more carefully all over his body and immediately rushed him to a different emergency hospital for he was black and blue over most of his entire little body.

This hospital did a thorough examination and informed her that her precious little boy would not make it past the day's end. He was afflicted with pneumococcal meningitis, which tends to affect young children and can be treated if detected early. No one can say for sure if her little boy would have lived, but that's a question she'll probably ask herself for the rest of her life.

—**Heather McNamara**

A FEW OF THE MOST COMMON LIMITING BELIEFS

If you really loved me, I wouldn't have to ask.

One of the most commonly heard phrases among couples is "If you really loved me, I wouldn't have to ask you." Well, it is not true. It is really possible that someone could love you and still not know what you want. The two don't necessarily go together! This romantic belief that if someone loves us, he or she will intuitively know and anticipate all of our needs has created huge amounts of disappointment and unhappiness.

Warning: Unless you are married to a bona fide psychic, it is very unlikely your partner will ever know what it is you want unless you have the courage and intelligence to specifically ask for it.

Just as the genie of the lamp cannot grant Aladdin a wish unless he first tells him what he wants, your spouse or lover

cannot fulfill your desires if he or she does not know what they are. If you want more romance, attention, affection or help with the dishes, you are going to have to ask for it.

The world is not a responsive place.

Your request for no MSG was ignored.   —Fortune Cookie

The oldest of ten children in an Irish-Catholic family, I was trained to be very responsible, even at a young age.

When I was six years old, my mother was driving me and my sisters to Vermont to visit my aunt. I was sitting in the backseat with my three sisters. The youngest, who was two months old, was having trouble breathing. I asked my mother to stop the car. She didn't stop. I said, "Something is wrong with Diana!"

She said, "Oh, she'll be fine," which is what my mother always said. When we got to my aunt's house, Diana was dead.

It didn't matter what I asked for—stop the car, stop the rat race, stop having more children, stop the Catholic Church from making it immoral for my mother to use birth control, stop my father from wanting to live life on the high side—listen to me, love me, care for me, take time for me—I never got what I asked for.

After a while, I stopped asking. In a few years I too had trouble breathing—with life-threatening asthma. It took ten years of healing to stop the asthma and start asking for what I wanted.   —**Marianne R.**

A father and his small son were out walking one afternoon when the youngster asked how the electricity went through the wires stretched between the telephone poles.

"Don't know," said the father. "Never knew much about the electricity."

A few blocks farther on the boy asked what caused lightning and thunder.

"To tell the truth," said the father, "I never exactly understood that myself."

The boy continued to ask questions throughout the walk, none of which the father could explain. Finally, as they were nearing home, the boy asked, "Pop, I hope you don't mind my asking so many questions. . . ."

"Of course not," replied the father. "How else are you going to learn?" —*Speakers Sourcebook II*

Sooner or later, of course, if the father doesn't seek the answers, the boy stops asking questions. Curiosity and the desire to learn are stifled.

My success will deprive someone else.

I think what happened was anytime I was desirous of anything there was always this sense that somehow my receiving was going to deprive someone else. It took a long time to learn that the universe doesn't operate that way. —Jane Bluestein

Most of us believe there is not enough time, money, food, or attention to go around. We believe that our getting what we want somehow deprives others of getting what they need. We assume that if we want something and we get it, there will be less available for someone else. We assume there is not enough food to feed everyone, so we had better not eat more than our share. We assume we have to suffer from boring work in a job we don't like because we're lucky to have a job at all. If we leave this one, we might not find another one.

If I get what I want, it will make me unhappy.

If a man could have half of his wishes, he would double his troubles. —Benjamin Franklin

Be careful what you ask for because you just might get it.
—Common parental statement

The prevailing myth is that if we ask for what we want and get it, we may ask for the wrong thing and then we'll be stuck with it. We learn as a child that with a puppy comes responsibilities—feeding it and walking it. If I ask for a man and get it, he may turn out to be an abuser. And, if I marry him, I'm stuck with him for the rest of my life. If I ask for a transfer, I might not like the new location as much as my current one. So, I'm better off not asking.

I can remember the exact moment in my life when I realized I had the ability to envision things, ask for them and get them. I was about fifteen years old, and I said to myself, "I can have anything I ask for!" And it frightened me because I had been told that you had to be very careful about what you ask for because you might get it, and it might really make you unhappy. From that moment on I was very afraid to ask for things because I had realized I was able to ask for what I wanted and I was afraid that maybe I would ask for something and I would get it and be terribly, terribly unhappy.   —Kay Walburger

3. FEAR

Only your mind can produce fear.   —*A Course in Miracles*

As a result of the negative, painful and shameful experiences of our childhood, we become afraid to participate, afraid to go after those things we truly want and desire. We become afraid of rejection, looking foolish, losing face and being vulnerable and hurt by others. As a result of these fears, we become passive. We settle for less than we really want and we sit in judgment of others who are getting what we want. We don't have the courage to ask for or the self-discipline to create. We end up using all of our energy to protect ourselves against boogey men we have created in our minds instead of using those energies to create what we want.

Fear of rejection

I want you to come to my house
and yet I don't.

You're so important,
but our screen door has a hole in it.
And my mother has no fancy cake to serve.
I want you to come to my house, teacher,
and yet I don't.
My brother chews with his mouth wide open
and sometimes my dad burps.
I wish I could trust you enough, teacher,
to invite you to my house.

—**Albert Callum**[1]

The main overriding fear that stops us from asking for what we want is the fear of rejection.

Man in a bar: What would I have to give you for a little kiss?
Woman: Chloroform.

I started asking myself, "What am I really afraid of?" Each time it came back to my sense of powerlessness—the sense that I would be powerless in any situation. I was afraid of rejection and rejection came in a hundred different faces. Like—I was never good enough, I would never do it right, and people would laugh at me. The number one fear was the fear of rejection, and at that time FEAR in my life meant "Forget Everything And Run."

—**Stan Dale**

When I was in high school I had a crush on a beautiful girl for years. She was the most beautiful and interesting girl in the entire high school. I was so intimidated by her that I could hardly speak around her. I ran into her a couple years later and she told me that she had had a huge crush on me and was dying for me to ask her out. I had wasted two years of my life because of my fear. When I finally asked her out, she said, "The trouble with you men is that you always reject yourself before you ever give us women a chance to. You're telling yourself no before we ever do. You should be braver."   —**John Taylor**

Being laughed at—humiliation and rejection—inadequacy—I don't know if I ever really believed that anybody would want to go out with me. That I was good enough.   —**Michael Hesse**

Fear of looking stupid

For many of us the paralyzing fear is, "If I ask for what I want, I'll come off looking stupid and then people won't like me."

In school I would never ask questions, ask for guidance, or ask the teacher to slow down, because then you would look stupid. I would never say, "Slow down, I don't know what you are talking about."   —**Tim Piering**

Asking teachers for help was another thing I was afraid to do because I had been identified as gifted. Therefore, I thought I was supposed to know everything, and that if I raised my hand, then I wasn't really gifted. Quite often I got into a lot of trouble academically because I couldn't raise my hand and couldn't ask.   —**Hanoch McCarty**

I just can't talk to my mom. I'm afraid to ask her to even talk about this issue because I'm afraid she'll get mad at me or she won't understand. I'm afraid to ask my teachers for help with my homework because they'll think I'm stupid. I'm afraid to raise my hand in class and ask for clarification because the other kids will think I'm dumb, and maybe the teacher will, and then I'll get a lower grade. I don't want to look stupid. I'm afraid to ask other kids for help on my homework, because then I'll look needy and they'll use that against me.   —**High school student**

I was at a ten-day meditation retreat, and about seven days into it, they conducted private interviews with everyone to make sure we were staying sane. The whole retreat was done in silence with no eye contact, discussion, journal writing, or reading. You just meditate, walk, eat, and sleep.

I remember the instructor asking me how I was doing. I said, "I think I'm flipping out. Everything I ever believed in doesn't make sense anymore. Everything I ever thought was reality I'm no longer sure of."

I thought he was going to say, "Okay, go eat some meat and get out of here. Watch some TV, put your feet in the dirt, or something like that." Instead he said, "That's good."

I was shocked. I was thinking, "How can that be good?"

He said, "Most of what you believe isn't true anyway. You must empty yourself of all your preconceived notions so that you can become acutely aware of what is really there. All your belief structures are dissolving so that you can enter a space of pure awareness." I left the interview feeling as if my head were spinning. I went out onto the porch of the large Georgian mansion we were in and wrapped my arms around this huge column, as if I were holding on for dear life. I felt as if I were no longer sure of anything. It was a state of "I don't know."

Then I had this huge flood of memories of times in my life when it was not okay not to know—like when my dad said, "Where's the hammer?" ("I don't know.") "You damn well better know, you had it last." It wasn't safe not to know. I remembered my first year of teaching, when my students would ask me questions I didn't know the answers to. It wasn't okay not to know, so then I started faking it—pretending to know, pretending to have read books I hadn't read, laughing at jokes I didn't understand, nodding my head in understanding when I was lost. I became afraid to say, "What does that word mean?" or "Could you explain that again?"   **—Jack Canfield**

Fear of being powerless

Asking people for stuff makes you vulnerable. In a way, it means they can hurt you by denying you the things you want. I don't like giving anyone that kind of power over me.

—Kevin Smith

Fear of humiliation

Many of us were humiliated, made to feel shame and embarrassment, for asking when we were children. The simple act of

raising your hand to ask to go to the bathroom can be a humili-
ating experience in some classrooms.

"Do you have to go number one or number two?"
"Do you have to go bad?"
"Are you sure you can't hold it?"
"Is it an emergency?"

Fear of punishment

I was one of the most frightened people on the face of this
planet. I would be hit by my mother if I asked for anything. She
would say, "What is the matter with you? Are you stupid?" That
was her favorite one. I got punished left, right and center for
any simple little question. My father was mostly absent so I
couldn't ask him for anything, and when I asked, I was always
afraid to hear "No!" "No" was the most devastating thing anybody could say to me because it took all of my courage to gird
my loins—so to speak—to be at the place of finally asking for
something.

It didn't matter what I asked for. Asking meant I was selfish,
self-centered, and egotistical—all of the negative things. The
litany of attempts to cut me down to size was profound. As a
result, it became easier either not to ask or to beat around the
bush, than to ever ask straight out for what I wanted.

When my mother was eight years old, she was a violin virtu-
oso in Russia. One night when she was practicing for a concert
her drunken stepfather took her violin and smashed it against
the wall. Something cracked inside her, and she made a decision to hate all men. Twenty years later when she was supposed
to be a mother who loved and nurtured her children and her
husband, she just couldn't do it. Her inner child was screaming,
hollering, kicking, and hating all men—including me, her own
son!

—**Stan Dale**

When my friend was eight, his father said, "Go back the boat
into the water." He basically screwed it up and damaged the
boat, because his father had skipped a whole bunch of instructions like how to start the car, how to steer the car to keep the
boat straight, etc. And my friend didn't ask because, in his family, he would get hit for not knowing. Asking for information
was punished by violence, followed by a comment such as "I
already told you how to start the car once."   —**Kelle Apone**

Fear of abandonment

Women are taught that the act of asking, wanting, and yearning for something is a male characteristic. It's aggressive—not receptive. "Don't be too pushy, don't be too demanding. It's not ladylike, it's not nice. You're going to be called a bitch, and a man killer."

So we are taught that we should not ask, and that we should take what we can get. This is the greatest enemy of all women on every level of their lives: emotional, physical, sexual, and financial. Every woman has stories about wanting and not asking, about accepting something that was less than what they wanted. It's really sad, and men often have a very difficult time understanding our pain.

For example, a guy will say to his wife, "Why don't you just ask me for that? Why do you have to go through all this stuff of worrying and trying to figure out what I'm thinking?" Men don't understand what it's like to be a second-class citizen. Considering women couldn't even vote less than a hundred years ago, considering that women still are not honored for their work financially the same as men are, considering there are still levels of authority women cannot achieve in the business world, there is often a very strong consciousness in all women that says, "I am different. I am less than. I am seen as less than. I cannot and I dare not ask, and if I do, I'm going to pay the price."

When you put that all together, and you are sitting around thinking that you want to say to your husband, "I need more attention," it catches in your throat no matter how enlightened you are, no matter how strong you are, no matter how aggressive, no matter how much you can talk about it to other people. There are thousands of years of programming screaming, "No, don't say it. If you say it, you'll be kicked out of the cave and you'll be alone and you'll be eaten up by the wolves because there are a lot of other women where you came from to replace you."

—**Barbara De Angelis, Ph.D., Creator of Making Love Work,**
Author of *Real Moments*

Fear of endless obligation

Some people are afraid that if they ask for what they want from someone, they will become encumbered with a future obligation that may go on forever.

I asked if both our kids could stay overnight at the house of a friend one night, when only one of our kids was invited. The parents agreed. Later, those same parents went away for their anniversary and asked if they could have their girls spend the night at our house.

When they came back, they brought a gift. Now I feel obligated to get them a gift, and I am afraid that this cycle will continue, of me owing her, then her owing me, on and on forever.   —Patty Hansen

4. LOW SELF-ESTEEM

According to several recent studies, only one out of three of us has high self-esteem.[2] "Look to your right and look to your left. Only one of you is okay!" is the standard line we use in our seminars. One out of three! We are suffering from a national epidemic of low self-esteem.

Most of us feel unworthy of love, happiness and fulfillment and inadequate to create the kind of life we want. We suffer from inferiority complexes, neurotic guilt and a lack of self-confidence. As a result, we don't believe our needs and wants are important and worthy of pursuing. We become codependent from our belief that other people's needs are more important than our own—especially the needs of men, our children, our aging parents, our boss, the homeless and the needy. We sacrifice our own fulfillment on the altar of taking care of others.

I was happy to be wanted by anybody.

In my past, if somebody liked me, I automatically had a relationship with him because he wanted me. I didn't even ask myself, "Can I do better?" or "What do I want?" It was more "Wow, somebody wants to be with me." This is absolutely the reason for several of my marriages, very quickly one after the other when I was in my twenties.

When my first husband asked me to marry him, I was not even in love with him. I didn't ask myself if this was the perfect person for me. I never asked myself anything. I just went along with it because somebody wanted me. In my work, I would hire people because they really wanted to be around me. I never asked myself, "Are they capable? Are they intelligent? Can they do a good job? Do I like them?" I just acknowledged from their side that they wanted me. It cost me a lot of pain and disappointment.   **—Barbara De Angelis**

A feeling of unworthiness

During World War II I led a company of men up the Rhine River. After a terrible battle that lasted three days, I realized I was the only survivor. I had lost every man in my outfit. I was devastated. These were the men I was responsible for and they were all dead. Why had I alone survived? I felt like a total failure. I felt guilty to be alive when everyone else was dead.

When I returned to Miami, I went on a three-day drinking binge and then I joined the Benedictine Monastery, satisfying my own needs and desires. I didn't feel worthy of experiencing the pleasures of life any longer since none of my men could either.   **—Name withheld by request**

I believe the fear of unworthiness is the greatest obstacle that prevents people from asking for what they want. When I know I'm worthy, it's easy to ask.   **—Diane Loomans**

I think every time a woman asks for what she wants, she has to go to war against thousands of years of genetic programming. It's very, very deeply genetically ingrained. It comes from the sense of women being helpless on our own, a sense that we cannot support ourselves, a sense that as women we will be taken advantage of, and therefore we need to hang on to whatever it is that's more powerful than us—the man, the job, the friend—it doesn't matter what. We need to hang on to something other than ourselves for our own safety. Therefore you don't want to jeopardize your safety, that's your survival, and therefore you don't mess with it.   **—Barbara De Angelis**

African American women are fifteen times more likely to get AIDS than their white counterparts.

In conducting research with this population, the connection between self-worth and self-care seemed evident. One woman was asked whether she always uses a condom when she has sex. She said no because she's into a relationship with her man and she couldn't possibly ask him to put things between her and him, and besides, whatever he has—(presumably including sexually transmitted diseases)—is hers as well. So, in a way, being in a relationship is more important to her than her own life. Fear was also a factor. She felt she could not ask him to do something that would help protect her because he would get upset, and strike out at her.

One of the other participants—a woman in her late forties—broke into tears during the interview. When asked why she was crying, she said, "This is the first time in my life anyone has ever cared enough to ask me what I think or how I feel about something." She was obviously deeply moved that we valued her opinion. After all, forty plus years is a long time to be discounted.   —Frank Siccone

My needs are not important.

I don't want you to go to any trouble for me.
Now, don't put yourself out.
I don't want to make any extra work for you.

When we don't get what we want from the important people in our life, we often conclude that what we want is not important. In fact, we may go even further, into a codependent state where we believe other people's needs and wants are more important than our own. Then we stop asking for anything.

I can't tell you how many times my ex-husband asked me what I wanted for my birthday and after I told him, he would get me something else. When I asked, "What made you decide to get me this instead of what I originally wanted?" he would say, 'I just thought you would use this more often.' "   —Patty Aubery

I am not worth it.

I remember needing some luggage. My dad was in the furniture business and had a lot of connections with people in stores so he asked me what I wanted. I said I had seen this blue American Tourister set that I really liked. He went out and came home with this set of green Crown luggage. The same pieces, the same kind of thing, but it wasn't what I had asked for. I had told him what I wanted, and I ended up getting something less. It was a couple bucks cheaper.

When I said, "This is really nice, but I wanted those blue American Touristers," I got this huge lecture about how lucky I was to have luggage.

"There are a lot of people that have to take their stuff in pillowcases." That kind of stuff. I realized that was one event in a series of events of kind of getting what I had asked for, but not quite.

What I noticed happened after that, was that for years, if I would go out to buy things, I would find what I wanted and then get the next worse thing. If I was looking for a TV, I would find the one I wanted, and then get the one right below it. If I was looking for clothing, I would never quite get exactly what I wanted. Because in my belief system I was lucky to have anything.

One of the rules of the family was "don't want!" I've been trying to figure out where that came from and I think having parents who grew up poor made me feel fortunate just to have anything. "You're lucky it's not worse, you're lucky this, you're lucky that, you should be grateful, etc."

It just gave me the message that I wasn't quite worth getting what I really wanted and I didn't really quite deserve to get the best. **—Jane Bluestein**

Because my father was very rarely around and because he made a lot of promises he never kept, my experience was that if you ask, you'll be disappointed. So don't ask and take whatever you can get. For me it was beyond scarcity consciousness. It was desperation consciousness. It was "I'll take the universe's leftovers." **—Barbara De Angelis**

I remember the first time I asked for $500 as my speaking fee. I literally had to take a drink of water because I couldn't get it out of my mouth. The woman who hired me said, "Yeah, that's fine."

I just stared at her and she said, "You didn't think we were going to say okay, did you?" I was thinking "Am I that transparent?" She said, "You're worth $500!" **—Jane Bluestein**

The fear that rejection will confirm some deep-seated core belief about myself.

Reprinted by permission of National Forum, Inc.

5. PRIDE

Many of us, especially men, get stuck in our pride. We become too arrogant to admit we need anyone or anything. We will not stop to ask for directions, advice or help. We are convinced we need to do everything ourselves—usually perfectly and usually on the first try—or we risk the loss of respect, friendship, and our own sense of adequacy.

> *You couldn't just say, "Hey, mister, could you help me?" No! It would take you off your high horse!*
> —**Clark Gable to Claudette Colbert** in *It Happened One Night*

I hate to ask for directions. It's like admitting I don't know what I'm doing. I figure that if I just drive around long enough, I'll eventually figure it out.   —**Jeff Aubery**

My family and I were on a vacation in Sedona, Arizona, and we decided to go horseback riding. I called the stables to make the reservations and to get directions. The directions I was given were skimpy, but I figured I could find the place. On our way out of town my wife asked me if I would pull over and call the stables again to ask for better directions. If I did that, I would appear helpless and incompetent, so I declined and sped on.

We drove for what seemed like miles while my wife became more agitated and upset. I continued to look for the one road

"Because my genetic programming *prevents* me
from stopping to ask directions—*that's* why!"

sign I had written down. I finally found the sign on the left side
of the road, not on the right side of the road as I had been
told. At that point I "caved in" and pulled into a small housing
development and asked a man who was working with a hammer. He didn't have a clue as to what I was saying as he spoke
only Spanish and I speak only English. However, somehow we
communicated "horsies, horsies" and he gestured down the
road.

By this time my wife was fuming. "Why didn't you ask the
stable owners?" she demanded. I was starting to seriously
doubt if I would find the stables and we were already late. I
turned up a dirt road that looked promising and "lo and be-
hold," there were the stables! "See," I said to my wife, "you just
didn't have any faith in me. I knew I could find it all along!" So
I got to be right, but what was the price I had paid for being
right?

The beautiful morning with my family had turned into a
tense nightmare. My wife was mad at me and my kids were
crying. The easiest thing to have done was to have said to the
stable owner when I made the reservations, "I'm sorry, can you
clarify your directions? I don't know my way around here.
Would you repeat how far it is?" I would have had to admit I
needed more help than I had already been given, and my pride
wouldn't let me.   —**Mark Victor Hansen**

Better to ask twice than to lose your way once.

—**Danish proverb**

I'm afraid to appear less weak and needy.

I suppose that on a lot of levels I don't like to ask. I'm a male, a former marine, a big strong guy and sometimes I think, "Why do I need other people to help me?" As with many people, I like to give more than to receive because I don't want the obligation of receiving. First I was burned and four and one half years later paralyzed. With the paralysis, it is virtually impossible not to depend on other people for some things. It is very hard to admit sometimes that I can't do everything that everyone else can do. I think most people like to help "people who are disabled." What they need to understand is how much it robs the other person of their independence when they are able to do the task but not given the opportunity. My advice—watch, then ask, then listen, then help.   **—W Mitchell**

I started a small restaurant about seven years ago, and after two years I went bankrupt. I never really developed the decor the way I wanted and we never had the money to do the advertising we needed to do. I suppose I could have asked my dad to lend me the money I needed, but at the time my ego was in the way. I wanted to prove I could do it on my own, but what I really proved was that I needed more assistance than I asked for.   **—Steve Parker**

When it comes to anything that shows they have a need, men are supposed to have everything, not need anyone, be self-reliant, so asking for what you want implies you don't have it. Asking implies need, need implies weakness, and weakness implies you are not a man. Therefore, if I ask, I am not a man.
                                        —Barbara De Angelis

Fear that people will judge me for not already having it

Hanoch McCarty tells us the following joke that his mother used to tell all the time. It illustrates the point of being afraid to ask because it will somehow expose our limitations.

An older man is standing in line for a bus and there is a young fellow behind him who says, "Excuse me, have you got a light?"

The older guy answers somewhat angrily, "No, I don't!"

The younger guy thinks, "Don't bite my head off," and gets a light from someone else. A few minutes later the older guy in front lights up a cigarette himself! So the young man behind him says, "Hey, buddy, why did you tell me you didn't have a match when you obviously did have one?"

The older guy says, "Look, if I had given you a light, you and I would probably have started talking. And, if we had started talking, we probably would have ended up sitting on the bus together. And, if we were sitting on the bus together, we would have ended up talking to each other. You look like a very nice fella, and I probably would have really started to like you. And then I might have invited you to get off at my stop to come to my house for dinner . And, if you came to my house for dinner, you would probably have met my daughter. And, if you would have met my daughter, you probably would have gone out with her. And, if you went out with her, who knows, one thing leads to another and you might have ended up marrying her, and I don't want her to marry someone who can't afford a lighter!"

—Hanoch McCarty

We are programmed in pride.

> *Guts!*
> *Guts!*
> *Pride!*
> *Pride!*
> *Loyalty!*
> *Loyalty!*
> *One, two, three, four,*
> *United States Marine Corps.*
> —Marine Corps cadence count

In the military the cultural norms are don't ask for help, don't be a wimp, and don't ask for special treatment. In the movie *A Few Good Men* we see a marine killed in his bed because he can't hack it due to a medical condition that made him unable to keep up with the rest of the troops.

I remember in the Marine Corps, these colonels or majors would say, "Hey, if you have any problems, my door is open; you can come in." But if you came in with a problem, it meant you were weak. In the Marine Corps, the underlying culture is "You take it and you handle it yourself. Don't come to me crying. Pull your own weight. Don't ask for help. You should be able to hack it yourself."

—**Tim Piering**

We are supposed to be able to figure it out by ourselves.

This belief that we are supposed to be able to figure it out by ourselves is so much a part of our culture that when we buy a VCR, we put it together without looking at the instruction manual. We only look at the manual as a last resort if we can't make it work by ourselves. Why is it that almost every VCR has a flashing 12:00 on the control panel? We won't even look up in the manual how to program the clock!

We only consult the manual for our computers when we have exhausted every other possibility. We are a nation of loners and self-sufficient do-it-yourselfers trained to suffer stoically in silence to the end.

This belief so permeates our culture that it has become a stigma in many quarters to ask for emotional and psychological support. The fact that Senator Thomas Eagleton from Missouri had once sought psychological help cost him the Democratic nomination for vice president in 1972. The belief was that if he had once sought psychological help, he could not be trusted to be stable and competent under pressure. Why is it that we can't get mental health covered in our insurance and national health care programs? We believe real people—especially men—just suck it up and handle it by themselves.

There was this incredible pressure in my family to always be "fine," to look good, to be perfect and to not make mistakes. That wipes out any idea of asking for help. My father was a self-made man who had survived the Depression all by himself. His operating assumption was that you do not ask for help because it makes you look vulnerable. And, if you're vulnerable and people see that you're not perfect, people will hurt you.

—**Jane Bluestein**

◆

"Oh," said Aladdin, "So now I understand why I haven't been asking for what I want. So, if I start asking for what I want, how will my life change?"

◆

A WHOLE NEW WORLD:
The Benefits of Asking

◆

*Man who waits for roast duck to fly into mouth must wait
very, very, long time.*
—Chinese proverb

If you don't ask, you don't get.
—Ghandi

◆

"Aladdin, you ask how your world will change? Listen, and be
amazed.

"All of your desires will be clearly known and understood. All of
your requests will eventually be granted and all of your dreams will
come true. You can ask for as much as you want, just the way you
want it, whenever you want it, from whomever and whatever you
want . . . and get it.

"It is possible to have your seemingly impossible dream if you
learn and apply the principles and techniques I will show you."

◆

Think of the benefits of knowing how, when and whom to ask
for everything you want: fewer disappointments in relationships, more effective team efforts at work, cleaner negotiations
at the bargaining table, the money you need to start a busi-

ness, fewer fights with your parents and children, the extra instruction and support you need, less suffering in the silent despair of loneliness, and the causes you support receiving the funding they need to continue their good works. Literally a whole new world can open up to you and everyone you care about.

You can ask for anything.

You can ask for a hug, comfort, listening, forgiveness, attention, time, intimacy, caring, respect, love, nurturing, a massage, healing energy, prayers, an explanation, loyalty, sexual fidelity and a 100 percent commitment.

You can ask for a helping hand around the house, a favor, someone to keep a secret, help with your homework, the loan of a sweater or jacket, private tutoring, information, help with a project, your kids' cooperation, someone to baby-sit, swimming lessons, money for the movies, participation in a car pool, help with a flat tire, the loan of the family car or compliance with rules.

You can ask to make a difference, get rich, become famous or lose weight.

You can ask for a better table, a substitution on the menu, your food to be reheated, more butter, a special diet, food cooked Pritikin style, a nonfat substitute or a special meal.

You can ask for volunteers, participants, donors, contributors, supporters, den mothers, troop leaders, teacher's aides, advisors, board members and assistants for your organization!

You can ask for an allowance, a loan, investment capital, an extension, better terms, lower interest rates, refinancing, a better deal, a price reduction, a raise, a promotion, more responsibility, less responsibility, a vacation, time off, a change in policy, equal opportunity, severance pay, shorter staff meetings or less paperwork.

On May 31, 1995, I received a letter from a woman in Illinois. Over a year earlier, she had called me at Jack Canfield's office to see if I had Roger Crawford's phone number. Roger Crawford is a phenomenal motivational speaker/author, who was born with seven fingers missing. This letter touched me so deeply, I had tears in my eyes when I finished it. Here is the letter in part . . .

Dear Kim:

. . . last year I called your office and sought your help in contacting Roger Crawford. You were kind enough to look up his phone number and address. I'm writing to let you know how everything turned out.

You might recall that I had ordered [the tape album] *How to Build High Self-Esteem,* after attending a seminar. Now, I never listen to self-improvement tapes, so the fact that I ordered the tape set, and started listening to it when it arrived, is amazing in and of itself.

The next day, I received a call from Children's Home Society; they had received our adoption application, which stated that we would consider adopting a child with missing digits. They asked if we would consider twenty-one-month-old Igor, who was born with only one finger on each hand and two toes on each foot.

I started praying real hard for divine guidance, with a request that God shout in my ear, as I'm usually pretty dense.

. . . I was listening to the tape album, and I got to the part about Roger Crawford . . . It occurred to me that he would be a good person to talk to about living with a hand difference. Then I realized that God was shouting in my ear. The creator of the universe had arranged for me to have that tape at that time so that a small boy in an orphanage in Volgagrad would join our family in America.

I called you . . . then I called Roger Crawford's number. It was out of service, so I tried directory assistance for the city. They had a listing for Roger Crawford, and I dialed the number. A lady answered, and I asked if this was the home of Roger Crawford, the speaker. She responded that this was his parents' home; she was Roger Crawford's mother! We had a long conversation, and she was very encouraging. I think God arranged that conversation also.

After several weeks of waiting for medical reports and pictures, we decided that this little guy was the right child for our family. (During this time, a five-year-old girl in Des Moines, Iowa, won a coloring contest. This led to a feature article in the local paper, because Hope has only one finger on each hand. My mother, who lives in Des Moines, sent the article to me, and I contacted Hope's mother. I don't think that it is just a coincidence that Hope won that contest at that time!)

On May 14, we boarded the plane for Moscow, and on May 27, Igor became Andrew.

Andy has been in our family for nearly a year now, and he is a delightful child, and the perfect kid for our family. After only two or three weeks, I stopped thinking of Andy as handicapped, as there is nothing he can't do. Andy gets along well with his five-year-old sister, who loves him dearly.

Kim, thank you for your help in finding the resources to make us a family. You really went the extra mile for a stranger. May God bless you.

Sincerely yours,
Holly K.   **—Kimberly Wiele**

YOU WILL TAKE CONTROL OF YOUR LIFE

The wind and the waves are always on the side of the ablest navigators.
                 —Edward Gibbon

◆

"When you decide, Aladdin, to take control of your life and be the captain of your own ship, you can accomplish anything your heart desires. Your self-esteem will unfold and you will believe in your dreams and your ability to achieve those dreams. No longer will you be a beggar child, dependent on others for what little good comes into your life—you will create your own good."

◆

Change Your Won't Power to Will Power!

I was working in the Hawaiian food business, which was a great job for somebody who weighed 255 pounds, when Richard Ney, a financial analyst, asked me, "If everything went perfectly for you in the next two years, how would you like to see your life change?"

I had never thought about it at all, so I just looked at him and said, "I don't know."

"Well, think about it," he said. "If you were going to have

food, some kind of a meal, wouldn't you think about what you were going to have?"

"Yeah."

"Well, how'd you want your life to change?"

"Well, I'd like to be a nonsmoker."

"That's good," he said. "Put that down."

"Okay, I'd like to weigh 185 pounds."

"Stop right there," he said. "I didn't ask you what you thought you could have. I asked you what do you really want?"

It suddenly dawned on me in that instant that the human mind will only say what it wants based on what it believes it can have. And that's all based on past conditioning. So I wrote down, "I want to weigh 145 pounds." Now, I hadn't weighed 145 pounds since I was ten years old. So I asked, "If I weighed 145 pounds (I'm five feet, five inches tall), what size would I wear?"

"Oh, about a size 32–33 pants." At that time I had a forty-six-inch waist, so for me to even conceive of being size 32 was something I couldn't believe. He asked, "If you were 145 pounds right now, how would your life change?"

So I really got into that, and from day one, even while I still weighed 255 pounds, in my mind I acted as if I was 145 pounds. I even went out and bought clothes that I would fit into at 145. It took me a year and a half to lose that weight, but I did eventually fit into those clothes. The most important thing was the belief factor.   —Ken Ross

YOU WILL HAVE BETTER BUSINESS AND PERSONAL RELATIONSHIPS

You train people how to treat you by how you treat yourself.
—Martin Rutte

A more fulfilling relationship is waiting for you with each person you know and those you come in contact with. You can have more cohesiveness between yourself and your co-workers and more intimacy at home with those you love. All you have to do is ask. Ask for time, ask for understanding and ask for co-operation.

Asking improves your chances of receiving by 200 percent.

When I was a kid, I was poor. I was a street kid. My mother and father didn't know very much about how the world really worked. I used to go into the saunas at the local "Y" and sit there with the local businessmen until I'd get dehydrated. I'd keep bringing these men water, being their water boy, basically, so I could sit in the sauna and listen to them talk business. I'd sit there for two hours a night.

They'd try and get me out of the sauna, saying it's not healthy for you to stay in the sauna two hours a night. But I didn't want to leave because I wanted to hear their stories and I wanted to ask them questions, which I did—lots of questions.

That's probably the most outrageous thing I've ever done. Across the street my friends were doing and selling drugs and here I was in the sauna listening to these guys tell great tales of success, health and family. **—John Assaraf, President, Re/Max of Indiana**

You get what you ask for.

The most important question I ever asked got me my first sales job. I was fifteen years old and I was working during the summer for a building products company in their warehouse. I loaded and unloaded trucks and had to lug heavy stuff all over the warehouse. It was sweaty and dirty and hard work in the warehouse. After a while I noticed there was another building—the office. And then I began to notice some important things about the office building.

One was that there was air conditioning and the people in there weren't sweaty and dirty. The second was that there were women inside the office building. I thought that was probably a better place to be. So I go inside one day because I needed to use the toilet. As I'm walking out of the toilet, I overhear the general manager of the company and the sales manager having a discussion about a problem.

Their best phone solicitor, who prospected on the phone for leads for the salespeople, was sick. They were short of leads and they were trying to figure out what they were going to do. When I heard this conversation, I stopped in the hallway and I looked over at this guy Ben Kramer, who today I affectionately call Uncle Ben, and I said, "Ben." He looked over and I said, "Why not let me do it?"

He just said, "Nah," and went on talking to the other guy. I didn't move. He looked back over at me and I said, "Why not?" That was the question that got me my first sales job. He stared me down, and I'll never forget this because he snapped his fingers at me and he said, "C'mon, kid," and he took me into the room and he taught me how to prospect. If I hadn't asked that question that day at that time, who knows how my life would have been different? **—Dave Yoho**

The greatest question I ever asked was when I had the chutzpah to ask my present partners if I could be their partner.

They said, "What exactly do you mean?"

I said, "Well, I'm willing to work, and I'm willing to create something. You want to expand and I could be an extension of what you're doing." That turned into a partnership, Re/Max of Indiana. We started in 1988, with a dollar volume of about fifty million dollars. Last year we sold 16,500 homes in Indiana at about one and a half billion. We should hit two billion this year. That one question has made me a multimillionaire.

—John Assaraf

The answer is yes . . . but you have to ask!

A salesman for a key-making machine entered a hardware store and gave the shopkeeper a demonstration.

"Isn't it a wonderful machine?" he asked.

"Yes, it is."

"It would be a marvelous investment and a great time-saver, wouldn't it?"

"Yes."

"Well, why don't you buy it?"

"Well," said the shopkeeper, "why don't you ask me to?"

—Dr. David A. Maclennan,
***Priming the Preacher's Pump**[3]*

There is a price for not asking.

A number of years back the University of Chicago received a million dollar grant from Mrs. Fields of the Marshall Fields Department Store fame and fortune. When the administration at Northwestern University read the headline in the newspaper, the people at Northwestern were shocked, How could this be? Mrs. Fields lived in Evanston, Illinois. Northwestern was in Evanston, Illinois. She had been a supporter in the past. Why hadn't she donated the money to Northwestern? Why had she given the money to the University of Chicago instead?

When the university officials called Mrs. Fields to discover why she had given the money to the University of Chicago rather than to them, she replied, "The people at the University of Chicago asked. You didn't."

"Oh, filled with hopeless longing. And you?"

For of all sad words of tongues or pen the saddest are these:
It might have been . . . —**John Greenleaf Whittier**

YOU WILL INCREASE YOUR PERSONAL POWER

There is no knowledge that is not power.
—**Ralph Waldo Emerson**

◆

"Only he who is knowledgeable and worthy," said the genie, "may enter the cave of wonders. Those who use their personal power have clarity of purpose, focus, and a passion for life that magnetizes others to them."

◆

She kept asking and she got it.

Shannon Rast and her husband had dreamed of placing huge clay pots filled with flowers at both ends of their new home's circular driveway. But other needs intervened.

Then Shannon saw four clay pots outside an out-of-business San Antonio motel. Thinking she might buy them at rock-bottom prices, she called a phone number on a sign in the motel's parking lot. She was told the structure, with three hundred rooms still full of furniture, was to be demolished and absolutely nothing could be released.

We'll see about that, she thought. After many phone calls she reached the California company that had bought the motel. They assumed the furniture had been removed. With the company's permission, Rast took charge.

Rast called Youth Alternatives, a facility for runaway and abused children, whose thrift shop desperately needed donations. She also contacted the Salvation Army, the Association for Retarded Citizens and several other organizations.

For ten days volunteers loaded trucks and hauled away furniture. Soon, the Youth alternatives store was filled to capacity and the other organizations received similar boosts.

Although Shannon Rast's original intention was personal, she fostered a new sense of pride among people who might never have worked together. And today Rast's circular driveway has four clay pots, two at each end.   —Debs McCrary

People will help you, but only if you ask.

This requirement was demonstrated in two field studies conducted by psychologist Thomas Moriarity and reported in the *Journal of Personality and Social Psychology.*

A young woman entered a cafeteria in New York City, placed her suitcase by a table where another person was eating, and went off to get some food.

While she was away, a young man came by, picked up her bag, and walked off with it.

In only one out of eight trials of this experiment did the customer at the table make an effort to stop him.

When the same woman again entered the cafeteria and placed her bag down by a table where someone else was sitting, but then *asked that person to keep an eye on it* while she got some food, her table mate stopped the young man when he began to make away with it *every time.*

On another day, the same young woman visited a beach, spread out her blanket, left a radio on it, and went off, either saying nothing to the nearest bystander or else asking that person to keep an eye on her things. Moriarity got the same results.

At both locations, nearly all of the bystanders she asked to watch her possession tried to stop the "thief," but of those she did not ask, only a few—one in eight in the cafeteria and one in five at the beach—did so.[4]   **—Pryor Report, February 1992**

So . . . if you want people to take responsibility for something, make an unambiguous request, and they'll probably come through for you.

YOU WILL HAVE AND GIVE MORE LOVE

If you miss love, you miss life.   —Leo Buscaglia

◆

"When we met," said the genie, "you told me that you deserved the riches of the kingdom. True riches are not only jewels and gold, but the richness of family and friends." The genie's voice mellowed and became as soft as a dove's wings. "Love is the ultimate answer to all of life's questions. I have seen what you hold in your heart for the princess, and it is of deep and abiding value. If we don't tell the ones we love and cherish about our silent yearnings, they will forever remain unfulfilled. Asking gives wings to our fondest dreams and desires."

◆

Ask for nurturing.

I remember when Bonnie first asked for a hug. It made such a difference in our relationship. Instead of resenting me for not offering hugs, she would simply ask.

It was such a gift of love to me. She began to understand that the way to love me best was to help me be successful in loving her. This is a very important advanced relationship skill.

I still remember the first day she asked for a hug. I was standing in my closet, and she was making different sounds of exhaustion. She said, "Ooohhh, what a day."

Then she took a deep breath and made a long sigh on the exhale. In her language, she was asking for a hug. What I

heard was a tired person and wrongly assumed that she probably wanted to be left alone.

Instead of resenting me for not noticing or responding to her
request, she took the big step to ask for what she wanted, even
though to her it seemed obvious.

She said. "John, would you give me a hug?"

My response was immediate. I said, "Of course." I went
straight over to her and gave her a big hug.

She let out another sigh in my arms and then thanked me for
the hug. I said, "Any time."

She chuckled and smiled. I said, "What?"

She said, "You have no idea how hard it was to ask for a
hug."[5]   —John Gray, Ph.D.

If you don't ask, you don't get.

*Gabriel looked her long in the face, but the firelight being
faint there was not much to be seen.*

*"Bathsheba," he said, tenderly and in surprise, and com-
ing closer: "If I only knew one thing—whether you would
allow me to love you and win you, and marry you after all—if
I only knew that!"*

"But you never will know," she murmured.

"Why?"

"Because you never ask."   —Thomas Hardy,
                                          Far from the Madding Crowd

When my mom was nineteen years old she was madly in love
with my dad. They had gone to school together their whole life.
My dad was "not ready" to ask my mom to marry him at nineteen, so she married the man who was not afraid to ask. A
year later he died from cystic fibrosis. My mom was a widow
at twenty.

When my dad found out that she was now a free woman he
desperately wanted to ask her on a date but his pride stood in
the way of his asking. My grandmother knew it was eating at
him. Here was his second chance, one that you don't normally
get in your life, but still, he didn't ask.

My grandmother finally called my mom's mother and together they made a plan. My mom was out with her mom and
my dad was out with his mom—and it just so happened—while
they were out, they ran into each other. They made it look coin-
cidental! Within months my parents were married.

                                          —Patty Aubery

YOU CAN ENRICH YOUR LIFESTYLE

Life is not lost by dying; life is lost minute by minute, day by dragging day, in all the thousand small uncaring ways.

—Stephen Vincent Benét

◆

"Knowing your own self-worth and believing in your dreams is part of life enrichment.

"Feeling worthy of having your food prepared how you like it, traveling in comfort and wearing the finest silks enhances your sense of well-being. When you include your ability to enhance other's lives through your own generosity, you will own all of the riches of the kingdom!"

◆

It's a funny thing about life; if you refuse to accept anything but the best, you very often get it. —Somerset Maugham

When I asked Jeff where he wanted to go for our honeymoon, he said, "Let's go to Maui. Make arrangements for something really special." So, I did! I reserved a beautiful suite at one of the nicest hotels on the island. When I told my husband where we were staying, he said, "Great. Did you ask if they have twenty-four-hour room service?"

I did ask, and they said it wasn't twenty-four-hour, but it was until 2:00 A.M.

When we arrived at the hotel, we checked in and immediately went to our room. We were both dying of thirst and couldn't wait to crack open the mini-bar. That's when we realized there wasn't one! We weren't happy about it but decided nothing was going to ruin this special trip. We would just forget about it.

I then decided to call room service. The person on the other end of the phone told me that room service was only available from 6:00 to 10:00 in the morning and 6:00 to 10:00 in the evening! My husband was not happy to say the least. I told him I would take care of the problem, and I went straight down stairs to see the manager.

When I met with the manager, I told her, "For $350 a day, I expect room service and a mini-bar. The brochure and the people I spoke with assured me I would have both."

She apologized and said, "But there is really nothing I can do. The kitchen is closed those hours and there are no mini-bars on the property." She started to get agitated with me.

I went back to my room and told my husband what had happened. This might not seem like a big deal to the average person, but when someone guarantees me something like this, I expect it. My husband said, "Honey, look, it's our honeymoon! Let's not let this bother us." I couldn't help it. I wasn't going to settle.

I said, "Look, it's late. I'm going to go to bed, but in the morning I am going back down there and I am going to ask for the manager's manager. Working for Jack Canfield for five years has ingrained it into my head—ask, ask, ask! I mean after all, what are they going to do to me? Worst case I have to spend a week in this suite without my mini-bar!"

The next morning my husband was almost embarrassed—he didn't even want to be present when I asked to see the "head manager." Well, the "head manager" ended up being the son of the owner. I introduced myself and I stated my case. I said, "I made it very clear to your reservationist that having room service and a mini-bar was important to me, and that person assured me it was no problem. Now I am here and it is a problem. What I want is the following: A room that will be able to supply me with food and drinks twenty-four-hours a day."

The manager then explained that the only rooms that had refrigerators were the villas on the water and they went for $895 per day. I then said, "Fine, that's where I would like to stay, and I would like it for the price of my suite." Five minutes later he came out of his office and said, "Here are your keys for the villa, Mrs. Aubery. I hope you enjoy your stay."

I thought my husband was going to fall over when I told him what had happened. I said, "See, Jack is right, you have to ask, ask, ask!"

—Patty Aubery

Another success story

During the Self-Esteem Seminar I participated in the "Ask, Ask, Ask, Ask, Ask Exercise" that you had us do. A week before the seminar my daughter Janna had been accepted to be an exchange student in Germany, and the fee for the year was $4,000. Being a single parent with three teenagers, I did not have $4,000 or any inkling of how I was going to get it. Financially, I was barely making ends meet. I had no savings, no credit for a loan and no relatives that could loan me the money. It felt as hopeless as if I had to raise four million dollars!

So during the exercise, that is what I asked everyone for, and I found it *very* difficult to ask the other participants—especially friends whom I knew from before the workshop—for money. At the conclusion of the exercise I realized that I did not have to "give up" other people's love and affection for me in exchange for asking for the money.

Based on what I learned at the seminar I decided to take some *action*. I made up a flyer with Janna's picture on it, her statement of why she wanted to go to Germany and a request for money. At the bottom was a coupon for people to tear off and mail their check to us by June 1. I asked for $5, $20, $50 or $100 and even left a blank space to fill in their own amount. I sent the flyers to family, friends, acquaintances, three local newspapers, ex-employers and fifty service clubs in our area. I only had two months to raise the money—which, from my perspective, seemed like a lot of money and not very much time.

But I also *consciously* decided to change my attitude towards the goal becoming a reality because I remembered that in the seminar you taught me that I "create, promote and allow" all events in my life.

I wrote out an affirmation: "I am joyfully receiving $4,000 by June 1 to pay for Janna's trip to Germany." I put the affirmation on my bathroom mirror and carried a copy in my purse so I could look at it every day. Then I wrote out an actual check for $4,000 and put it on the dashboard of my car. I spent lots of time driving each day and it was a visible reminder. I took a picture of a hundred dollar bill and enlarged it. I put the hundred dollar bill on the ceiling over Janna's bed so it was the first thing she saw in the morning and the last thing at night.

When I explained the idea to Janna, she was hesitant to do "this asking thing" and practice an affirmation, but she agreed to give it a try. The first gift we received was for $5. The largest was for $800. But most of the gifts were $20 or $50, some from people we knew, some from strangers. All the parts came together to make the whole.

By June 1 we had joyfully received $3,750! We were thrilled and so excited! However, while this was wonderful, I still had no idea where I was going to get the last $250. But I still had until June 5 to somehow raise the remaining money. On June 3 the phone rang. It was a woman from one of the service organizations in our town. "I know I'm past the deadline; is it too late?" she asked. "*No!*" I replied. "Well, we'd really like to help Janna, but we can only give her—$250."

Altogether we received gifts from twenty-three individuals

and two service organizations—we received *exactly* the amount of money we needed and we received it by the deadline!!!

This has been a wonderful and practical example to me and to Janna about using affirmations, creating your own reality, asking the universe for what you want, and believing in yourself and others. I know this "life experience" will be one that Janna will remember and build on for future situations in her life—and so will I!   **—Claudette Hunter**

YOU WILL MAXIMIZE YOUR TALENTS AND YOUR SKILLS

◆

"If you remain trapped in the marketplace for the rest of your days, Aladdin, you will not realize your true talents and have the time to sharpen your skills. The path to your freedom lies in the questions you ask and what you are willing to settle for. Think big, Aladdin . . . now is the time!"

◆

You create your opportunities by asking for them.

—Patty Hansen

Be outrageous.

I always wanted to be a producer, and I was constantly visualizing myself as a producer because I really wanted it. I got up very early one morning and was watching a show called *Today in L.A.* and Gloria Steinem was on promoting the paperback release of *Outrageous Acts and Everyday Rebellions.* She ended her segment by saying that if everyone could just promise to do something outrageous today, it would be a better world.

Three hours later, I decided to be outrageous. I just picked up the phone, called Gloria's office and got a meeting with her. I was just a kid in my twenties and I said to myself, "Oh my God, I did it."

I said, "I think you should be on morning television." She agreed. I then went to Steve Freedman, who was the executive producer of *The Today Show* at the time, and sold the idea of

Gloria being a regular on the show. We were there for a couple of years. That's how I got started as a producer.

—**Carla Morganstern,**
Television Producer

◆

"I understand, Genie, why I need to ask and what will happen once I do ask. My life and the lives of those close to me will forever change—for the better. Will you tell me more of those who have been successful in their asking?"

◆

THE MASTERS OF THE LAMP

◆

*And it shall come to pass, that before they call, I will answer
. . . and while they are yet speaking, I will hear.*
—Isaiah 65:24

◆

Throughout history, there have been many people who have mastered the art of asking for and getting what they want. These masters of the lamp overcame all kinds of obstacles and shaped their own destinies. Having mastered the principles of asking and receiving, they have created their dreams and contributed to the lives of others in countless ways.

◆

You have to do it by yourself, and you can't do it alone.
—Martin Rutte

Masters constantly ask for support in many forms.

*There is no such thing as a self-made man. You will reach your
goals only with the help of others.* —George Shinn

One of the things that distinguishes masters from others is
that they constantly ask for anything and everything they need.

They ask for time, assistance, instruction, mentoring and coaching. They ask people to show them how to sing, paint, juggle, tie a knot, set the timer on their VCR and fix their car. They stop and ask for directions. They ask people to share their recipes for their chocolate chip cookies as well as their recipes for financial success.

By following the advice of the masters, you too can discover your mission, clarify your dreams, reawaken your passion and learn to ask effectively, clearly, creatively and repeatedly for what you want.

Masters of the lamp ask for money, loans, grants and subsidies. They ask people to invest in their businesses, underwrite their projects, donate to their causes and finance their research. After being unable to secure an advance for his next book, a now successful author asked forty friends each to put up $1000, which he lived on for the year that it took him to write his book. The book became a best-seller and made him $400,000, from which he repaid all of his friends with interest.

Masters of the lamp ask for information, guidance, advice and lots of feedback. They are constantly striving to improve their grades, income, sales, results and performance. An Olympic pole vaulter who suddenly stopped improving approached the retired pole vault champion who held the world's record in the event and asked him for help. The world record holder responded by coaching him at his home for a week. The young man went on to win the gold and break the former world record.

At one time almost all of these masters of the lamp had trouble asking for what they wanted and needed. They had all the same issues of ignorance, fear, pride and unworthiness that the rest of us have struggled with, but they faced them, overcame them and got on with the business of creating the lives and the results they wanted.

If they can do it, so can you!

If someone else can do it, so can you. This has been proven by the thousands of people who have overcome their fears and self-doubts and gone on to get a scholarship to college, marry the person of their dreams, start their own business, publish a book, increase their private practice, expand their client base, get a part in a television series, double and triple their incomes, buy an expensive house with no money down, and take vacations in exotic places at virtually no cost to themselves.

A man's doubts and fears are his worst enemies.
— **William Wrigley, Jr.**

THE SEVEN CHARACTERISTICS OF THE MASTERS OF THE LAMP

I'm tough, ambitious, and I know exactly what I want. If that makes me a bitch, okay.   —**Madonna**

1. They know what they want.

The masters of the lamp know what they want. They are clear about their purpose, their vision and their goals, and they are able to communicate this to others.

A little kid down at our church in Huntington Beach came up to me after he heard me talk about the Children's Bank. He came up to me, shook my hand, and said, "My name is Tommy Tighe, I'm six years old and I want to borrow money from your Children's Bank."

I said, "Tommy, what do you want to do?"

"Ever since I was four I had a vision that I could cause peace in the world. I want to make a bumper sticker that says, 'PEACE, PLEASE! DO IT FOR US KIDS, signed Tommy Tighe.' I need $454 dollars so I can print one thousand bumper stickers."

"I can get behind that," I said. Once the bumper stickers were printed, Tommy's Dad whispered in my ear, "If he doesn't pay the loan back, are you going to foreclose on his bicycle?"

Tommy convinced his dad to drive him up to Ronald Reagan's home. Tommy rang the bell and the gatekeeper came out. Tommy gave a two-minute, irresistible sales presentation on his bumper sticker. The gatekeeper reached in his pocket, gave Tommy $1.50, and said, "Here, I want one of those. Hold on and I'll get the former President."

Next he sent a bumper sticker to Mikhail Gorbachev with a bill for $1.50 in U.S. funds. Gorbachev sent him back $1.50 and a signed picture that said, "Go for peace, Tommy," and signed it "Mikhail Gorbachev, President."

After Tommy's project began to take off, the Sunday edition of the *Orange County Register* did a feature story on Tommy. Marty Shaw interviewed Tommy for six hours and wrote a phenomenal piece. Marty asked Tommy what he thought his impact would be on world peace. Tommy said, "I don't think I am old enough yet; I think you have to be eight or nine to stop all the wars in the world."

Someone sent Joan Rivers a copy of the interview with Tommy. She loved the story and called Tommy to invite him to appear on her television show.

"Tommy, I want you on my TV show."

"Great!" said Tommy.

"I'll pay you $300," said Joan.

"Great!" said Tommy. "I am only eight years old, so I can't come alone. You can afford to pay for my mom too—can't you?"

"Yes!" Joan replied.

"By the way, I just watched a 'Lifestyles of the Rich and Famous' show, and it said you ought to stay at the Trump Plaza when you're in New York. You can make that happen, can't you?"

"Yes," she answered.

"The show also said when one is in New York, you ought to visit the Empire State Building and the Statue of Liberty. You can get us tickets, can't you?"

"Yes. . ."

"Great. Did I tell you my mom doesn't drive? So we can use your limo, can't we?"

"Sure," said Joan.

Tommy went on "The Joan Rivers Show" and wowed Joan, the camera crew, and both the studio and television audiences. He told such captivating and persuasive stories that the audience pulled money out of their wallets to buy bumper stickers on the spot.

At the end of the show, Joan leaned in and said, "Tommy, do you really think your bumper sticker will cause peace in the world?"

Tommy, enthusiastically and with a radiant smile, said, "So far I've had it out less than two years and I already got the Berlin Wall down. I am doing pretty good, don't you think?"

—Mark Victor Hansen

2. They believe they are worthy of receiving it.

In order to receive the gifts of life you must believe you are worthy of receiving them.

When I started my business, I had no money, so I decided to go to the bank for a loan. Technically I had no collateral because the house we're buying is on a real-estate contract, which means we don't get the actual deed to this house until we make the last payment. I got dressed up, took a copy of my book and went into the bank. I walked up to the loan officer and threw my book on his desk and said, "Look, you don't know me, I don't even have an account here, but I just started this business that is going to help a lot of people and I'm really smart and need some money."

He said, "How much?"

I said, "Fifteen thousand dollars." He gave me a check. As I walked out of there, part of me was thinking "Who the hell do you think you are?" Then the other part of me said, "I don't care, I've got fifteen thousand dollars more than I had an hour ago, perhaps I should have asked for thirty thousand."

—Jane Bluestein

3. They believe they can get it.

All masters of the lamp ask with certainty—knowing that they will receive what they ask for. Some call it faith, others call it self-confidence. In either case, it is the belief that this is possible that propels them into action.

My wife Linda and I had just started a self-esteem training program called Little Acorns in Miami, Florida. One day we received a brochure for an educational conference in San Diego. After reading the brochure, we knew we had to go. But we didn't see how we could get there. We were just getting started, we were working out of our home, and we had just about exhausted our personal savings with the early stages of the work. There was no way we could afford the airline tickets or any of the other expenses. But we knew we had to be there and we believed that somehow we could make it happen. So we just started asking.

First I called the conference coordinators in San Diego, explained why we just had to be there, and asked them if they would give us two complimentary admissions to the conference. They said yes. I told Linda we had the tickets and we could get in to do the conference. She said, "Great! But we're in Miami and the conference is in San Diego. What do we do next?"

We had to get transportation. I called Northeast Airlines and asked the president, Steve Quinto, to donate two round-trip tickets from Miami to San Diego.

He said, "Of course I will," just like that. It was that fast, and the next thing he said really floored me. He said, "Thank you for asking."

I said, "Pardon me?"

He said, "I don't often have the opportunity to do the best thing that I can for the world unless someone asks me to. The best thing I can ever do is to give of myself and you've asked me to do that. That's a nice opportunity and I want to thank you for that opportunity." I was blown away, but I thanked him and I hung up the phone. I looked at my wife and said, "Honey, we got the plane tickets."

She said, "Great! Where do we stay?"

Next I called the Holiday Inn Downtown Miami and asked, "Where is your headquarters?" They told me it was in Memphis, Tennessee. I called Tennessee and they patched me through to a guy in San Francisco who controlled all of the Holiday Inns in California and I asked if there was some way he could help us with the lodging for the three days. He asked if it would be okay if he put us up in their new hotel in downtown San Diego as his guest. I said, "Yes, that would be fine."

He then said, "Wait a minute. I need to caution you that the hotel is about a thrity-five-mile drive from the campus where the conference is being held, and you'll have to find out how to get there."

I said, "I'll figure it out even if I need to buy a horse." I thanked him and said to Linda, "Well, honey, we've got the admission, we've got the plane tickets, and we've got a place to stay. What we need now is a way to get back and forth from the hotel to the campus twice a day."

Next I called National Car Rental, told them the story, and asked if they could help me out. They said, "Would a new Olds 88 be OK?" I said it would be. We put the whole thing together in one day.

We did wind up buying our own meals for part of the time, but before the conference was over I stood up and told this story at one of the general assemblies and said, "Anyone that wants to volunteer to take us to lunch now and again would be graciously accepted." About fifty people jumped up and volun-

teered so we wound up having some of the meals thrown in
as well.   —Rick Gelinas

4. They are passionate about it.

At the last moment we decided we needed to be at the First
Earth Summit in Rio de Janeiro, Brazil. We only had two weeks
to raise the $8,000 we would need to pay for the transportation,
hotel rooms, food and printing of the booklets on self-esteem
we wanted to distribute to the conference participants. We also
needed to get passports, visas and our hotel registration
handled.

We knew deeply in our hearts that if people didn't esteem
and value themselves, there was no way they would esteem
and value the ecology that supports their existence. We felt we
needed to go to the summit and make sure people saw that the
environmental crisis we face was related to the crisis we all are
experiencing in our hearts and souls.

Because of our passion for sharing this important message,
we got on the phone and began calling people, asking them for
their support. One of the first phone calls netted us $500. The
next call was to a lady who said we had two minutes to talk
because she was leaving for the airport instantly. We had never
met this woman before and after only a few minutes of conversation on the phone she gave us $1,000. We didn't even know
her, but she picked up on the passion we had for our vision and
she wanted to support us. She actually broke down and cried
on the phone because she couldn't believe the deep feelings we
had stirred up in her. She said she was surprised that she was
so deeply touched and that she was so happy to do this for us.

When you hold your vision and know that what you are doing is important and will serve many, it is easy to enroll others
in supporting you. Just think—$8,000 in two weeks! By the
way, most of it was from people we had never met before.

—Jackie Miller

5. They take action in the face of fear.

All the masters of the lamp act upon their inner and outer
guidance. It is not that they do not have fears like the rest of
us; they all do. What sets them apart is that they take action
in the face of their fears.

One weekend a man named Malcolm, who lived in Vancouver, took his fiancée hiking through the north woods of British Columbia.

Somehow they managed to get between a mama bear and her baby cubs. The mama bear, wanting to protect her cubs, grabbed hold of his fiancée. Malcolm is just five feet two inches tall and the bear was enormous, but he felt courageous and managed to disentangle his fiancée, whereupon the mama bear grabbed him and proceeded to crush every major bone in his body.

She finished by sinking her claws into his face and ripping straight across it, back toward the scalp.

It's amazing that Malcolm lived. He was in restorative surgery for the next eight years. By that time the doctors had done all the cosmetic surgery they could do. It hadn't helped much and he saw himself as an ugly person. He no longer wanted to expose himself to society.

So one day Malcolm went in his wheelchair to the tenth-floor roof of his rehabilitation center and was preparing to push himself over the edge when his father appeared. His father had heard an intuitive voice telling him to go see his son.

Just in time, his father appeared at the top of the stairs and said, "Malcolm, wait a second."

Recognizing his father's voice, Malcolm turned around in his wheelchair.

His father said, "Malcolm, every human being has scar tissue deep inside him somewhere. Most of us wear it under a smile, some cosmetics and nice attire. You get to wear yours on the outside. But we're all the same, son. We've all been deeply wounded in some way."

Malcolm could no longer thrust himself off that building.

A short time later a friend of his brought him some motivational tapes to listen to. On one tape he heard the story of Paul Jeffers, who lost his hearing at age forty-two and went on to become one of the most outstanding salesmen in the world. Malcolm heard it when Paul said, "Setbacks are given to ordinary people to make them extraordinary."

Malcolm said to himself, "That's me. I am extraordinary!"

Malcolm had to confront his fear of being rejected because of his physical disfigurement. He woke up every day knowing that was a possibility, but he forged ahead anyway. Malcolm decided to become an insurance salesman—a position that would expose him to rejection many times a day. He decided to make his potential handicap an asset.

He put his picture on his business cards and when he gave them to people he would say, "I'm ugly on the outside, but I'm beautiful on the inside if you just get a chance to know me."

A year later, Malcolm became the number one insurance agent in Vancouver.   —**Mark Victor Hansen**

6. They learn from their experience.

Masters of the lamp know that they don't get everything right the first time they do it—including asking for what they want. They simply learn from their experience and apply what they have learned the next time.

One of the greatest lessons I ever learned was when I was a salesperson for a video warehouse store in Fort Lauderdale, Florida. We were paid on commission—a very small commission on the hard goods, things like televisions and video cameras, and a massive commission on the soft goods —batteries, bags and other accessories—because there was a massive markup on that stuff. One day a guy came in who was in a very big hurry. He was going to go on a trip with his family, which was waiting in the car, and he needed to get a video camera, and he needed to get it quick. He just trusted me and he said, "Okay, give me whatever you think I need because I'm going to spend $1,000 on a camera. Here's the check. Give me something I can use right away."

So I picked something out for him and I showed him how to use it. I didn't make any real money off that because it was a hard good. Instead of showing him any of the other accessories, I said to myself, "The guy's in a hurry."

About three days later the same guy comes back into the store absolutely fuming. He started screaming at me as if I had just killed his first-born. He said, "I trusted you. I wrote you a check for $1,000 as soon as I walked in. You were supposed to take care of me. I went to Disney World with my family for the first time, and within twenty minutes my camera battery ran out. If you were going to take care of me, why didn't you sell me an extra battery?"

I said, "Because you were in such a hurry."

He said, "You ruined my entire vacation." I just felt like death warmed over and I learned right there and then to never, never try to mind read or tell somebody else what they need. It would have only taken two seconds to ask, "Do you need an extra battery? Do you need a tripod?" And let him make up his own mind. Not only did I lose a customer, I lost a valuable commission. Now I always ask and let the client determine if it serves them or not.   —**Harv Eker**

7. They are persistent.

Several years ago I was in New York City during Thanksgiving with my new wife. She felt sad because we weren't with our family. Normally she would be home decorating the house for Christmas, but here we were, stuck in a hotel room.

I said, "Honey, look. Why don't we decorate some lives today instead of some old trees? Let's buy some food and give it to people who are financially unable to give a Thanksgiving dinner." I continued, "Let's go somewhere we can really appreciate who we are, what we are capable of, and what we can really give. Let's go to Harlem and feed some people in need. We'll go buy enough food for six or seven families for thirty days. We've got enough. Let's just go do it!"

Because I had to do a radio interview first, I asked my partners to get us started by getting a van.

When I returned from the interview, they said, "We just can't do it. There are no vans in all of New York. The rent-a-car places are all out of vans; they're just not available."

I said, "Look, the bottom line is that if we want something, we can make it happen! All we have to do is take action. There are plenty of vans here in New York City; we just don't have one. Let's go get one."

They insisted, "We've called everywhere. There aren't any."

I said, "Look down at the street. Do you see all those vans?"

They said, "Yeah, we see them."

"Let's go get one," I said. First I tried walking out in front of vans as they were driving down the street. I learned something about New York drivers that day: They don't stop, they speed up! Then we tried waiting by the light. We'd go over and knock on the window, and the driver would roll down the window, looking at us kind of leery, and I'd say, "Hi, since today is Thanksgiving we'd like to know if you would be willing to drive us to Harlem so we can feed some people." Every time, the driver would look away quickly, furiously crank the window up, and pull away from us without saying a word.

So we got better at asking. We'd knock on the window, they'd roll it down, and we'd say, "Today is Thanksgiving. We'd like to help some underprivileged people, and we're curious if you'd be willing to drive us to an underprivileged area that we have in mind here in New York City." That seemed slightly more effective, but still, no cigar. Then we started offering people $100 to drive us. That got us even closer, but when we told them to take us to Harlem, they said no and drove off.

We ended up talking to about two dozen people. Everyone said no. My partners were ready to give up on the project, but I

said, "It's the law of averages; somebody is going to say yes."
Sure enough, the perfect van drove up. It was perfect because it
was extra big and would accommodate my four partners. We
went up, knocked on the window, and told the driver. "Could
you take us to a disadvantaged area? We'll pay you a hundred dollars."

The driver said, "You don't have to pay me. I'd be happy to
take you. In fact, I'll take you to some of the most difficult spots
in the whole city." Then he reached over on the seat and
grabbed his hat. As he put it on, I noticed that it said "Salvation
Army." The man's name was Captain John Rondon, and he was
the head of the Salvation Army in the South Bronx.

We climbed into the van in absolute ecstasy. He said, "I'll
take you places you never even thought of going. But tell me
something, why do you people want to do this?" I told him my
story and that I wanted to show gratitude for all that I had by
giving something back.

Captain Rondon took us into the South Bronx, which makes
Harlem look like Beverly Hills. When we arrived, we went into
a store where we bought lots of food and some baskets. We
packed enough food for seven families for thirty days, then
went out to start feeding people. We went to buildings where
there were half a dozen people living in one room: "squatters"
with no electricity and no heat in the dead of winter, surrounded
by rats, cockroaches, and the smell of urine. It was both an as-
tonishing realization that people lived this way, and a truly fulfilling experience to make a difference for them, even in a
small way.

You see, you can make anything happen if you commit to it
and take persistent action. Miracles like this can happen every
day—even in a city where "there are no vans."

—Anthony Robbins

PART II

RELEASING THE GENIE

◆

You don't always get what you ask for, but you never get what you don't ask for . . . unless it's contagious!
—Franklyn Broude

4

KNOWING WHAT TO WISH FOR

◆

Dream lofty dreams, and as you dream, so shall you become.
Your vision is the promise of what you shall one day be; your
ideal is the prophecy of what you shall at last unveil.
—James Allen

◆

Aladdin sighed. "I want to be able to do the things that I want like the people you showed me. I know I want to be the Prince and I know I want the riches of the kingdom. I'm ready to start. Where is the beginning, oh Genie?"

◆

"Master, first you must have absolute clarity. Clarity is true and consistent power. The things I will share with you will help you obtain clarity of vision.

"During this part of our adventure, I want you to begin to weave your own magic carpet. To weave your carpet I will give you several tasks to complete. Each task is a thread of the carpet. The more tasks that you complete well, the more threads you will add to your carpet, making it stronger and more beautiful.

"The first thread that we need is the Wishing Thread. All else follows our wishes, dreams and desires. Once we clarify our wishes, our path becomes more sure."

THE FIRST TASK.

"You must first create your wish list. I want you to sit down with paper and pen in hand. Write 'I wish for . . .' and ask for one hundred and one wishes. I will not accept ninety wishes or ninety-nine wishes. The correct and magical number is One Hundred and One."

◆

Aladdin started to scribble furiously. The only sound was the scratching of his pen across the paper. All of a sudden he stopped and wailed, "I cannot do it! I have never had permission to wish for much. A good meal, a warm bed and my dreams of grandeur. But that doesn't fill out One Hundred and One wishes!"

◆

The genie spoke with conviction. "This is the real beginning of the task. To convince your mind to expand, to give yourself permission to thoroughly explore what you really want and what you don't want is difficult for most of us. I never told you that the task would be easy . . . but you must complete this in order to progress to the next task. Begin, Aladdin. Search for your dreams and write them down!"

◆

You can't ask for what you want unless you know what it is. A lot of people don't know what they want or they want much less than they deserve. First you have to figure out what you want. Second, you have to decide that you deserve it. Third, you have to believe you can get it. And, fourth, you have to have the guts to ask for it.
—**Barbara De Angelis**

The First Task: Make a List of 101 Wishes

Just as Aladdin was asked to make a list of 101 wishes, we ask you to make a list of 101 wishes you have. Our experience is that this will take several hours, perhaps even several days to complete. If you are serious about getting more of what you want in life, stop and make your list of 101 wishes now.

When you make your list, be as specific as possible. If you

want a new car, specify which make and model. If you have a
color preference, write that down, too. If you want a better job,
specify exactly what kind of job you want. Be as specific as
you can with each wish.

John Goddard made such a list when he was fifteen years
old. His father, a successful businessman, would invite associates for dinner at their home once a week, every Friday evening. Young John Goddard was very impressed with the
conversation overheard during these dinners. His father and
their guests would eventually discuss their life's regrets—all
the things they wished they had done in their lives and never
gave themselves a chance to complete, much less begin. After
one such dinner as this, he became determined not to end up
like his father's friends when he was their age.

John went to his room and wrote down 127 things he wanted
to accomplish in his life. Now, in his sixties, John has accomplished 115 of his 127 goals. This list has provided a structure
for his entire life that has taken him to over one hundred countries, facilitated meeting many world leaders, including the
Pope, and helped him achieve many personal dreams. He has
visited the Great Wall of China, explored the Nile River, rid-
den a horse in the Rose Bowl Parade and learned to fly forty-
eight different types of airplanes.

◆

*"Done," cried Aladdin! "I never thought I could wish for
so much!" His face was shining with the glow of accomplishment, for now his mind was glowing and growing.*

◆

Before you can ask for something, you have to know what it
is that you want and you have to believe it is possible to get it.

Anything at all

I took a ten-evening course on goals and on the first night she
gave us a blank booklet and said, "Write down a goal you

have." And then she said, "Okay, write down another one." This went on for about ten minutes and we were all getting a bit bored. And then she said, "Write down another one." This went on for the entire three hours! All she did was say, "Write down a goal." "Okay, write down a goal." "Don't use the fact that you can't think of another one to not write down the next goal. Just keep writing." For three hours!

When it was all over she said, "Okay, now I want you to do a special thing. I want you to write down 'a goal,' but this one is special. On this one you can wave a magic wand, and write down anything you want. It doesn't have to obey the law. It doesn't have to obey gravity. It doesn't have to live up to any requirement of anything. Just imagine you have a magic wand."

Now remember, I had been writing down goals for three hours. Everything I could think of—money, health, relationships, travel—anything I could think of for three hours. So I said to myself, "Okay, it doesn't have to obey the law? Okay! I want to live in a whole house full of beautiful naked women." It was embarrassing, but that is what I wrote down. I didn't tell anybody this for ten years, but that's what I wrote down. I had been dredging my mind to think of anything I could for three hours, so I just made up that.

Sandra, the instructor said, "Okay, I'll meet you back here one week from today for the next class, and, by the way, that last one is the one that will get fulfilled." Everyone in the room gasped.

When we returned to class a week later, I was absolutely shocked because during that week I had met a woman, Carla, who later became my second wife. We went on a date and I went nuts over her and asked if I could stay overnight. She said, "Yes."

I stayed overnight, and in the morning, her daughters—she had two little girls—came running in bare naked and of course Carla was in bed with me naked. I said, "Oh my God, I'm in a whole house full of beautiful naked women." Except of course two of them were two and four years old! I guess I forgot to be specific enough in my request.

So I come to the class, and the instructor says, "Put up your hand if you remember the very last goal that you wrote down, that was totally outrageous and didn't obey gravity or the law or anything. Put up your hand if it has already come true in one week!" Fifty of us—one quarter of the people in the room—put our hands up.

She said, "I've done this many times. It's the last one you just wrote that always comes true. It's because I am the teacher and because I said it with total conviction. I didn't try to convince you of it, in which case you could be skeptical; I just announced it as an obvious fact." Of course none of us had believed her at the time, and yet one-quarter of the people in the room had achieved their goal.

We had goose bumps because people jumped up and said what their goals had been. They wanted their income to go up by a factor of ten. They wanted a sixty-foot yacht, and meanwhile they were just a social worker or teacher. And in the intervening week some relative they didn't know had died and they inherited a sixty-foot yacht. Our jaws dropped open for every one of them because originally Sandra had specifically said, "Make sure it doesn't obey gravity, or have any restrictions of law or anything." So we went totally wild.

Then she said something even more shocking. She said, "By the way, it happened because you all believed me." I stood up and said, "Sandra, I want to understand something. If you had said a different one, then that's the one that one-quarter of us would have had fulfilled?"

She said, "Yeah! Sometimes I say it's the third one that you wrote down." Everybody in the room opened their books to read the third one because we could just as easily have had that instead. We were sitting there totally stunned.

There were people in the room who were crying. She had told us on that second evening that there's nothing out there. There are no rules, and there's no law. It's not that we're lawless, it's rather that you create with your mind so powerfully. It's all in what you believe is possible.　　**—Raymond R.**

The only way to discover the limits of the possible is to go beyond them into the impossible.　　**—Arthur C. Clarke**

The Second Task: Clarify your vision.

The vision exercise is a good way to clarify what you want. It helps you to delve deeper into your unconscious and connect with the true desires of your heart. The key here is not to think about whether or not something is possible, but simply whether or not you want it. Once you commit to having something and use the principles and techniques outlined later in the book, your mind will figure out how to get it.

The paradox of life is that we are often not shown how we can get something until we first commit to having it.

The best way to do this exercise is to put on some relaxing music, close your eyes, do some deep breathing to get relaxed and then ask your unconscious mind, your heart or your inner child to show you in the form of ideas and images what it is you truly desire in each of the following arenas:

- Marriage and love relationships
- Family and friends
- Home, apartment or other living space
- Furnishings and other possessions
- Car and other forms of transportation
- Clothes, jewelry, etc.
- Job and career
- Money and finances
- Achievements
- Health and physical fitness
- Recreation and free time
- Personal and spiritual growth
- Things you would like to contribute to your community

When you are finished reflecting on and visualizing the ideal picture in each of these arenas of your life, open your eyes and write them down in as much detail as you can.

These are the things that you now want to go after in your life. Some will require study and preparation. Some will require concerted effort over many years. Some you will be able to get right away.

Another useful step is to go back and make a list of all of the things you can begin to ask for that would help you get each of the things on your list. Then put the names of individuals and institutions that you could ask for each of those things. Next place a date by each item that you will commit to asking by. Now you have a game plan for beginning to take positive action toward the things you want.

The Third Task: Complete the perfect day fantasy.

The best way to do this exercise is to find a comfortable place to sit or lie down, make sure you won't be interrupted, put on some pleasant music, close your eyes and relax. Then go through the following exercise from memory or have someone read you the cues, pausing for at least fifteen seconds after each one. You could also record the cues onto a cassette tape and then play it back for yourself to react to.

Close your eyes, get relaxed and let yourself create your ideal day. Start with waking up in the morning. Who would you wake up to? What would your house look like? What would you do then? Would you exercise, pray, meditate, eat a gourmet breakfast, get a massage? What does your ideal car look like? How do you get to work? Do you drive? Are you driven? Where do you work? What does the office look like? What kind of work are you doing? What kind of people do you work with? What is your salary or income on this ideal job? What do you do for lunch? Dinner? After work? Do you go to a health club? Do you play tennis? Do you go shopping? Do you meet friends or your spouse? Do you go out dancing? Do you spend quality time with your family? Fill in all of the details of your ideal day.

The Fourth Task: Complete the "I want" process.

This exercise is one of the fastest and most powerful ways to surface what you really want. You will need a partner to do this exercise. It is best that the person is someone you feel safe with and who will not judge your responses in any way. You will each get a turn to do the exercise. Make sure you have a pen or pencil and a pad of paper.

Sit facing your partner. Whoever is going to go first should close his or her eyes and take a few deep breaths to get relaxed. It is helpful to read the following words to the partner with the eyes closed to deepen the state of relaxation before you start.

"Just relax and remember a time when you were really relaxed . . . a time when you were very, very relaxed. Perhaps it was a time in nature or a time when you were lying on the beach or on a vacation somewhere. Or maybe it was when you were sitting in a hot tub or getting a massage. (Pause) Just let yourself go back to that time when you were very, very relaxed. (Pause) That's right, very good. (Pause) And from this place of relaxation, just let yourself get in touch with that part of you that knows what you truly want without any barriers of fear, guilt or limiting beliefs. And from this place deep in your heart, keeping your eyes closed, just let yourself answer this question: What do you want? (You record your partner's answer on a piece of paper.) What do you want? And so on. Continue this process for ten to fifteen minutes, then reverse the process. At the end of the exercise, review your list of answers. You will probably find that the answers that come later in the process are more truly what you want. Now make a commitment to do whatever it takes to get them.

The Fifth Task: Stretch your imagination.

Here is a set of questions that can stimulate further thinking about what it is that you want in your life. We suggest you take out a pad of paper and write down all of the answers that are stimulated by these questions.

- What would you most like to accomplish before you die?
- What things do you want to own that you currently don't own? Do you want a new car? A boat? A new stereo system? A VCR or a camcorder? New clothes? More jewelry? A mountain bike? A motorcycle? A cat or a dog? New carpeting?
- What are you dissatisfied with in your primary relationship? In your relationship with the members of your family? In your relationships at work? Do you want someone to spend more time with you? Leave you alone? Visit more often? Do you want to feel closer? Stop fighting? Improve your relationship? Feel more comfortable sharing your feelings? Get something off your chest? Ask for forgiveness? Share your dreams?
- What is broken that you need to get fixed?
- What do you need or want from your spouse? Your best

friend? Your parents? Your children? Your brothers or sisters? The people you work with? The people you go to school with? Your next-door neighbor? Your baby-sitter or housekeeper? The people in your church or synagogue? The people in your support group?

- What do you need from your doctor or dentist? Your lawyer? Your financial planner? Your accountant? Your teacher at school? Your coach? Your mentor? A consultant? A counselor, psychologist or psychiatrist? Your minister, rabbi or priest? Your mayor, congressman or senator?
- Whom do you envy and what is it that they have that you want?
- Do you need time off? A vacation? A promotion? A raise? More instruction? More appreciation? More recognition? More support? Better equipment? Someone to listen to your idea? Someone to help you solve a problem? Less backbiting? More cooperation? More understanding? Less stress? More room?
- Do you need more sleep? Better food? More time to play? To go dancing? To stop smoking? To lose weight? To get fit?
- Would you like to travel more? Go out more often? See more movies? Go to a concert? Play a sport? Throw more parties?
- Would you like to learn a foreign language? Take a course at the community college? Attend a seminar? Learn how to use the computer? Get onto the internet? Read more books? Learn how to cook? Learn to golf? Play an instrument? Learn to paint or sculpt? Write poetry? Learn to type? Take an acting class?
- Do you want to make a contribution to the world before you die? Raise money for a favorite charity? Help your kids achieve their goals? Run for office? Serve on a committee or board? Eradicate illiteracy? Stop unplanned teenage pregnancies? Solve some problem in your community? Help bring about peace in the world?

◆

"Aladdin, now that you have clarified your wants and desires, let us look at the next step in weaving your magic carpet that can take you anywhere you want to go!"

◆

5

LIGHTING THE LAMP

◆

Success isn't a result of spontaneous combustion. You must set yourself on fire.
—Arnold Glascow

◆

"Aladdin, the glow on your face illuminates your soul! You are transforming before me from a street urchin to a man of ideals. Your passion for life is beginning to show. Look once again at the lamp in your hands. The lamp cannot fulfill its purpose in life without two very important ingredients. Do you know what they are?"

◆

"Sure, one is the fuel. The other is the fire. Until both are combined there is no illumination from the lamp," explained Aladdin.

◆

"I knew I had a smart master! You, like the lamp, must have both fuel and fire to fulfill your purpose. Your ensuing tasks will help you complete this. When you learn to believe that what you want is possible, your belief will be your fuel. And when you release the passion inside of you to accomplish your dreams, then the fire inside of you will burn brightly enough to accomplish all that you desire and nothing will stand in your way."

◆

DEEPENING THE BELIEF AND RELEASING
THE PASSION

"Once you know what you want, Aladdin, you have to believe it is possible to get it or you will not have the courage to ask for it. So, you need to deepen the belief. The most powerful way to deepen the belief in your life is to see the result that you want as having already been achieved, and to consistently see yourself as having already accomplished the goal. This builds up a mental force in your mind that eventually turns into motivation which propels you into the necessary actions to achieve your dreams.

"Close your eyes, Aladdin. We are going to the palace!"

◆

Aladdin waited. Nothing happened. He waited a few minutes more and then opened his eyes. "We're not at the palace! I thought that you were taking me there!"

◆

"I thought that you were taking us both there," said the genie.

◆

"How could I do that? I'm not the genie here, you are!"

◆

"This is the beginning of the sixth task . . . learning to see what you want inside your head. When you can see with clarity and strength that that which you desire is already yours, your passion for your desires will be kindled and your belief that your desires are obtainable will be instilled. Close your eyes again, Aladdin. Do you remember in the second task, we talked about taking some deep breaths and talking to your mind? We are going to do the same thing now, and when you are ready I want you to tell me what the palace looks like, sounds like, feels like and smells like."

◆

*Aladdin closed his eyes and took three deep breaths.
"The first thing I notice is the quiet. It is always so noisy*

and dirty in the marketplace, yet the palace is quiet and clean. It smells like flowers and mint. I hear only soft music floating in the air. Everywhere I look, the walls gleam like jewels and there is so much room! The halls look like they go for miles and the columns that hold the ceiling almost touch the sky! There are soft colors on the walls and beautiful carpets on the floors. I love it here! This is where I belong. This is where I want to be!"

◆

"See yourself in the palace room, Aladdin. See yourself straighten a picture on the wall. See yourself in royal garments. See yourself being served the finest fruits by a smiling servant. Claim ownership of your dream, now! And when you do, it will become achievable."

◆

All who have accomplished great things have had a great aim, have fixed their gaze on a goal which was high, one which sometimes seemed impossible. . . . —Orison Swett Marden

The Sixth Task: Visualizing your dream.

Take time each day to visualize your desired outcomes as already having been achieved or completed. If your goal is to have your Ph.D. in psychology, visualize yourself sitting in your office with the diploma hanging on the wall. If your dream is to have a relationship with a kind and loving person, visualize yourself in a relationship with a person that is expressing those qualities. What does his or her voice sound like? What does his or her touch feel like? What do you talk about? And how does he or she listen to you?

We recommend doing this at least twice a day—when you first wake up in the morning and again in the evening before you go to bed. Make this into a daily discipline. At first you may need to put little notes on the bathroom mirror to remind yourself to do it, but after a while it will become as natural and habitual as brushing your teeth.

In New Orleans, Louisiana, a self-made oil millionaire wanted to give something back to his community. He adopted an inner city middle school that had a drop-out rate of 84 percent. That means that 84 percent of the kids from this middle school never graduated from high school. He told the students that if they stayed in school, got good grades, and had a 95 percent record of attendance, he would pay for their college education. Knowing something about lighting the lamps in children, he not only made the promise, but he created the image clearly in their minds.

The students were taken to several nearby universities, where they each spent an entire day shadowing a college student. They attended classes, went to the gym, hung out in the student union, ate in the cafeteria, and went to the library with their assigned student. By the end of the day, each student had a clear picture of what it looked like to be a student at a college or university. They could now "see" themselves being there. Before this experience, they had no picture. Without a picture, they could not imagine it.

Then, every morning for the next several years, the teachers would have the students close their eyes and imagine being a college student. This continually rekindled the flame of belief in the students. By the time these kids graduated from high school, the drop-out rate had dropped to less than 20 percent—almost a complete reversal of the earlier statistic!

In 1983, the Australian sailing team won the America's Cup for the first time. When the coach of the team was interviewed about the victory, he explained that he had read the book *Jonathan Livingston Seagull,* and it had inspired him to make a cassette tape of the Australian team beating the American team. He had recorded a narration of the winning race over the sound effects of a sailboat cutting through the water.

He then gave a copy of this tape to each member of the team and asked them to listen to it twice a day for three years. That's 2,190 times! Before they ever set sail in San Diego harbor, they had beat the American team 2,190 times. The flame of belief had been deeply instilled in each member of the team.

For the four years leading to the Olympics, Peter Vidmar, U.S. Olympic gold medalist in gymnastics, and his training partner would stay in the gym for an additional fifteen minutes of practice after everyone else had left. They would imagine that the Olympic gymnastic meet was down to the wire, and the last event, which they were about to perform, would decide the gold medal. They would visualize themselves performing a perfect 10, winning the medal and standing on the victory stand to receive their gold medals—every day for four years! The flame of belief got stronger every day. No wonder they won the gold.

Ken Ross explains how he used the same technique to help Valerie Brisco-Hooks win her second Olympic gold medal.

In July of 1982 I was sitting down with Valerie Brisco-Hooks and her coach Bobby Kersee. Bobby said to me, "I think she has the ability to make the Olympic team but she doesn't have the confidence."

So I said to Valerie, "It's July of '84 right now and you are standing on the floor of the Coliseum and one hundred thousand people are standing and cheering for you. You just won the 200-meter dash. How has your life changed?" As I spoke, I watched goose bumps begin to rise on her arms, and in that moment I looked at her and said, "The flag is going up, the national anthem is being played and your family and friends are sitting in the stands. How has your life changed?" And suddenly tears began to pour out of her eyes.

In July of '84, after Valerie won her second gold medal, ABC was interviewing her and asked her what it was like standing on the platform. And she said it was just like every other day. Because every day before she would go out there and train, she would feel the experience of the success as if she'd won.

—Ken Ross

◆

"You may open your eyes, Aladdin. You are doing well. One more thread for your magic carpet has been woven into the fabric. The next task is something for both your eyes and your hands to accomplish."

The Seventh Task: Creating your dream.

If you either don't visualize well, or simply want to accelerate this process, you can create external goal pictures for each of your desires. If you want to have that doctorate in psychology, copy a doctoral diploma and print your name on it. Frame it and put it on your wall. If you want to take a vacation in

Hawaii, go to a local travel agent and get a travel brochure on Hawaii. Cut out a picture of yourself and glue it on the picture of the sunset or the snorkeling boat. Then place the picture somewhere you will see it every day, such as the refrigerator door, the bathroom mirror or above your desk at work. Each time you see it, it will become more and more of a reality in your mind.

You can also make a dream book by cutting out pictures of all of your goals and pasting them into the pages of a notebook or a scrapbook. Make sure to go through your dream book at least once a day. The results can be nothing less than miraculous.

Delight Thyself also in the Lord, and He shall give thee the desires of thine heart.   —Psalms 37:4

When Mark and I got married, we both wanted to have children right away. I was 35 at the time and my biological clock was really ticking!

After one year of having a lot of fun, but still not having any children, we started going through the routine of testing, hormone therapy, temperature taking . . . the whole nine yards. After about six years of unsuccessful results, we did two things that I believe helped create our perfect family.

First, we decided that we would allow ourselves to be open to our children coming to us from other sources than ourselves. We agreed that adoption would be an option we could embrace.

Second, we created a dream board. Mark and I spent hours, both together and separately, going through magazines and cutting out pictures of our ideal children. We were very specific with what we wanted. We included hair and eye color, body type, styles of furniture for their rooms, family sports activities, places we would visit together, vacations, and pets. I had always wanted two little girls, so I cut out a picture of two little girls holding hands.

Three months after the completion of our dream board I received a phone call from a young lady that started with, "I hear that you and Mark are looking to adopt a baby, and I want you to be the parents of my child." I almost dropped the phone! I truly believe that our darling Elisabeth was conceived that very day that we completed our dream board!

Not only have we been blessed with one perfect and beautiful daughter, but our family was completed in 1987 with a phone call that was the addition of our second and equally perfect daughter.

Ninety-eight percent of all the things Mark and I pasted on our dream board have come true. And all of what has happened is even better than we imagined! Both of our children look like they were born to us, and people are always astounded when we tell them that our girls are adopted. Once, when Melanie was about four years old, she was in a donut shop with her Dad and me. The lady behind the counter said, "Oh, you look just like your daddy!" "No, I don't!" Melanie stoutly replied. "I don't have a bald spot on the top of *my* head!"

The concept of a dream board is a wonderful project for kids as well as adults. Clarifying dreams and desires, and then using the dream board as a tool to re-inspire us daily is a very powerful use of our imaginations.　　　　　**—Patty Hansen**

When people think of buying a house, most will first think of the criteria they desire, then they work with a real estate agent until they find what they want. This is the traditional way it's done. Well, we aren't traditional.

During the early 1990s, we were busy building our business and weren't in the market to buy a home. But, my wife, Tere, had said for two years as she weekly perused the Sunday Homes for Sale section of newspaper for enjoyment, "I know we will have more house and amenities than we think possible, and it will be an incredibly smooth and easy process. It will seem unreal, but will actually be an amazing miracle. I have this strong feeling about this."

As we developed our yearly Goal Book for 1993 on New Year's Day, we decided to include our dream home that year. Being students and practitioners of positive thinking and clear goal-setting, we approached our house hunt creatively. After all, our goal-setting strategies had proven effective repeatedly, with the most important instance being that we had met each other after we each had listed and asked for specific qualities in a partner and relationship!

Both of us had ideas of our house preferences for years. We discussed, negotiated, and listed these criteria, then we decided on the area. We were very specific and clear that we wanted a: 2,000+ square foot two-story 4 bedroom, 2-½ bath stucco home with vaulted ceilings, white and open space, fireplace, carpet and ceramic tile, lots of windows, ceiling fans, nice low-maintenance landscaping, pool and spa, two-car garage, with pleasant neighbors, easy access to thoroughfares, and close to the beach in a nice area of Huntington Beach, California.

Next, we added this list: a map, and a colorful collage of pictures that represented our desires to our Goal Book. We developed an affirmation statement, each created a visual picture, set the accomplishment date for 5:00 p.m. on July 31, 1993, then closed the book for the day. We had asked, now we were ready to take action and receive.

We reviewed our Goal Book often, and I joined Tere as she continued her Sunday Homes for Sale ritual. Initially, I decided to cover our bases and work with a realtor. We went through three . . . and still no dream home. Some came close, but we knew none we had seen were "it" and we weren't going to settle for anything else. Tere kept saying, "We'll know it when we see it, like when we met, we knew."

After five months, some excitement and some exasperation, we re-evaluated what we were doing. We had a very busy summer schedule planned with trainings and producing an audio cassette album. I told Tere, "I'm done. Let's have them find us. Let's place an ad in the paper HOUSE WANTED, EXCELLENT CREDIT, etc. It's out there, and it can find us."

We received four phone calls responding to our ad. The first call was "it"! As we walked in to view the home, our hearts pounded a little faster. Tere had a sparkle in her eyes. The house was 2,000 square feet, beautiful, and had absolutely everything we had asked for except the ceiling fans. The front yard was gorgeous, and the back was all concrete with a stucco and tile fence around the crystal blue pool and spa. Our first thoughts were, "This is way out of our range. We won't be able to swing this one." It seemed more like a house that would be our second or third, not our first. Then we considered possibilities. After all, the law of attraction was at work; we had asked and here it was.

We negotiated some then left to think about it because we still felt a little stretched. The seller called us the next day, saying she believed the house was supposed to be ours and offered to substantially decrease the price, to actually below the market value, which gave us that much more equity. We came to an agreement, and closed escrow in four days! The date was July 9, 1993 at 5:00 p.m. Our dream home was ours! Talk about easy! It did seem unreal.

Today, we still live in and enjoy our miracle dream home that we clearly asked for, and yes, we've installed the ceiling fans. We respect the awesome power of setting clear, specific goals, and we know that the thoughts we think draw things to us. We're still clear and careful about what we ask for, because we know it will probably come to pass!

—**Bob and Tere Harris**

Love is a canvas furnished by Nature and embroidered by imagination.
            —Voltaire

◆

"You have completed all seven tasks set before you. You have now made a wish list, clarified your vision, fantasized a perfect day, figured out what you want, and you have stretched your imagination. You lit your own lamp with belief and passion by visualizing your dreams and creating a dream book. With the completion of your tasks you have completed the magic carpet that will take you from where you are to where you say you want to go. Wrap yourself in the carpet, Aladdin, and wish whatever you may!"

◆

Aladdin wrapped himself in the carpet and visualized himself in splendid new clothes of the finest silk. He could smell the newness of the fabric. And when he unwrapped himself from the carpet, the memory of his experience was like a caress that lingered.

"This is how it is meant to be for me; I was born to be such as this! To wear the finest silks and to enjoy the riches of the kingdom is my pleasure. This will be mine and I know it to be true with each passing moment. . . ," Aladdin exclaimed.

◆

"And I too know it will be true for you. Your voice is strong with the ring of authority. However, there is one last obstacle you must overcome before the kingdom may be yours. And this will be the hardest of all."

◆

6

CONQUERING THE LABYRINTH OF FEAR

◆

Do the thing you fear and the death of fear is certain.
—Ralph Waldo Emerson

First you jump off the cliff and you build your wings on the way down.
—Ray Bradbury

◆

"We are now at the beginning of the greatest obstacle that most people ever face . . . the Labyrinth of Fear. You will enter on this side of the Labyrinth, think with your head and follow your heart through the maze, and exit on the other side. You are allowed to take your magic carpet with you, and the lamp for illumination."

◆

"You are coming with me, are you not, my Genie?"

◆

"I will meet you on the other side. Your own fears must be over-come by you and you alone. No one can help you for no one knows your fears as well as you. However, inside the maze you come upon certain gates. Each of these gates is there to help you. When you enter a gate, you will be told of the process that must take place in order to pass through that particular gate. Once you have success-fully gone through all of the gates, the way out of the maze will become instantly clear to you.

"Another thing, Aladdin. Remember that most fear is self-cre-ated. Most of us live under the illusion that things outside of us are causing our fear. When you are exploring the Labyrinth of Fear, and you come into contact with something that creates within you the experience of fear, you will believe the fear is real, but it is not. You may feel many sensations—rapid pulse, dizziness, sweaty palms, shaking, shortness of breath or muscular tightening. But remember, while the experience of the fear will be very real to you, the source of the fear is in your own mind.

"Another thing. I have a gift to give you before you enter the Labyrinth."

Around Aladdin's neck there appeared a chain with links of gold, and attached to the chain was a medallion. Aladdin looked down at the beautiful object around his neck, and saw an inscription on one side. It read F E A R. He turned it over, and on the other side he read

> Fantasized
> Experiences
> Appearing
> Real

◆

"This is beautiful, Genie. Thank you!"

◆

"It is more than beautiful, Aladdin. It holds an eternal truth. Whenever you become afraid in the maze, look at your medallion and you will be reminded of the truth—all fear is created by fantasized experiences appearing real. It will give you the courage to go on. Remember to stay in the present or to use your power of imagination to create only positive pictures, which will motivate you to be bold and clear in your search. All it takes is awareness and intention, both of which you have. Remember, Aladdin, you are in charge!

"The entrance to the Labyrinth of Fear is in front of you, Aladdin! Go now, and conquer all that stands in your way!"

◆

Aladdin entered the maze, and as soon as he made the decision to turn to the right, he came upon the First Gate.

◆

THE FIRST GATE:
REALIZE THAT YOU CREATE ALL YOUR FEARS

We have met the enemy . . . and they is us.

—Pogo (Walt Kelly)

Complete the awareness process.

Make a list of completions for the following sentence:

When it comes to asking for what I want, I'm afraid to _____.

For example, such a list might include, "I'm afraid to _____:

- ask my mother to stop criticizing me as a parent and trust me.
- ask my boss for a raise.
- ask Janet out for a date.
- ask my grandmother to help pay for my college education.
- ask my husband to spend more time with me and the kids.
- ask someone to critique my writing.
- ask my wife for more frequent sex.
- ask my boss for a day off.
- ask the doctor to change my medication.
- ask my dad for a loan.
- ask my neighbor to help me with the electrical work.

The next step is to go back over each item and change the structure of the sentence to:

I would really like to _____ and I scare myself by imagining _____.

Notice that the key words here are **I scare myself by imagining.** Here are some examples:

- I would really like to ask my mother to stop criticizing me as a parent and trust me, and I scare myself by imagining that if I do, she will stop coming over to visit.
- I would really like to ask my boss for a raise, and I scare

myself by imagining that if I do, he'll get angry with me and take it out on me in some way.

- I'd really like to ask Janet out for a date, and I scare myself by imagining that she would say no.
- I'd really like to ask my grandmother to help pay for my college tuition, and I scare myself by imagining that my dad would get mad at me and yell at me.
- I'd really like to ask my husband to spend more time with me and the kids, and I scare myself by imagining that he would fly into a rage or withdraw even further.
- I'd really like to ask someone to critique my writing, and I scare myself by imagining they'd tell me I have no talent and that I am wasting my time.
- I'd really like to ask my wife for more frequent sex, and I scare myself by imagining that she will criticize me for never being home and not being very romantic and it will end up in a fight.
- I'd really like to ask my boss for a day off, and I scare myself by imagining that if I did, he would rant and rave about how I am not committed enough to the job and he might even use it against me in some way later.

Once you complete the exercise, you will see more clearly and specifically how *you* scare yourself. It is me making up all of these negative scenarios that have not really happened. The sad thing is that my body cannot tell the difference between a real event and a vividly imagined event, so I will actually feel scared—in some cases, even petrified. And yet it is all my doing. It is all me scaring myself by making up these horrible outcomes.

So what to do? There are three solutions.

1. Come back to the present.

The first solution is to simply stop fantasizing negative futures. Come back to what is actually happening in the present. Nothing all that terrifying. Concentrate on your breathing. Notice the sights and sounds around you. Get out of your head, and get back into reality. Come back to your true senses (sight, touch, sound, taste and smell).

Take a moment to articulate what you see, hear and feel. For example: I am aware of seeing the leaves of the tree outside my window fluttering in the breeze. I am aware of hearing my son's voice in the other room. I am aware of the sensation of feeling my back against the back of the chair. I am aware of hearing the sound of my own breathing.

This will bring you back into present time faster than any other method. Take a few seconds and do this now and notice how you start to become more centered and relaxed. Taking a few deep breaths before you begin will also enhance your state of relaxation.

2. When in doubt, check it out.

A second solution is to check out your fantasies. Ask the other person how they would feel about being asked for those things. Share with them your worst fantasy and ask them if it is true. Here are a couple of examples based on the situations described above.

"Mom, when you come over to my house and criticize the way I am raising Jessica and Christopher, I feel belittled and I get angry at you. I have been thinking about discussing this with you, and I have been scaring myself by imagining that if I bring this up, you will feel criticized and get angry with me, and you'll choose to stop visiting us anymore, and I would be hurt and miss you if you did that. Do you think that is really how you would react, or am I out in left field on this one?"

"Boss, I would like to discuss asking you for a raise, but I have been scaring myself by imagining that if I did, you would get angry with me for asking. I realize I don't know how you feel about employees asking you for a raise, and I'm also not sure how you would like such a raise request to be submitted. I also realize that I am not sure what your criteria for granting a raise are. What would I have to do to merit a raise? Can we talk about this?"

"Dad, I was thinking about asking Grandma for some money for college, and I was imagining that if I did that, it might upset you in some way. Would it?"

3. Imagine the desired outcome.

The third option is to use the power of your imagination to picture the outcome that you want. For example, actually close your eyes and imagine asking your mother to no longer criticize how you raise your children. Imagine her responding, "I'm sorry, I had no idea you were feeling criticized. I was just trying to offer my help. Perhaps there was a better way I could have done it that wouldn't have made you feel like you were doing it wrong. Next time, I'll just ask if you are interested in any feedback or suggestions. Would that be better?"

Now you may not get that exact response when you ask, but it doesn't matter. You will have visualized the positive outcome you want, and that will give you the necessary psychological boost to actually go ahead and ask your mother to be more sensitive in her feedback. Even if she is a little defensive at first, she will have heard the message that you wanted her to get. You can also add to your visualization that if she does get defensive, you will tell her that you still love her and you still want her to come around. You just want her to be more sensitive to this area of the relationship. You can even instruct her on how to give you suggestions so that they don't feel like judgmental put-downs. You can even rehearse in your head how you would like to react to any objection or upset she might have. This actually lays down a blueprint in your nervous system that assists you to act that way later in the actual situation.

◆

Completing the process of Gate Number One was exhilarating for Aladdin. He actually felt better than when he entered! He walked slowly on through the maze feeling confident in himself. He saw a bridge, and as he began to pass over it, the bridge started to shake and roll beneath his feet.

"Who goes there, on my bridge?," said a voice that sounded as if it had been made from splinters of glass.

"It is only I, Aladdin, who wishes to cross."

A beast slowly rose from the mist below and slithered across the other end of the bridge. It was the ugliest thing that Aladdin had ever seen and the disgusting smell that came from it wrinkled Aladdin's nose. Then the thing opened its mouth to show rows and rows of razor-sharp teeth.

"If you dare to come any closer, I will scratch you and rip you into small pieces. I promise you, it will be extremely painful, as I will shred your body a little at a time. And then I will devour you."

"I don't believe in you. You are nothing to me," said Aladdin. He started toward the monster.

The monster reached forward with a slashing motion and ripped Aladdin's coat sleeve from his body, leaving a bloody gash on his arm.

"This is real," Aladdin screamed. "This is not my imagination. I am hurt, I am bleeding!" He scrambled back to safety on the other side of the bridge. He looked at his arm, and as he did, he noticed his medallion. Grabbing it in his hand, he advanced once more toward the beast. The monster backed away from the bright and shiny object in Aladdin's hand. Aladdin moved more surely across the bridge and reached the other side safely.

He had overcome the Fear of Physical Harm. Aladdin entered Gate Number Two.

◆

THE SECOND GATE: ANALYZE YOUR FEARS

Most fears can not withstand the test of careful scrutiny and analysis. When we expose our fears to the light of thoughtful examination they usually just evaporate.

Ask yourself, What is the worst thing that could happen?

When you find yourself afraid to ask or afraid to take action, stop and take a deep breath. Then rationally ask yourself,

"What is the worst thing that could happen? Is it really that bad? Can I survive it?" If you think you can, and what you want is important, then go for it!

One day it suddenly dawned on me. I was standing in the hall outside the door of someone I wanted to get an appointment with. I was having trouble getting in to see him. The secretary had just told me that the person was busy and that I could not go in. I figured that she was just doing her job of protecting her boss from time wasters. I, however, didn't feel that what I had to offer was really a waste of time. I knew that my service had the potential of saving this man a lot of time and money over the years.

I also knew that if I simply opened the door and went in anyway, the worst that could happen is that the man would throw me out of his office and I would be back in the hall. I figured I was *already* in the hall, so it couldn't get any worse than it already was.

So, I opened the door and walked right in. And, you know what? I got the account. The buyer said, "I figure anyone that is that determined to get an order will probably be that determined to meet our needs."

—Successful salesman who asked to remain anonymous

Super salesman Murray Slaughter makes another cold call.

Could you survive it?

Albert Ellis asked me, "What's the worst thing that could possibly happen and could you survive that?" When fear starts to overcome me, I think, "What's the worst thing that could happen?" Usually, it's no big deal! By this time next week I won't even remember it.   —Thea Alexander

"What's the worst thing that can happen?" That's always been my thing when I'm trying to go for something. What's the worst thing that can happen? And, if it will not kill me, it's not the worst thing. I have no qualms about calling Oprah or anyone else. I just call and ask. My attitude is "If they say no, that's fine. It's not going to kill me!"   —Judith Briles

Realize you haven't really lost anything.

Remember that the rejection is really an illusion. Consider this: If I ask Janet to go to dinner with me and she says no, I didn't have anyone to eat dinner with before I asked her, and I don't have anyone to eat dinner with after I asked her. I didn't really lose anything. I didn't have it before and I don't have it now. There was no real loss. It didn't get worse. It stayed the same.

If I apply to Harvard and I don't get in, I wasn't in Harvard before I applied, and I am not in after I applied. It didn't get worse. It stayed the same. Since I am already handling that—not having dinner with Janet or not being a student at Harvard—what's the big deal? I know I can cope with that reality because that already is my current reality and I am just fine.

What I point out to people is that it's silly to be afraid that you're not going to get what you want if you ask. Because you are already not getting what you want. They always laugh about that because they realize it's so true. Without asking you already have failed, you already have nothing. What are you afraid of? You're afraid of getting what you already have! It's ridiculous! Who cares if you don't get it when you ask for it, because, before you ask for it, you don't have it anyway. So there's really nothing to be afraid of.   —Marcia Martin

What's the best thing that could happen?

The next step is to ask yourself, "If I ask for this thing, what is the best that could happen?" Wow! Think about it! You could actually get what you ask for—perhaps even more.

Take time to really think about and examine the best possible outcome you could get. The boss could say yes. Your mother could agree to stop criticizing you. Your dad could say, "I'd be delighted if your grandmother loaned you the money for your college tuition." Your wife might say, "I've wanted to create more intimacy, romance and sex in our relationship too. Let's work on it together."

What's most likely to happen?

Finally, ask yourself, "Based on everything I now know, what is most likely to happen?" You will find that if you take yourself through this type of analysis—in most circumstances—what is most likely to happen is not such a big, hairy deal. In fact, it will usually turn out to be pretty good. Armed with this new awareness, you can simply go ahead and ask.

Complete second awareness process.

One of the best ways to break through the layers of denial and lack of awareness around asking for what you want was developed by psychologist Nathaniel Branden. He developed the technique of rapidly and repeatedly providing endings for incomplete sentences. The process is a simple one, but oh, so powerful! Make sure you actually take the time to do these. It will literally transform your asking.

Set aside about fifteen minutes every day for a month. Sit down with a notebook and a pen, or at your typewriter or computer, and, as rapidly as you can and without stopping to think about what you are writing, write down five to ten endings for each of the incomplete sentences that appear below:

- If someone had told me my needs and wants were important . . .
- If I were willing to ask for what I want . . .
- When I ignore my deepest desires . . .
- If I were 5 percent more assertive in stating my desires . . .

- If I deny and disown my needs and wants . . .
- If I am willing to listen to my deepest yearnings and desires . . .
- If I were more accepting of my needs and wants . . .
- If I were willing to act on my preferences . . .
- If I believed I could really have what I want . . .
- One of the things I need to ask for is . . .

Remember to write as quickly as possible, without stopping to think about what you are writing and without evaluating the answers in any way.

At the end of each week, reread all that you have written during the week and then write five to ten endings for this sentence:

- If any of what I have been writing is true, it might be helpful if I . . .

According to Dr. Branden, doing these sentence completion exercises stimulates the unconscious integration of new ideas. It helps brings our fears out into the open where they can be examined and challenged . . . and it helps us tap into new levels of awareness, knowledge and readiness to action that we may not have previously realized we possessed.[6]

◆

Upon the exit of Gate Number Two, he was in a dark and spooky forest. Huge trees bent over him, pulling at him as he walked on. No light from a moon lit this night, so Aladdin took out his lamp and held it aloft to guide his way. All of a sudden, it seemed as if a hand snuffed out the light in his lamp, and he was totally alone in the dark.

"This is the Fear of Abandonment. I don't want to be left, alone in the dark. I am truly afraid. Please, Genie, do not let me suffer!" There was no answer from the genie. Aladdin decided he felt better just hearing himself talk out loud. So he started to sing a tune he had learned as a small child from the washerwomen in the marketplace. When the song ended, he began again. That is when he

heard a creaking in the trees, and the path opened to reveal . . .

◆

THE THIRD GATE: USE POSITIVE SELF-TALK

"Oh, Little Blue Engine," cried the dolls and toys. "Will you pull us over the mountain? Our engine has broken down and the good boys and girls on the other side won't have any toys to play with or good food to eat, unless you help us. Please, please, help us, Little Blue Engine."

"I'm not very big," said the Little Blue Engine. "They use me only for switching trains in the yard. I have never been over the mountain." . . .

Puff, puff, chug, chug, went the Little Blue Engine. "I think I can—I think I can—I think I can—I think I can—I think I can—I think I can—I think I can—I think I can."

—*The Little Engine That Could*
by Watty Piper

One of the most effective techniques for motivating ourselves is positive self-talk. We think almost fifty thousand thoughts a day. Many of those thoughts are about ourselves and many of those are negative. "I'll never get what I want. What was I thinking? Who do I think I am? Who am I kidding? They'll just say no. What's the point of trying. I never get what I want. They'll just reject me again. This is too hard. I'm not good enough. I don't know what I am doing. I don't know why I am bothering. Nobody ever gives me what I want. He's never going to say yes. If I ask, he may get mad at me and fire me. He may think I'm being greedy. If I'm too pushy, I could lose the sale here. If I ask her, it might ruin the mood." And so on.

These thoughts stop us from making the requests and taking the actions we need to take to achieve our goals and fulfill our dreams. We need to replace this negative self-talk with positive self-talk.

Use the law of replacement.

There is a law in psychology that says you cannot get rid of one thing without replacing it with something else. Since nature abhors a vacuum, if we just try to eliminate the negative without replacing it with the positive, the vacuum created will eventually suck the negative back in. If we are not careful and conscious, we sometimes end up just replacing one negative with another negative. A good example is that when people stop smoking, they often start to gain weight. The reason? They have replaced smoking with eating. There are better solutions like replacing smoking with deep breathing, stretching, getting a hug, expressing our feelings and sharing our needs and desires.

Similarly, in dealing with our negative and limiting self-talk, we must replace the old fear-based and self-deprecating statements with positive, affirming and self-empowering statements. For example, "They'll never listen to me" is replaced with "I can learn to capture their attention and hold their interest." "I'll never get what I want" is replaced with "I am joyfully and skillfully creating what I want in my life with the support and aid of others." "What's the point of trying?" becomes "With each attempt I make, I am getting closer and closer to my objective."

A powerful technique is to make a list of all the negative self-talk you have around the issue of asking. Write out a positive counter to each statement. Write each statement on a separate three-by-five card. Carry these cards in your coat pocket or purse and read them several times a day. If you read them out loud, that is even better. Take advantage of times like sitting in the doctor's office, waiting for an appointment, waiting for your lunch to arrive, before you go to bed at night and again when you first wake up in the morning. The constant repetition of these statements will slowly begin to crowd out and replace the negative thoughts and beliefs.

Another use of this technique is to create an affirmation card for each of the things that you want to ask for. If you need to ask for financial support for school, write the following statement on a three-by-five card and add it to your pile of cards to repeat daily. "I am joyfully asking for and receiving a full scholarship to Ohio State University." Other possibilities include "I am enjoying country line dancing with my husband every Friday night." "I am comfortably asking for and happily receiving a raise of $200 per month." "I am enjoying my extra week of summer vacation at our cabin in Vermont."

This is a useful technique in becoming an effective and successful asker. You must align your thoughts with your intended outcomes and the performance of the necessary actions that will produce the result you are seeking. Your mind is a creative tool that you direct by the exercise of your will. Simply put, you are responsible for monitoring and choosing your thoughts so that they support the manifestation of the results you desire in your life.

Realize that everybody else is afraid too.

It is very liberating when you realize that everyone else is walking around just about as afraid as you are. Knowing that everyone else is afraid gives us an edge. Knowing that most people want the same things that we want—safety, acceptance, inclusion, recognition, and an opportunity to express themselves—gives us the edge because we can stop waiting for them to give it to us and we can give it to them. Once we do this, we get out of our fear and into service. The natural benefit of that is these same people then want to give back to us.

It all changed when I realized I'm not the only one on the planet who's scared. Everyone else is, too. I started asking people "Are you scared, too?" "You bet your sweet life I am." "Aha, so that's the way it is for you, too." We were all in the same boat. That's probably what is so effective at our workshops. When I ask, "Who else feels like this?" the whole room of hands goes up. People realize they are not the only one who feels that way.

—Stan Dale

Somebody in one of the trainings said, "I'm really afraid to approach attractive women." The trainer asked, "How many men are afraid to go up to attractive women?" They all raised their hands. He said, "The secret is that everyone's afraid to go up to attractive women, but some people do it anyway." I thought, "Whoa!" It was one of those profound sort of moments. I started realizing that, whatever I felt, the only way I was going to get what I wanted was to go and ask them out anyway.

—**Michael Hesse**

The thing I point out to my students is that they may think that they are the only person in life that's afraid of everyone else. Looking out of their eyes they think, "Oh, that person over there is so strong, they are so confident, they have all the answers, they've got everything and I mean nothing to them." We all have our internal fears and self-doubts and we think everyone else doesn't have any. We think everyone else is just perfect. Then I point out that everybody else is just as afraid.

In a large group I ask, "Which of you is sure that the other people in the group are totally confident?" They all raise their hands because everybody is always sure that the other people are totally confident. Then I ask, "Well, which of you is the confident one?" Nobody raises their hand. So then I point out that everybody is scared to death. That kind of levels the playing field. Once we realize everybody is at the same level—we are all scared to death—that gives us a little bit more courage to go for it and make some requests.

—**Marcia Martin**

◆

As Aladdin exited Gate Number Three, there was a small path to his left.

Aladdin followed the path, which meandered back and forth inside the maze. As he walked, he felt as if someone were watching him. And it wasn't someone kind. He felt as if his every movement were being studied and judged. And then he heard a snicker. Followed by another, and then full laughter roared from behind him. Aladdin spun around, and yet saw no one. From behind him again, more laughter, and then from the other side, more laughter again with comments . . .

"Just look at him, who does he think he is?"
"A foolish street child, who is nothing!"
"A dirty little imp!"
"He is so ugly, he looks as if he wet himself!"
"Stupid worthless Aladdin!"

Laughter bounced from every wall. Aladdin put his hands over his ears and shouted, "You will not stop me! I am not afraid of you trying to shame me . . . this is the Fear of Humiliation, and the Fear of Feeling Foolish. I will not be afraid!"

As he ran down the path and turned a corner, he faced the Fourth Gate.

◆

THE FOURTH GATE:
FEEL THE FEAR AND DO IT ANYWAY!

Fear only sticks around if you hang on to it. It's very interesting. I think of fear as a very boring, very ungracious guest, who will stick around only as long as I entertain him. The best thing to do with fear, is to let it go. If you laugh at your fears, then they just disappear. The only way I've ever been able to get rid of fear is to laugh it away.

I realized that two things can't occupy the same space at the same time, and, if I take the space that fear previously occupied and fill it with positive intention and specific goal-oriented action, the fear can no longer occupy that space.

I realized that there are two paths you can take in life. One is seeing life as a series of problems, fears, and failures. The other is seeing life as experiences, opportunities, and adventures. It is exactly the same life. It's just that the perspective is different. You can either walk path A or path B. The choice is always yours.

—Thea Alexander

Just do it!

If something is to happen, you need to ask. Many business people and employees—all types of people, in fact—shortchange themselves by failing to ask for what they need.

You gain strength, courage and confidence by every experience in which you really stop to look fear in the face. You are able to say to yourself, "I have lived through this horror. I can take the next thing that comes along." You must do the thing you think you cannot do.   —Eleanor Roosevelt

It doesn't matter what you are thinking or what fear you have, if you just do it. Action is the only thing that matters. Whenever I put myself in a position where I have taken action, even though I've been afraid, I always feel extra good.

What allows me to move forward so that I don't let the fear stop me is seeing the result so clearly that I'm really hooked on having it. Then all of my considerations mean nothing. It's just acting. Taking the action is all that counts.

I can see that at the end of my life, I'm going to look back and say, "Gosh, I wish I had taken more action."

—Diana von Welanetz Wentworth

Action conquers fear.   —Peter N. Zarlenga

How to confront your fear of looking foolish

Feel the fear and do it anyway.   —Susan Jeffers

I did some work with a therapist named Steve Heller. In addition to doing work in the office, we had to do real world exercises. One of them, which seemed kind of dumb at the time, was to walk down a big street and stop somebody and ask them where that street was. If I were on Wilshire Boulevard, I would stop a complete stranger and ask, "Can you tell me where Wilshire Boulevard is?" The two things that I experienced were:

(1) In spite of feeling like a complete idiot for asking that question, people didn't treat me like I was stupid. In fact, people usually smiled and were friendly. They were very nice and seemed happy to be asked. They'd say, "You're right on it" and I'd say "Uh, thank you." I'd go on and that would be it. It wasn't like anything terrible happened by asking a "dumb question."

(2) I discovered people actually enjoy being asked if they know the answer. I guess it reaffirms their intelligence and usefulness.

You could do the same thing in front of a 7–Eleven store. "Can you tell me where a 7–Eleven is?" They would say, "There's one right there." Then I'd simply say, "Oh, that's right, thank you."

The purpose was to overcome your fear of being foolish or looking foolish asking a question, and it worked for me.

—Michael Hesse

◆

When Aladdin had completed the fourth process, the gate opened and he passed through into what seemed to be a huge room. As Aladdin walked from one end of the room to the other, it became darker and colder inside the room, and the wall on the other side of the room seemed to retreat before him, instead of getting closer. Aladdin became very frightened. He didn't know what was happening, but the room was changing before his very eyes and he felt out of control. Completely powerless, he sank to the floor. This was the Fear of Change, the Fear of Feeling Powerless. He started to sweat, and then he heard: "What is the worst thing that can happen to you?"

And before him on the facing wall, was the Fifth Gate.

◆

THE FIFTH GATE:
BUILD UP TO THE BIG STUFF SLOWLY

The trick to building up your asking muscle is to start out slowly with little steps. Celebrate your little victories. They are the stepping-stones to the bigger conquests. Each day do a little more asking. Build up your strength step by step. Each day ask for something a little bigger. Ask someone a little bit harder. Keep stretching into bigger and bigger challenges. You learn to be a better asker by practicing asking. Practice all of the principles and techniques you will learn in Part III. Practice with your children. Practice with your spouse. Practice with your parents, friends and colleagues at work. Practice, practice, practice.

Start out slow with safe people.

Self-confidence is the result of a successfully survived risk.
          —Jack Gibb

I would want to start with people around me that were safe and loving that I could practice with—people with whom I could say, "I'm just learning how to ask and I need to practice and have you support me and give me feedback on how I could improve my asking so that I can get better at it." You need to surround yourself with individuals or join an organization where you can be vulnerable and be yourself without having anybody put you down. **—Helice Bridges**

Do the thing you fear to do and keep on doing it . . . that is the quickest and surest way ever yet discovered to conquer fear.
—Dale Carnegie

Remind yourself why you are asking.

In order to overcome your fear, it is useful to remind yourself why you are asking. What is the bigger purpose? What will be accomplished if you ask for and get what you want? Will you be able to send your kids to college? Will you be able to feed your family? Will you be able to retire in comfort and security? Will you be able to feed the homeless in your community? Will you be able to graduate and get a better paying job?

Once you connect with the higher purpose, it often makes your fears seem petty in comparison to the good you will accomplish by asking.

Ask yourself these two questions:

1. How will getting this benefit me?
2. How will getting this benefit the others that I care about (my family, friends, team, school, church, company, community, state, country, etc.)?

Conquer the fear of change—a little at a time.

If you don't like the outcomes you are currently producing, start changing your thoughts, images and behaviors today a little at a time. You can't keep doing the same things you're doing and expect your life to change. As the popular saying goes,

If you keep on doing what you've always done,
you'll keep on getting what you've always got.

Another way of putting this is that if your current actions were enough to produce more of what you want, more would have already shown up. Probably the most potent expression of this principle is the twelve step programs' definition of insanity:

Insanity is continuing the same behavior and expecting a different result!

There are only three ways that you can improve the quality of your life:

1. Find out what is working and do more of it.
2. Find out what is not working and stop it.
3. Try out new things and see which ones work and which ones don't. Incorporate the ones that do into your behavior.

Why people resist change and growth

If all of the ideas and behaviors discussed in this book are so good for us, why do so few people really ever change? Why do we resist the very things that would make us free? Well, the answer is that we are creatures of habit. We get used to being a certain way, even if it doesn't work very well. Try a little experiment.

You will need to put this book down in such a way that you have your hands free and can still read the book. Fold your hands in your lap. Notice which thumb you have on top—left of right? Refold your hands so that the other thumb naturally ends up on top. This involves moving every finger in the previously lower hand up a notch. Notice how that feels. Does it feel awkward, uncomfortable, strange, weird or "wrong"?

Notice what your body wants to do. Does it want to go back

to the first position, your "normal" position, your habitual condition? Let yourself do that. Go back to the original position. How does that feel? Does it feel better, right or comfortable again? Is it a relief to be back to this position?

In that little exercise is contained the basic reason why most people never experience the quality of life they secretly yearn for. They would rather be comfortable than uncomfortable. They would rather be comfortable than do what is required to produce the desired result. They get stuck in what psychologists call their "comfort zone."[7]

Comfort zones are plush lined coffins. When you stay in your plush lined coffins, you die.   —Stan Dale

Growth and development requires some discomfort. As one young ski enthusiast once told us, "If you want to get good at skiing, you've got to get comfortable being uncomfortable."

Many of the things that are required to build and maintain high self-esteem may sometimes be uncomfortable. Saying no, asserting your rights and needs, asking for what you want, expressing your true feelings, saying positive things about yourself, letting someone nurture you, with a hug or a massage—these may all be things that are uncomfortable at first. So what! Do it anyway! One of the ways to get through the discomfort is simply to do the thing you are uncomfortable doing.

Winners are those people who make a habit of doing the things losers are uncomfortable doing.   —Ed Foreman

Do you remember when you first learned to ride a bicycle or drive a car? More than likely you were uncomfortable. You had to go through the awkward stage. When each of our five children was learning to walk, he or she went through the awkward stage. They wobbled, they were unsteady, and they fell down a lot, but they were also determined to have more mobility and greater mastery of their body. Now they run so fast you can't catch them.

We all have to go through the awkward stage of any newly acquired behavior. And, if you missed the awkward stage as a child, you have to go through it now. Many of us remember how uncomfortable we felt during our first public speech, first dance, first date, first job interview, first musical performance, first confrontation of an authority figure, first sexual experience or the first time we took a stand against the crowd. Many of us have handled those and gone on to other firsts—first day on a new job, first child, first start-up of a company, first client, first bank loan, first mortgage, first radio interview, first TV talk show and so on.

Many of us still need to handle some of those earlier firsts that we avoided due to fear, lack of encouragement and support or low self-esteem. And the process never ends, does it? There will be more firsts that we will encounter in which we will feel awkward for a while, until we get the hang of it. The first death of a loved one, the first friend we know who gets cancer or AIDS, the first unwanted pregnancy, the first time we have a major illness or accident, the first divorce, the first signs of aging, the first time you have to write a will, the first lawsuit, the first time a child has a brush with the law or doesn't get into the college of his or her choice and so on. Life is a series of new experiences. They can be seen as unwanted pains or as potential adventures. It is all up to you.

Give yourself permission to be awkward.

Anything you want to learn, you are going to be awkward at it at first. Give yourself permission to be a beginner, a learner. New territory is where we experience our greatest sense of aliveness if we don't numb ourselves out to it.

I was afraid to go bowling unless I already knew how to do it. Because I was a good athlete in some areas (football, basketball, volleyball, rugby and track), I felt I had to appear to be good in all sports. I was so afraid to look like a klutz! It literally ran me. As a result I missed out on a lot of fun and growthful experiences. I finally realized that I had to give myself permission to be a learner—a beginner again like I was in the fifth grade.

I remember the first time I fell off the ski lift at the top of the mountain in Sun Valley and a four year old went by me with all the style and mastery of an Olympic skier. I had to remind myself that this was my first day of lessons and he had probably been skiing for over a year. I had the right to be awkward.

I also had the right to seek out and get good instruction. Over the years I've noticed some people engage in sports and never improve. They don't seek out coaching. We all need to be willing to utilize coaches and mentors. Every time I take a skiing or tennis lesson, I get better. I'm always amazed at how much I improve, especially if I practice in between.   —Jack Canfield

Give yourself permission to be a learner.

No matter what you want to learn, you are going to be awkward at it at first. This is true of dancing, driving a car, bowling, giving a speech or asking for what you want. You may be uncomfortable and awkward as you first learn how, but starting small will give you the confidence to go for the bigger thing. Whether it is the first time you ask someone out for a date, the first time you apply for a bank loan or the first time you ask your boss for a raise, you will probably do it awkwardly. That is okay!

Give yourself permission to go through the awkward stage. It is a required step in the journey toward mastery. You must be willing to go through it if you are to become more proficient at getting what you want. See each experience of asking for what you want as just that—an experience to learn from and get better at.

Each time you ask for something, you will get a little bit better at it. Your subconscious mind is constantly monitoring what you do and the response it elicits from the other person.

♦

When he came out of Gate Number Five, Aladdin felt a little cold. As he walked, he felt colder and colder, colder

than he had ever felt before. There had been nights in his life when he had gone without shelter or bedding but never a time when his body and mind felt as if they were slowly freezing as they were now. As he continued, he saw icicles hanging from the ceiling of the cave and he felt his bones shake. "When people are rejected by all who see or know them, this must be what happens to their hearts. This must be the Fear of Rejection!" And when he named the fear, the floor beneath him opened, and he saw the Sixth Gate.

◆

THE SIXTH GATE:
RE-FRAME THE MEANING OF REJECTION

You must remember that there are two domains in the mind. One is fact and the other is meaning. Human beings seem driven by the need to make up a meaning for every fact and every event—including rejection. The truth is that all facts are just facts and all events are meaningless. You are the one who makes up the meaning, and once you make the fact or event mean something, it becomes an unexamined box that can limit and disempower you.

Once you make up a meaning, you have to produce new facts or experiences in life that validate that meaning or else you go insane. So if you are rejected as a kid, you decide it means you are inadequate. The truth is that you are not really inadequate, but once you believe you are inadequate, you will gather more data to prove to yourself that you are, which, in turn, will further deepen this belief.

When you are rejected, you usually make up the meaning that there is something wrong with you that makes you unworthy of acceptance. You make up the meanings that you are inadequate, unlovable and a failure, and that the world is not a safe place, and that other people are self-centered and uncaring. Rejection does not mean any of these things—unless, of course, you decide that it does.

If you decide a neutral event means something negative about yourself, you can just as easily undecide it and redecide it. The choice is always there. It is simply up to you to exercise that choice. If you can make up one meaning, you can make up another. In both cases it is you making it up. So, why not make up a meaning that empowers you to ask for and create what you want in your life rather than one that cripples and paralyzes you? Again, the choice is always yours.

Remember, a no doesn't mean anything about you.

Most people think that rejection means they are a bad person, a failure, no good, inadequate, worthless, etc. It doesn't mean that at all. In fact, "It don't mean nothin!"

Fact: I didn't get everything I wanted from my parents.

Meaning: (which I made up) I am inadequate and unworthy of receiving. (After all, I reason, if I were lovable, my parents would have given me everything I needed and wanted. If I had been worthy of receiving, I would have got it. And since I didn't get it, it must mean that I am unworthy.)

Behavior: I sit back and do not participate. I do not ask for what I want. I do not get what I want. I settle for less than I desire and am capable of having.

Don't take no personally

Remember, you are just an extra in everyone else's play.

—Stewart Emery

One of the early students in my model and talent school was a woman who was probably five or ten years older than I. At the end of her course, she went on her first interview. After learning that she had not been hired for the job, she resigned from the Agency.

"Why would you quit after one interview?" I asked.

Her answer was "I looked as good as I possibly could, I performed the best I could, and I still did not get the job. I cannot suffer this kind of rejection—I give up!"

In vain, I explained that she could look and do her best, and still not get the job perhaps because she was not the "look" the client was seeking. Perhaps she was the wrong age, her eyes were the wrong color, or maybe she resembled the interviewer's aunt (that she hated). Her rejection could have come from many different things that had nothing to do with her preparation or performance.

I reflected that the same experience had occurred during my first week of professional modeling. At the initial interview I was told that I was "too all American," yet at the next I learned I was "too exotic." The following found me "too short" and another "just too tall" for the job in question. It seemed that each interview was a contradiction of a prior one. The woman, not having been prepared to deal with repeated rejection could not be dissuaded.

From then on, we taught our students to thrive on rejection in advance. We encouraged them to look on it as a challenge to expect and overcome. The models and talent learned that rejection can be an opportunity to grow and an incentive to never, never give up.   **—Betty Mazzetti Hatch**

In every negative event is the seed of an equal of greater benefit.   **—Napoleon Hill**

FRANK & ERNEST

My first book, *State of the Art Selling*, was turned down by twenty-six publishers before one finally bought it. Talk about rejection. Now I know why so many talented writers don't get their work published. When they're constantly exposed to that type of rejection, their confidence and their perseverance get worn down. Sure, after the first rejection I was disturbed, but not devastated. Five or six rejections later, however, I was starting to get very concerned.

Then I called my agent and asked what the problem was. He said that there were just so many other books out there on sales, publishers were hesitant to take on another one. But I knew I had a fresh approach and important ideas to add to an admittedly crowded field. So after the next rejection, I called the publisher and asked what I could do to improve my chances. What was missing from my book? What did it need to make it stand out and invite acceptance?

I followed the next rejection with a similar phone call, and the next and the next. Suggested changes were made. Now I was looking forward to each rejection. Without even knowing it, these publishers were helping me write my book!

The valuable lesson I learned was not to equate rejection with failure. When the twenty-seventh publisher bought my book, he was not getting a manuscript that had failed twenty-six times. He was getting a manuscript that had benefited from the advice of twenty-six talented, knowledgeable professionals. Rejection is just one person's opinion. You cannot take it personally, or it will destroy your confidence and keep you from moving on.

—Barry J. Farber,
Author, *Diamond in the Rough*

You can never learn less, you can only learn more.
—R. Buckminster Fuller

◆

"*The seventh and final gate awaits me if I can only find it. I feel so lost and so tired, I can barely drag myself forward. If I could only sleep for a while, I could do it. If I don't find the gate, I will fail. I have come so far; to fail now is more than I can bear.*" *Aladdin felt as if he were going to cry . . . but a man doesn't cry . . . and he was almost a man. His body felt as if there were no strength left in any muscle and all he wanted to do was sleep. He lay down, and gazed up to the sky, as if the answer could be found in the great expanse above. And then he saw the impossible thing of beauty. The Seventh Gate was in the clouds above. With joy in his heart, he climbed upon his magic carpet and was flown to the opening of the Seventh Gate.*

◆

THE SEVENTH GATE:
REMEMBER—IT'S A NUMBERS GAME!

You have to kiss a lot of frogs to find a prince.
> —**Phrase embroidered on a silk cushion on Princess
> Diana's bed**

First, let's be clear about what we mean by "success in asking."
Babe Ruth struck out 1,330 times. But we remember him as "The
Sultan of Swat" because he hit 714 home runs. So it is with me.
Each time I ask somebody to make a contribution to our work,
and I strike out, I get closer to the home run I will eventually
score by continuing to step up to the plate.
> —**Rick Gelinas,
> President, Delphi Foundation,
> who has raised millions of dollars to support his
> organization.**

When I was doing real estate on the side, I realized that it's
definitely a numbers game. I watched these tapes where they
said you have to go out and constantly get yourself in front of
people. And that's exactly what I did. There were a thousand
homes and I continuously canvassed those homes. I gave them
flyers, I showed up on their doorstep, and I gave them pumpkins
at Halloween. Pretty soon, they remembered me. I just constantly got myself out of in front of them.   **—Tim Piering**

Thanks for the twenty-five dollars!

I brought to my first selling job a belief that was bound to get
me into trouble: everybody should always love me. Obviously
there are two things wrong with that belief; "everybody" and
"always." And as I started selling, I began to get immediate
and powerful feedback relative to my belief. At the time, it
amazed me to what extent people would go to avoid an insurance salesman. They would see me coming down the hall and
they would turn and walk the other way. That hurt. My ego
really beat me up.

My selling day would go like this: I would try to sell John, he
wouldn't buy. I'd put him on my back and go see Ellen. She
wouldn't buy, and so on. By the time I got to Bill, I had all these
people, courtesy of my ego, on my back. Obviously, the meeting
with Bill wasn't a success. I seemed locked into that pattern.

So I made a decision. I decided to quit. No loss to the insurance industry, but admitting failure seemed pretty traumatic to me.

Fortunately, right when I needed it, a friend of mine gave me Victor Frankl's *Man's Search for Meaning*. That book opened my eyes to the power of beliefs. It helped me examine my own beliefs about myself and my work. A very lucky learning experience. And I made a couple of simple but powerful belief changes. I made the conscious decision to believe that no one sale would determine who I was or who I would become.

Then I went a step further. At that time, I had to see about twenty prospects to make one life insurance sale. The average commission from that sale was $500. Five hundred dollars divided by twenty calls is $25 per call.

This is how I changed the belief game. I would call on Mary, and she wouldn't buy. Instead of putting her on my back, I'd mentally say, "Thanks for the twenty-five dollars." I would do the same thing with the next eighteen prospects. Each time they said no, I'd mentally respond, "Well, thanks for the twenty-five dollars." When I got to the twentieth prospect, and he bought, again I would say, "Thanks for the twenty-five dollars."

What happened was that fairly soon the twenty prospects became ten and the $500 commission became $1,000. At that point I could hardly wait to go out and say, "Thanks for the twenty-five dollars."

I didn't really change the way I was selling. I simply decided to change my beliefs. I stopped believing that when a prospect said no it was an indication of failure. And then I listened to that more rational, empowered part of myself that kept reminding me that my self-worth was never on the line in a selling situation. This became a daily ritual. I kept repeating to myself, "I cannot fail, my self-worth is not on the line."

What I was doing was controlling my self-talk, challenging the voice of my ego and choosing more appropriate beliefs. That made all the difference.[8]
                                                          —Larry Wilson

The "25 bean technique" of W. Clement Stone

Practice, practice, practice until you eventually get numb on rejection.
                                                          —Brian Klemmer

W. Clement Stone, the founder of Combined Insurance and one of the motivational geniuses of our century, was one of the masters at teaching salespeople how to get over their fears of asking. He knew that they would probably quit after ten sales calls if they didn't have a technique to keep them going until they got a yes. So what he did was to give them twenty-five navy beans, which he instructed them to put into their left pants pocket. Every time they made a sales call, they were to move one of the beans from the left pocket to their right pocket. They were not to quit for the day until they had moved all twenty-five beans to their right pocket.

Because they were required to keep going until all twenty-five beans were transferred from one pocket to the other, the salesmen didn't quit. By the end of the day, they invariably made a sale, which motivated them to keep on going. They became able to handle the rejection because they learned they would eventually get a yes.

This simple but powerful technique helped thousands of salespeople—many without a high school diploma—get over their fear of rejection and build lucrative careers in sales. Think of how you could apply this same principle to your life.

The magic formula of all successful askers:

SWSWSWSW!
Some Will, Some Won't, So What! . . . and . . .
Someone's Waiting!

What that means to you is that you may have to ask a lot of people a lot of times to finally get what you want. Some people will say yes and some will say no. So what! Keep right on asking. You may hear a lot of no's, but it often only takes one yes to make all the rest of your efforts worthwhile. And remember, someone out there is waiting for you to ask them. You simply have to ask enough people in order to find them.

Remember, you've got to ask, ask, ask! . . . So, go for it— starting today—right now!

I found my wife through Great Expectations, the video dating service.

First of all I had to write a statement. I took that statement and showed it to everybody I knew. I asked for feedback on how to improve it and make it more interesting. When I had to take the pictures, most people took the photographer they had over at Great Expectations, but I went to this Hollywood photographer who did head shots for actors and actresses. He shot three rolls of film until we got one really good picture, and then he touched it up, took out the wrinkles and made me look younger. I'm not a homely person, but it really helped to have a good picture.

Then for the video I went in with a friend because I figured instead of just talking to some stranger who was interviewing me, I would have somebody I could talk to and feel more comfortable with. I got myself into a situation where I could ask lots and lots of women out, but I also tried to package myself well to give myself the best chance to get a yes.

At first the calling up and asking out was a little uncomfortable, but I decided it was a numbers game and I went out with probably two or three women a week just to get experience. The more I practiced, the more comfortable I got with the whole process. I think I went out with about forty people before I met Marianne, who became my wife.	—Michael Hesse

Don't wait for the perfect moment.

If you wait until the wind and the weather are just right, you will never plant anything and never harvest anything.
			—Ecclesiastes 11:4

You miss 100% of the shots you never take.   —Wayne Gretzky

Don't wait. The time will never be just right.   —Napoleon Hill

Do the Evening Review Exercise

A powerful tool for the acceleration of behavioral change is the Evening Review Exercise. It is very simple to do and will produce very profound results. Every evening find a few quiet minutes by yourself. You can do this in bed if that is the only time you can find. Take a few minutes and relax yourself by taking a few deep breaths. Then ask yourself the questions listed below and notice what you become aware of. Your answers may come in the form of an image or they may come as words. Either way is fine.

- What did I want that I did not ask for today?
- Who could have helped me today if I had asked?
- Where could I have asked for what I wanted and got it today?
- How could I have asked more effectively?

Once you receive an answer, create a new image of yourself actually asking for what you wanted. Visualize yourself asking for it more effectively. See yourself doing it the way you would have liked to have done it had you not been so shy, frightened, prideful or defensive. You will be surprised how readily both the circumstances and the "corrections" will come to you.

What this daily activity does for you is heighten your awareness—which is the first step to all behavioral change. It also programs your unconscious to act more assertively and effectively in the future. Make this a daily ritual until you see your behavior changing.

Oh, what the heck, go for it anyway!

A helpful technique for taking action in the face of fear is to utilize the following phrase sung as a little chant.

"O-o-o-o-o-o-o-o-o-o-o-o-h what the heck, G-o-o-o-o-o-o-o-o-o-o-o-o-o for it anyway!"

Whenever you are afraid, close your eyes, take a deep breath, and (out loud if possible) repeat this little chant. Sing it several times. Sing it like a Gregorian Chant. It is amazingly powerful.[9]

Two weeks after taking your seminar, I was in the bank making a deposit. On the way out the door it occurred to me that I should ask the bank to contribute money to the school I run. As I headed back into the bank and up the stairs to where the executive offices were, all my nagging doubts and fears began to surface.

"You don't have an appointment. You're not dressed professionally enough. They probably have a formal application process for their grants to schools. You don't even have a brochure
on the school with you."

Listening to all of this in my head, I turned around and
started walking back down the stairs to leave. As I reached the
bottom stair, I heard a voice in my head singing, "O-o-o-o-o-h
what the heck, g-o-o-o-o-o-o for it anyway!" I laughed to myself
and said, "What the heck, go for it!" So, I turned around, went
back up the stairs, and after a ten minute wait, got in to see the
president. I presented the case for our school and asked for a
$10,000 donation.

He said, "Normally, we would ask you to fill out an application, but your passion for what you're doing is so strong and
your commitment is so obvious, that I can give you a check for
$2,000 today, and if you call me back next week, I'll talk to the
board of directors and see if I can't get you the other $8,000."

A week later I received a check for $8,000. I am so glad I
didn't walk out of the bank without asking!   —Elaine Stevens

Getting unstuck

We asked Rick Gelinas, one of the most effective askers we
know, "How do you overcome your fear of asking?" His response is an interesting one:

You don't. There are days, many of them, when the fear of
being rejected absolutely paralyzes me. I sit and stare at the
damn phone as though it were a ticking bomb. I can do nothing.
Usually that doesn't last more than a day. But that fear *can*
sometimes go on for *many* days. Once about five years ago, it
went on for *weeks*, and I became completely inactive and sodden with hopelessness. Depression set in and I spent endless
days and nights watching television mindlessly. Finally, when
I began to doubt my sanity and the depression had started to
affect my breathing and the other systemic functions of my
body, I began to think I might actually die from depression and
inactivity. Soon I became so frightened of dying that this fear
drove me back to work. I had decided that I either had to get
back to work, get back to asking, or die. The fear of dying had
become greater than the fear of asking. I guess sometimes it
has to come to that.

Like I said, it only got that bad once. Usually, I enjoy working
ten or twelve hours a day, seven days a week. But there are

milder mini versions of that depression occurring from time to time, and these are just expressions of the fear of rejection. I tell myself people aren't rejecting me when they decline my invitation to "make an *investment* (read *donation*) in our children." I know that to be true, but hearing the big "NO" too many times in a row does get wearisome. As I climbed out of my severe depression that time years ago, I tacked a little scrap of paper on the wall above my telephone. On it I addressed a brief message to myself to ward off depression when my fear of rejection lasts too long:

> Rico,
>
> The next time you get severely depressed, remember that you always feel better the moment you start working again.
>
> Love,
> Rick
>
> —**Rick Gelinas**

Remember, most people want to give.

Basically most people want to give. They almost encourage you to ask. —**Brad Winch**

If you can't speak, write a letter.

Sophie Androyovna, I cannot go on in this way. For the last three weeks I have been saying to myself: "I shall tell her today," and yet I keep on going away feeling the same mixture of sadness, regret, fear as well as happiness in my heart. Every night I go over the day and curse myself for not having spoken to you, and wonder what words I would have used if I *had* spoken. I am taking this letter with me, so that I can hand it to you if my courage fails me yet again.

—**Leo Tolstoy, in a letter to his future wife**

Focus on the other person's needs.

We all fear rejection. As I listen to my speech introduction, I mentally fill the auditorium with klieg lights of love by concentrating on the needs of my audience, not myself. Care about them with your whole heart. And when you speak one-on-one, tell of the benefits for THEM, visualize them using it, enjoying it, loving it. They will see the bright picture you project in the theater of their mind, and gladly do what you ask.

—**Dottie Walters, International Speaker**

◆

As soon as Aladdin completed the process of Gate Number Seven, he felt the very slightest of breezes across his cheek. Turning, he saw a beautiful butterfly with wings of amber and burnished gold that alit on his shoulder. In a voice like that of musical chimes, the butterfly said, "You must follow me, Aladdin, for I will lead you from the maze. You have successfully conquered all the fears presented to you and finished all the processes through the gates. Your life, like the path before you, will unfold in splendor. You have blessed yourself with your own endeavors." Aladdin looked down and saw that he had become clothed in the very set of silks that he had imagined earlier.

"Is this real now, and mine to keep?"

◆

"This is only the beginning, Aladdin. All that you wish for can now be yours."

◆

With that, the butterfly lifted herself and floated ahead of Aladdin leading the way past glorious flowers and melodious brooks that tumbled sweetly over rocks of sparkling gems. Everywhere he looked, the trees, the flowers, the path, the brook—all seemed to be washed in shimmering and glistening golds and silvers. Entranced, Aladdin stepped through the outlet of the Labyrinth of Fear.

"Where are you, Genie?" Come to me at once . . . I have so much to share with you!"

◆

"What do you wish, Master?"

◆

Aladdin started, the voice of the genie so close to his ears, it seemed to fill and echo inside his head.

"Oh, Genie, I had the most incredible adventure, and met the scariest monster! This butterfly . . ." Aladdin turned to see that the butterfly had disappeared.

"Where did she go?"

◆

"The butterfly, like all that you experienced inside the Labyrinth of Fear, was of your own making. She was there to show you that you can create and uncreate all that you believe is real, both negative and positive."

◆

"What is next, Genie? I have my new clothes . . . my magic carpet, my lamp, my wish list, dream book, and I know what I want."

◆

"It is now time for you to make your very first wish . . . the one that will form the outcome of all the wishes that will follow. This is your direction, your path, it will hold the treasure that will be yours. What is your greatest desire, Aladdin?"

◆

Aladdin opened his mouth and then quickly shut it. This was not a question that could be easily answered. There was so much that he wanted! With the vision process he had learned to visualize, he had created sharp focus and clarity of his desires. He had learned to believe that what he chose could be obtained as long as he used the tools and techniques the genie had taught him. He knew that he would continue to have fears come into his experience, but now he knew that each fear did not need to be a stumbling block to what he wanted. He could create passage by overcoming his fears and he knew how to do that. Aladdin closed his eyes and took a deep breath.

◆

"Are you all right, Master? Do you have a problem?"

◆

"I'm fine, Genie." Aladdin opened his eyes. "I needed to become quiet so I would know what is most important to me right now. There is so much, and I feel like I can have it all! I just wanted to make sure that I know where I want to start."

◆

"During your travels through this adventure, you have gained much wisdom, my son. Had I asked you the same question before our adventure began, I think you might have asked for a good meal and that would have been it!" the Genie chuckled. "You now know that asking the right question of the right person at the right time is the key to the kingdom. I shall name it 'The Aladdin Factor.'"

◆

"Thank you, Genie. I have so much to thank you for, I don't really know where to begin."

◆

"*This is an important principle, Aladdin. Asking for what you want and receiving that which you have asked for is only part of the Aladdin Factor. The third part is gratitude. When you are grateful to the people in your life, the circumstances surrounding your achievements and the world at large, it completes the circle. You then live in a state of blessed reality.*"

◆

"*That is why I have decided to ask for what I am now going to ask you for. My question is,*
   "*What is your fondest wish, oh my Genie?*"

◆

A profound silence ensued. Then a sigh from the genie. "I wish only for one thing. I wish for my freedom. If you would give me my freedom, I would be the happiest genie in the world."

◆

With the blink of an eye, Aladdin said, "I grant you your freedom."
   The air hung heavy with the silence that followed the granting of the genie's wish. Aladdin's eyes filled with tears. Had the genie felt so little for him that with his freedom, he had disappeared? With all that they had gone through together, and all that the genie meant to him—mentor, teacher and friend—Aladdin had hoped that the genie would stay . . . even if he were free.
   "*Oh, Genie . . . my friend, my teacher, I must now go forward on my path without you. I know I will miss you . . . I prayed you would stay with me. Genie . . . where are you now?*"

◆

"*Here, Aladdin. I am here.*"

◆

"*Where?*" *Aladdin spun around and looked behind him,*

looked to the right . . . . looked to the left. "Where are you? Where are you?"

◆

"Here, Aladdin. Look again. Look into the deepest part of your heart, into your innermost being. For I am here within you, your teacher and your friend. You will never be alone, for I am with you always. I am here inside of you . . . Where I have always been."

◆

PART III

How to Ask, Who to Ask and What to Ask For

◆

You've got to ask! Asking is, in my opinion, the world's most powerful—and neglected—secret to success and happiness.
—Percy Ross

HOW TO ASK

◆

I was thinking to myself, "If the world were just perfect and you didn't have to ask for anything, if people were just sensitive to all of our needs, that would be much easier."
—Jeff Aubery

Don't wish it were easier, wish you were better.
—Jim Rohn

◆

1. ASK AS IF YOU EXPECT TO GET IT

Expect your every need to be met.
Expect the answer to every problem,
expect abundance on every level . . .   —Eileen Caddy

The first and most important principle in asking for and getting what you want is the "ground of being" from which you ask. By ground of being we mean your state of thinking in regard to your level of certainty about getting what you are asking for. If your expectation is that you will get what you are asking for, it will affect everything else—your body posture, your eye contact, your tone of voice and your choice of words.

In order to create a positive ground of being, ask your self the following questions. "How would I be if I knew for sure I was going to get what I wanted? What would I be saying? How would my body feel, stand and move? What kind of language would I be using? How would my voice sound if I absolutely knew for certain I was going to have what I wanted?"

Once you get in touch with that, then come from that place and make your request or ask your question. Otherwise you are putting yourself in a state of thinking "I'm not going to get what I want." If you are anticipating rejection, then you will be manifesting that on the outside. So it is important to start with a state of "I already have what I'm asking for. It's already mine. I've already gotten a yes. It's a done deal."

We find what we expect to find, and we receive what we ask for.
                                                        —Elbert Hubbard

Ask with a positive expectation.

We tend to get what we expect.   —Norman Vincent Peale

I was in San Francisco at a major hotel and I realized I didn't have any cash with me. As I considered cashing a check at the front desk, I realized I had two problems. The first was that I was not a registered guest in the hotel, and I knew that represented a problem because hotels don't cash checks unless you're a guest of the hotel. The second problem was that I didn't have my driver's license with me. It was in the process of being sent through the mail and I hadn't received it yet, so I really didn't have the form of identification that is generally needed in order to cash a check. I had these two big strikes going against me.

I imagined the normal thing of me walking up to the desk and saying something like, "Gee, do you think you could cash a check for me? I'm not a guest at the hotel and I haven't got my driver's license, but I would really appreciate it if you could cash it." Of course that situation always produces "No, of course we can't cash that check. You don't have your driver's license and you're not staying here." So I knew that I needed to be in a different place to have something different happen.

I created the image in my mind of what I would be saying and how my body would be walking and how the tone of my voice would sound and what the words of my request would be if I absolutely knew they were going to cash my check. I vividly imagined all that in my head and got myself totally into that place of certainty. Then I just came from that place and did what I had seen in my mind.

I walked up to the reception desk as if everything were great. As I was talking to the person at the desk, I put my hand into my purse and took out my checkbook at the same time. I knew that in a situation where I knew I was going to get a check cashed, I wouldn't bother to wait to take out my checkbook. I would be taking my checkbook out the same time as asking. As I did that, I looked directly at the person at the desk, and instead of asking "Can you cash a check?" I said, "What's the most amount of money that I can cash a check for?" As I put my checkbook down on the counter in front of him, I took a pen out and started to write the hotel's name on the check. He was so with me at this point that he didn't even ask if I was a guest of the hotel. I guess he just assumed I was from my manner.

He said, "A hundred dollars."

I looked at him, smiled a big smile and said, "Great! That will work perfectly." That's what I knew I would say and how I would say it if I were going to get a check cashed. I wrote down $100.00 and handed him the check.

He said, "We need to have a driver's license."

I said, "Great, no problem." I reached into my purse and pulled out an ID card which obviously wasn't a driver's license. I gave it to him and said, "Here, this will work." I just handed it to him and didn't say anything. I didn't try to explain it. I was just giving him something coming from the ground of being that this will work.

He looked at the card and said, "We need a driver's license."

I said, "Okay, fine. No problem." I didn't resist what he was saying at all; I totally accepted it and said, "No problem." Then I just reaffirmed what I had stated before, coming from the same place I had come from before. I said, "Well, use that, it's like a driver's license. It will work the same way as a driver's license. That will work." I simply handed it to him again.

He took it again and it was funny. He looked at it like he was trying to see a driver's license. He looked at it and one more time made a weak attempt. "Well, I really need a driver's license."

I just smiled at him and said, "Well, use that. It will work."

He got a big smile on his face; he looked at it and then he looked at my check, back and forth, and I could see that he was really trying to see a driver's license, and I guess eventually he saw one because he looked up and said, "Okay," and handed me one hundred dollars.
　　　　　　　　　　　　　　　　　　　　—Marcia Martin,
　　　　　　　　　　　　　Executive Trainer, Seminar Leader

See it the way you want it to be.

We usually get what we anticipate.　　　　　　　**—Claude M. Bristol**

Here is another example of the power of a positive ground of being.

One of the great thrills of my life was working with Andy Banachowski at UCLA. Andy's the greatest women's volleyball coach of all time and has won six NCAA championships. Andy said, "You know, your program is really great. The U.S. women's volleyball team could really use this, but the coach is Israeli and he is very arrogant. He will never listen to this. But I'll tell you what. Go over and see Chuck Erbe at USC."

So I went over to see Chuck Erbe at USC and he said, "This is a great program. We really need this here. And you know what? You should go see Arie Selinger, but he's Israeli and very arrogant. He'll never listen to you.

And then I began to think, "Wait a minute. Something's not right in this picture. It suddenly dawned on me that I was doing the opposite of everything I teach. I needed to create a picture of Arie Selinger excitedly waiting for my call and being totally available to meet with me. So I put myself in the right state by imagining Arie Selinger desperately needing me, waiting expectantly by the phone for my call. Then it would be easy to call. After all, he's waiting for my call.

In my mind I have Arie Selinger sitting by the phone. He's sitting there with his hands praying, "Ken, please call. I'm waiting for you. I really need your help to get our team right."

So I picked up the phone and called. I said, "This is Ken Ross, can I speak to Arie Selinger, please?"

The voice came back, "Who's calling, please?"

"This is Ken Ross. I was referred to you by Chuck Erbe at USC and Andy Banachowski at UCLA. They both thought you'd be very interested in the program I'm doing with them."

All of a sudden I hear this real thick Israeli accent come on the line and I told him what I was doing. The voice says, "We're using Denis Waitley. Are you familiar with Denis Waitley?

"Oh, yes," I replied. "I'm very familiar with Denis Waitley. He's got great programs, but if you don't take the time to see what I'm doing, you're not going to know what the best program is."

He said, "What's three o'clock look like for you tomorrow?"

I got off the phone and I must have gone four feet in the air because I realized that's all I wanted to do. I wanted to get in front of him and I had accomplished that. So I got in front of him and showed him the program I had put together. Afterwards, I didn't hear anything for a week. I figured I had given it my best shot and they just weren't interested. Then I got a call and he said, "We unanimously decided we want your program!"

—Ken Ross

Life . . . tends to respond to our outlook, to shape itself to meet our expectations.

—Richard M. DeVos

Ask with conviction.

One morning a young woman applied for registration at my modeling school, whose first impression was very unattractive. She was tall, thin, and clean, but that is about all you could say about her physical beauty. Her complexion, hair, posture, and clothes were all problematic. Trying to be honest and kind, I suggested she go across the street and enroll in a business course. I encouraged her to learn the skills to get a regular job, and suggested she might return thereafter and consider modeling. Her eyes looked directly into mine as she responded firmly, "Mrs. Mazetti, if you will let me take your course, I will be the best black model you ever have." She knew what she wanted, was confident of what she could do, and was determined to do it. I signed her up immediately. After completing her training, correcting her skin problems, redoing her hair, and perfecting her posture and walk, this new model began accepting professional assignments. She modeled with such grace and style that people who watched her at restaurant fashion shows put down their forks to admire her. This unforgettable woman in fact became the best black model I ever had.   **—Betty Mazzetti Hatch**

When I called Zig Ziglar's office to request an interview with him, for my book *America's Greatest Speakers*, their first response was "No, he is too busy."

I said, "Can you imagine a book called *America's Greatest Speakers* out on the market and Zig's not in it? I can't even fathom that; can you please tell him I called? I'll get back to you." It was that kind of positive attitude—the fact that I wouldn't take no for an answer, the conviction that he had to be in there—that finally got me a yes.   **—Michael Jeffreys**

There was another asking exercise that my therapist had me do. I was to go into an ethnic restaurant and seriously ask for absolutely the wrong kind of food. So I'd go into a Mexican restaurant and ask for fettuccine Alfredo, or I'd go into an Italian restaurant and say, "I'd like a beef burrito with cheese."

One experience I had was really strange. Because I asked

with confidence, rather than the waitress saying, "That's a stupid question," she completely bought into my reality. I was in
an Italian restaurant and I asked for a burrito. The waitress said,
"I don't know. Let me check." She actually went back to the
kitchen to see if they had burritos. Then she came back and
apologized because she didn't have any. Because I asked with
confidence, she completely bought into the reality of my request. Even though it was an absurd request, it suddenly became her reality too.   —**Michael Hesse**

Imagine the person you are asking is desperately looking to
give someone what you want. For example, pretend they have
just returned from a medical clinic where they have been told
they will die of a physical heart attack if they don't open their
emotional heart and be of service to someone else. They are
sitting there thinking, "How can I possibly be of service to
someone? What can I possibly do?"

That's when you arrive and say, "I have to move all of my
furniture out of my apartment this weekend, and I need someone to lend me a van and to help me with the moving. Would
you be willing to help me out on Saturday?" Imagine they are
waiting for the request and will celebrate you as the solution
to their problem. "Thank you for asking!" they'll say. "I was
looking for a way to be of service."

When we were interviewing all the people for this book, the
response we heard over and over again was "Thank you for
giving me the opportunity to explore the arena of asking questions and making requests with you. I learned a lot from the
interview!" Now think of it for a moment. We make all the
money. We get all the glory, and yet they are thrilled to be part
of the process of creating the book.

Assume you can.

Too often we assume that we can't afford it, can't get a discount, can't get a scholarship, can't return it without a sales
slip, can't bring the children, can't leave the children, can't
have pets, can't get a raise, can't have support, can't hire a
temp for the day, can't get a table by the window, can't get a

better room, can't get tickets at this late date or can't find a place to stay when there is a convention in town.

A friend of ours who is a professional speaker arrived at a hotel where he was supposed to speak at a convention the next morning, only to find that his room had been given away to someone else. They offered him a room in a hotel that was about twenty minutes away, and he said, "No, I have been traveling all day and I am too tired to go any further. Besides I have a confirmation for sleeping space in your hotel, and I intend to sleep here tonight. Since you say there are no rooms left, I will sleep on the couch in the lobby. And I feel it is only fair to inform you that I sleep in the nude, and I have no intention of changing my habits tonight." With that he began to loosen his tie.

The dismayed clerk said, "Wait a minute. Let me see what else I can do." There actually was a room that someone had checked out of earlier that had not yet been made up. With the help of a security guard, they prepared the room for our friend, which he was happily sleeping in less than twenty minutes later.

Start with the assumption that you can get what you want.

2. ASK SOMEONE WHO CAN GIVE IT TO YOU!

Don't ask a naked man to give you the shirt off his back.

Before you ask someone for something, make an assessment of whether or not they will be able to give it to you. If you're looking for people to invest money in your project, ask them if they are in a position to make an investment before you spend an hour sharing your business plan with them.

If you are asking someone to listen to your problem and help you solve it, make sure they have the emotional maturity and the ability to help you.

If you are asking someone to love you unconditionally, make sure they have the capacity to do that before you demand the impossible of them. Otherwise, you may end up wasting many years of your life pushing someone to give you what they are unable to give.

It would be stupid to ask the receptionist at a major corporation to make a hundred-thousand-dollar buying decision. It would be equally futile to ask your three-year-old to always remember to pick up after herself. It may also be just as futile to ask your parents to love you and accept you just the way you are.

In our workshops we will sometimes illustrate this principle by having someone stand up and yell the following sentence at the wall: "I want you to become a car!" After a few minutes they get that they can yell at the wall all day long, and it is never going to become a car. There is nothing they can do to make that wall into a car. It is always going to be a wall.

Sometimes it is the same way with people. They are simply not going to change and give you what you want. It simply isn't in them to do it. They have no desire to do it. They are not skilled enough to do it, or they are too wounded to do it. Now you come up against some tough choices. You may need to leave the company, team, unit or relationship in order to get what you want. That is not always an easy thing to admit. It may require taking some very uncomfortable actions and risks. But it is better than continuing to hope for something that is impossible to get from the person you've been asking for it.

There is a big difference between being unreasonable and unrealistic. For instance, it is not unreasonable to want your husband to understand your feelings, but if your husband is an engineer who has never ventured into his right hemisphere or emotions in his entire life, it is just unrealistic, meaning it is unlikely.

It's not that your feelings are not worth being understood. It's just that he doesn't have the capacity. He's strong in some other area. So part of what you need to do is to direct those needs to the people and the places that can satisfy them, as opposed to just expecting one person or one situation to take care of every need.   —**Mark Goulston**

Realize that some people aren't capable of delivering.

It is important to know who is capable of giving you what you want and who is not, and to not expect it from a source that can't supply it. Just because you want it or just because you're asking, doesn't mean he or she is capable of giving it to you.

If you ask your husband for something over and over and he does not give it to you or doesn't do it, you have to stop and consider the fact that he simply doesn't want to. If he doesn't have it in him or if he has no interest in growing in this particular way, that is his prerogative. He's not withholding it because he's trying to hurt you. He just can't do it.

Ask yourself, "Is this person capable of giving me what I want? Have I seen any evidence in their life that he or she is capable of it? Or am I just in love with the potential that is there?" I may want my partner to be open and romantic, but I see no evidence in his life that he is ever that way with anyone. If he's never been that way and shows no interest in being that way, why am I expecting him to be that way?

If this is an issue in your relationship, you need to sit down with your partner and say very bluntly, "Here are the commitments I need from you in this relationship," or "I've been asking you to talk to me about this for three months, and you're not doing it. You don't want to, do you? Do you have any desire or willingness to have the kind of discussion I'm talking about or not? I just need to know if you're simply not willing to do this."

Give the other person the option to not give you what you want and to acknowledge that they don't want to. That's a hard thing to do. In many cases, that's when you leave.

—Barbara De Angelis

Ask someone whose business it is to know.

I was attending a dinner at a winery in San Jose. Because of the wine and the great conversation, I lost track of time and missed the last plane to L.A. by about fifteen minutes. I had no luggage, no toothbrush, no anything. I called around and could not get a room at the usual places that I stayed when I was in San Jose. Then I called some other places near the airport and they were all booked solid. It seems there was a computer convention in town and every room was booked.

As I was about to resign myself to sleeping in a chair at the airport, a taxi driver approached and asked me if I needed a ride. I said, "No, what I really need is a room, and everything in town seems to be booked." He told me to wait a minute, called a place and got me the last room. The hotel actually paid for my cab fare to the hotel and provided me with a toothbrush, toothpaste, and a razor. It was not the Ritz, but it had a bed and a shower. Now, whenever I'm stuck, I don't give up. I start with the assumption that I can get what I want, and just start asking the people whose business it is to know.   **—John Taylor**

I got tickets to the Rose Bowl game three years ago two days before the game. Everyone said, "There won't be any tickets left at this late date."

"Well, let's ask and find out," I thought. My wife had been in a therapy group with the president of a local ticket selling company, and I asked her to call him and see if there would be any tickets left, how we would locate them, and what we should be prepared to pay. We ended up with tickets on the 45 yard line, row J. They were fabulous seats and my son and I have memories and pictures that we will always treasure.

—Kyle Robertson

Ask people who are qualified and motivated to help.

In his book *Ask for the Moon and Get It*, Percy Ross tells the following story about Bel Geddes.

One day, with just $5.83 in his pocket, Bel Geddes sat down on a park bench and noticed a magazine lying next to him. He picked it up and flipped through the pages. One of the articles caught his eye. In it, a prominent banker, Otto Kahn, was quoted as saying, "Millionaires should help artists."

Bel Geddes stood up, excited. He rushed to a Western Union office and spent a good part of his $5.83 on a telegram to Kahn, asking for money. He explained his situation and his desire to produce plays and design sets. The next day, Kahn wired Bel Geddes $400.

With this stake—and Kahn's vote of confidence—Bel Geddes went to New York and got a job designing opera sets. He went on to become one of Broadway's best producers. He also earned an international reputation as a designer of auto bodies, chairs, refrigerators, and other consumer items.

Bel Geddes took a long shot. But he also asked the right person.[10]   **—Percy Ross**

Ask the experts.

Recently we were asked to speak to the salespeople of a major optical company. Before our talk we identified the top five sales producers in the company. During our talk we asked the salespeople to write down the names of the top five producers. We then asked them to raise their hands if they had ever approached any of these top five people and asked them how to do it. Had they ever asked them to share their secrets of success? To give them some guidance, pointers or tips? Only three hands out of one hundred and fifty went up.

"Why haven't you asked?" we asked.

"I'm too busy." "Why would they want to help me out?" "I'm not sure they'd say yes." "I've only been here one year. What would I have to offer back?"

What a waste! The very best people that have the best information on how to do it are not being asked to share it. Have the courage to ask the people who have earned the right to talk about it.

The way to be successful is to hang out with successful people. Ask them how they got to be where they are. Most people love to talk about their successes and how they created them.

Reconsider who is an expert.

Virginia Satir, a pioneer of the fields of social work and family therapy, was hired as a consultant to make a series of recommendations on how to reform the social services department of a midwestern state. She spent one month traveling around the state asking the front-line social workers what needed to happen to make the system work better. At the end of the month she compiled all of their suggestions into a report and submitted it to the State Department of Social Services. They were ecstatic about the report, which they thought was brilliant.

All she had done was go to the people working in the system and ask them how to improve it. They were all too glad to tell her. The State Department of Social Services could have done the same thing, but it never occurred to them. No, better to pay an outside "expert" tens of thousands of dollars for a report.

Why not ask the people in your organization, church, family

or business to share their point of view with you. They usually have lots of recommendations and useful ideas.

By the way, one of the best people to ask in any organization is the receptionist. She is often considered one of the most lowly people, but think about it for a minute. She interacts with all of the customers who call in. She listens to their complaints, listens to what they think about not being able to reach you, and so on. She hears the comments of people coming and going all day. People will often vent their feelings with the receptionist because she often has the most free time available to listen. She interacts with UPS, clients who are waiting, suppliers, salespeople, even the delivery people. You'd be surprised how much she knows.

Get the other person's full attention.

Before launching into your request, be sure you have the other person's full attention. Don't ask your five-year-old to clean her room up while she is in the middle of watching Barney on television. Don't ask your husband to fix the toilet while he's watching the NBA playoffs. And don't ask your boss for a raise while he's walking out the door.

Make sure you have someone's full attention before making a request.

- Do you have a minute?
- Can I talk with you for a moment?
- Can we turn the TV off for a moment? I have something important to ask you.
- Can I set up an appointment with you?
- Can I schedule some time to talk with you about something that is very important to me? What would be a good time for you?

3. BE CLEAR AND SPECIFIC

Be specific in your requests.

Two ministers died and went to Heaven. St. Peter greeted them and said, "Your condos aren't ready yet. Until they're finished, you can return to earth as anything you want."

"Fine," said the first minister. "I've always wanted to be an eagle soaring over the Grand Canyon."

"And I'd like to be a real cool stud," said the second.

Poof! Their wishes were granted.

When the condos were finished, St. Peter asked an assistant to bring back the two ministers. "How will I find them?" the assistant asked.

"One is soaring over the Grand Canyon," St. Peter replied. "The other may be tough to locate. He's somewhere in Detroit—on a snow tire."

Here's another example of someone not being specific enough in their request:

In our workshops, we'll often ask people to make a list of what they want that they currently don't have. When we ask people to share their lists, invariably somebody says, "More money."

At that point we'll reach into our pockets, pull out a quarter and give it to them. "So now you have more money. Are you satisfied?"

"No. I want more than that."

"Well, how was I supposed to know? How was anyone supposed to know? How is your brain supposed to know? How is God supposed to know? You have to be more specific in your asking. How much more money do you want?"

"Oh, I don't know. Twenty thousand dollars."

"Well, you gave it away in your first phrase of that sen-

LOOK, LADY— YOU'RE THE ONE WHO ASKED FOR A FAMOUS MOVIE STAR WITH DARK HAIR, STRONG NOSE AND DEEP SET EYES...

tence—'Well, I don't know.' See the problem is that you don't know, because you've never really sat down and figured out exactly how much money you need to lead the kind of life you think you want. You say you want a home on the ocean in Santa Barbara, but have you ever checked out what they cost? Do you know what the annual real estate taxes would be—the annual insurance costs? Figure it all out and then you'll know exactly how much you're going to need to finance that dream."

Most people don't get clear about what they want because they don't see how they could afford it now, so it seems like it would be a waste of time. What they don't realize is they are working backwards. If you get clear about what you want and what it will cost you, then your brain will figure out how to make it happen.

It works the same way with people. You have to be specific in what you ask for. People don't know unless you tell them. Let's look at some common examples.

WRONG: I want a raise.
RIGHT: I would like a raise of $500 per month.
WRONG: I want you to dress more hip.

RIGHT: I want you to buy those new long skirts everyone is wearing and wear them with your boots.

WRONG: I want to spend some time with you this weekend.

RIGHT: I want to go out to dinner and a movie with you on Saturday night. Would that work for you?

WRONG: I want you to finish the Mitchell Report.

RIGHT: I want you to finish the Mitchell Report and leave it on my desk by Thursday at 3 P.M.

WRONG: I want more help around the house.

RIGHT: I want you to do the dishes and take out the garbage every night after dinner.

"This is what I get for requesting an office with a window."

Be careful what you ask for.

A story is told about a man who owned a Chrysler dealership back in the days right before Lee Iacocca took over the chairmanship and it looked like Chrysler might actually go bankrupt. Because of the dismal forecast of Chrysler's future, sales at the dealership began to drop off and the dealer became very despondent. All of his life's dreams had been pinned to the success of his business. He became so despondent, in fact, that eventually his wife left him and took the children. This added to his depression until finally his whole dealership became dysfunctional and he eventually went bankrupt.

In order to start over and get his life back on track, he moved to Santa Monica, California. He was unable to start another business so he took a job in a Ford dealership there. At this time foreign cars with better gas mileage were all slowing down the sales of American cars, and the man just couldn't seem to get his new sales career off the ground. So, one day, in a deep fit of depression, he decided to take his own life. He walked out to the edge of the Santa Monica Pier with the intention of jumping off head first at low tide so as to break his neck on the sand far below.

As he stood on the edge of the pier preparing himself to jump, he noticed a bottle floating on the surface of the water. It seemed to be almost glowing. It piqued his curiosity so much that he temporarily forgot about his suicide attempt. He climbed down the ladder on the edge of the pier and waded into the water to retrieve the bottle. As he opened the strange-looking bottle, a genie popped out and told the man that he could have one wish. He suggested he take his time and craft the wish very carefully.

"Oh, no," said the man. "I know exactly what I want. I have been silently wishing for it for a long time. I want to wake up tomorrow morning and be the owner of a foreign car dealership in a major metropolitan area."

Poof! The next morning he woke up with a Chrysler dealership in Tokyo!

Yes, it is a funny story but it's also tragic, isn't it? Obviously, he had violated one of the cardinal rules of effective asking. He had not been specific enough in his request! Well, the same is true for the wishes and requests that you make. They need to be specific if you want them to be granted.

So—one last time, be very specific in all of your requests!

When making any request, whether it be of yourself, the universe or another person, be as specific as possible. The two important aspects of specificity are *how much* and *by when*. How much do you want and by when do you want it? You may not get it exactly when you want it, *and* you may! But in either case, everyone involved is now clear.

What doesn't work is any of the following:

- Whenever you can get around to it.
- Whenever it is convenient.
- Sometime soon. (What's soon? Today? Tomorrow? Next week? Next month?)
- Next week sometime.
- Later today.
- Whenever.
- You know.
- Surprise me.

Here's what works:

"Hi, we're looking to buy a dishwasher for under $600 today and we need to have it installed on Monday. Is that something you can do?"

"I want you to fill out these forms, make two copies and have them all on my desk by two o'clock this afternoon."

"I told my parents I had to have a phone
in my room so they moved all of my stuff into
the living room."

Ask for what you want, not for what you don't want.

WRONG: I don't want you to yell at me anymore.

RIGHT: I want you to stop yelling and talk to me in a normal tone of voice. If you start to lose control, I want you to take a time-out for five minutes and come back when you've calmed down.

WRONG: Don't slam the door when you leave.

RIGHT: Please close the door softly when you leave.

The reason this is important is that when you tell someone what you don't want, their mind creates a picture of the words you use. "Don't slam the door," evokes a picture of a door slamming. "Close the door softly," evokes a picture of closing the door softly. Psychologists tell us the unconscious mind filters out all negative words. So again, "Don't slam the door," becomes "Slam the door." Now you can see why it is important to ask for what you want instead of what you don't want.

When feelings are involved, use the following formula:

When you _____,
I feel _____,
and what I want is _____.

Let's break that down a bit.

Be specific and descriptive. Be neutral, not judgmental. For example:

WRONG: When you act like a jerk . . .
RIGHT: When you get drunk and start flirting with other women . . .
WRONG: When you get defensive . . .
RIGHT: When you start telling jokes and changing the subject instead of listening to me . . .

So, here's what the whole formula might sound like:

WRONG: You are such a jerk around other women.
RIGHT: When you get drunk and start flirting with other women I feel scared that you are going to leave me, and what I want is for you to dance and talk to me at parties and reassure me that I am the one you love.
WRONG: You are so inconsiderate.
RIGHT: When you play your radio that loud, I can't hear myself think. I feel frustrated that I can't concen-

trate on finishing my report, and what I want is for you to either turn the volume way down or wear your headphones.

It's possible to be too specific.

A fellow came into a diner and said to the waitress, "I want a club sandwich with one slice of white bread, one of pumpernickel, and one of whole wheat, toasted medium. Put the bacon and cheese on the bottom layer, the chicken, lettuce, and tomato on the top layer. Put mayonnaise on each layer. Trim the crusts and cut it up into fourths, with a sliced pickle on each part, and a toothpick to hold each part together. Got it?"

"Gotcha," said the waitress. Then she yelled into the kitchen, "One club—for an architect. I'll be right in with the plans."

—*The Best of Bits and Pieces*

4. ASK FROM YOUR HEART

Speak from your heart and don't worry about how it's going to be taken and ask with the intention of it doing the highest good for everyone involved. **—Dr. Gary Arthur**

Ask with passion.

You can have anything you want if you want it desperately enough. You must want it with an inner exuberance that

erupts through the skin and joins the energy that created the world.
                                                    —Sheila Graham

When I was in Chapter Eleven, and I was asking my creditors to go along with my reorganization, I started with "Look, here is my mission. Here is something that is burning in my gut that not only have I been doing but I want to be able to continue doing. Here's my track record and here are the kind of things that have happened as a result of the books we have published. We have books out there that have been on the *New York Times* best-seller list. We are reaching millions of people out there."

People could get ahold of that and say, "Yes, I see what you're doing. Yes, I believe in what you're doing." The second thrust was to say, "These are the consequences. I am willing to bare my soul to you. Here is where my finances are right now and here are the scenarios that could proceed from here. It could go this way or it could go that way." If you're coming from a place where you are trying to do something good, you have exhausted all of your other options, and you show people what can happen if you are funded or supported, and it's not just a selfish thing but something that really helps others, then as I said before, people want to feel like they are doing something good.   —Brad Winch

Have unbridled passion for your purpose, project or goal.

He who clings to life shall lose it—but losing it in a right cause will gain it.
                                                    —Anonymous

Another secret, if it can be called that, is to have passion. Unbridled, unembarrasing, unflinching, foolish, undying passion! I am absolutely driven by what I do. It's the most important thing in my life. I am a fool for my mission, and I love being that fool! Let me explain why I am so passionate.

I got into the work I do to try to "recreate" my son. He was killed by a man too stoned on cocaine to know his car had hit a little boy on a bicycle. My grief nearly killed me. Linda, my wife, and I decided to heal ourselves by dedicating our lives to helping children avoid growing up into the kind of adult who can do that. See, I don't regard what I do as work. It's a dedication, passion and mission.   —Rick Gelinas

Ask with urgency and passion.

Enthusiasm moves the world.   —J. Balfour

I was taking a course on how to create bigger results faster, and I had a coach by the name of Doris. She was unbelievable. I wanted to get an Apple computer so I could write my book. This is when the first Macintosh had just been developed. It was not even out in the market yet. Every place I went they had a list of people who were waiting for a computer. The earliest I could get one was forty-five days.

When I called Doris to report in on my progress toward getting the computer, she started yelling at me, "You are more powerful than that. You can get that computer. I know you can." I told her I had already gone to five or six places. She said, "If you had to get the computer, you could get it."

I got off the phone and my ear was burning. I had never been treated like that before. I started making calls and started with the Apple Computer's company headquarters. When the lady answered, I said, "I *have* to get a computer." It was a whole different slant on things. Because of my conviction and my urgency, the lady on the phone got enrolled in it.

She said, "Here are all the local distributorships."

I started calling the distributorships, and when I'd get a salesman, I'd say, "I have to get a computer."

The usual response was "Well, we only have one demo model and there's a wait for the rest." On about the fifth call, the salesman said, "You know, I only have two demo models, but I'll sell you one." By Saturday morning, I had that computer.

I said to myself, "Whoa, there's something really amazing going on here." I realized that when you get a spirit behind it, it enrolls people. It was for a bigger purpose, too. I wanted to write a book that would uplift and empower people. People get enrolled in that. That's when asking starts to get powerful—when you ask with passion.

I've noticed the same thing when I've been on the receiving end. When I was a real estate agent, I had a piece of rental property and I had all these applications. This woman called me on the phone and said, "I've just got to have this house. I love this house. I sat out in front of it, it was so cute. I have to have it." I had no choice. I had to give it to her.   —**Tim Piering**

Ask with eye contact.

The eyes are the landing strip to the heart and for me the heart is where the soul is.
                                            —**Stan Dale**

When you are making a request of someone, maintain eye contact with them. If you avert your eyes, they are less likely to trust you. Also, by maintaining eye contact, you can see their nonverbal reactions to your request. If you look away, you miss out on these important nonverbal cues.

Ask in a kind voice.

> Your voice is like music. Ask in a harsh, brash way, "Give me that!" and you ask for conflict. Think of music. Say in a kind, smiling tone, "You are so thoughtful and generous to allow me to have it. Thank you with all my heart." You show appreciation, which always means to increase in value.   **—Dottie Walters**

Ask politely.

In our interviews with salespeople, investors and foundation executives, we heard one thing over and over and over. People are much more prone to go out of their way to help people who are friendly, considerate and polite.

Ask with respect and admiration.

The most effective technique I've found is to let people know how fascinated you are with them. There is nothing more flattering than to say to somebody, "I think you are important. I think what you have to say is worth recording. May I ask you some questions?" It's hard for people to say no to that kind of a request.   **—Michael Jeffreys**

5. ASK WITH HUMOR AND CREATIVITY

Before going on vacation, donate blood. Mosquitoes don't give coffee and doughnuts—we do.
    —Sign outside Red Cross Building, Minn., MN

Ask with humor.

The shortest distance between two people is laughter.
    —Source Unknown

Bob Swilnard was a lifeguard with an attitude.

A clever, imaginative, humorous request can open closed doors and closed minds.
                                                    —Percy Ross

One of the most powerful ways to move people is to use appropriate humor. Humor captures our attention and breaks down our defenses. It floods our brain with endorphins and makes us feel better. It disarms our resistance and opens our minds to new possibilities.

Here is a card Jack found in the bathroom of a hotel he stayed at:

More great examples of creative asking:

An army chaplain posted the following sign on the door of his quarters:

If you have troubles, come in and tell us about them. If not, come in and tell us how you do it.

Veteran American League baseball umpire Bill Guthy was working behind the plate one afternoon and the catcher for the visiting team was repeatedly protesting his calls. Guthy endured this for a number of innings, and then called a halt. He said:

> *Son, you've been a big help to me in calling balls and strikes today, and I appreciate it. But I think I've got the hang of it now, so I'm going to ask you to go to the clubhouse and show whoever is there how to take a shower.*[11]
>
> —*The Best of Bits and Pieces*

Ask creatively.

At a dinner for Commonwealth dignitaries, a chief of protocol approached Winston Churchill, who was presiding, and whispered in his ear that one of the distinguished guests had been seen to slip a silver salt shaker into his pocket. Churchill promptly pocketed the matching pepper shaker. At the end of the meal he slid up to the offending guest, murmuring, "Oh, dear, we were seen. Perhaps we had both better put them back."[12]   —*The Little Brown Book of Anecdotes*

> *Imagination is more important than knowledge.*
>
> —**Albert Einstein**

The chief buyer for a thriving company was particularly inaccessible to salespeople. You didn't call *him*. He called *you*. On several occasions when salespeople managed to get into his office, they were summarily tossed out.

One saleswoman finally broke through his defenses. She sent him a homing pigeon with her card attached to one leg. On the card she had written, "If you want to know more about our product, just throw our representative out the window."[13]

—*The Best of Bits and Pieces*

As an instructor and agent for models and talent, I stressed the importance of becoming the part to get the job. As a result, when one of our movie and television character actors, Hank

Underwood, went on an interview for the part of a construction worker in a commercial, he dressed in his hard hat, work clothes and wore his tool belt. At the reception desk, he announced, "Hank Underwood here, what would you like for me to do?"

The receptionist said, "Oh, I'm afraid you have the wrong building, the construction is going on next door."

He replied, "No, I'm here for the part of the construction worker in the commercial." Of course, he got the job.

—Betty Mazzetti Hatch

When I was in the first grade living in the deep south, my parents and I went to get a "Crystal hamburger" after the movies. A little boy, younger than I, was selling newspapers to the customers and asked my dad if he would like one. Dad said, "Nope, I've already read it."

"What about your wife?" the boy persisted. "Would she like one?"

My dad laughed and joked, "Oh, she can't read!"

Immediately, with sparkling dark eyes, the youngster shot back, "Well, put one in her back pocket, and maybe she won't look so dumb!" Taken by surprise, we laughed 'till we hurt. It was a quick, positive, and clever response to the "no" he had received. My dad was impressed. He bought the paper.

—Betty Mazzetti Hatch

A story that drives home this point is one that Dale Carnegie used to tell (there's a version of it in *How to Win Friends and Influence People*). Years ago Bethlehem Steel paid Charles Schwab, its dynamic president, a salary of $1 million a year. This was back in the days when a million went a long way. Schwab earned his pay because he knew how to get results from people.

One day, the story goes, he came upon three of his workers smoking, in violation of company regulations. He had every right to reprimand them with the warning, "No smoking, men. You know the rules." But Schwab knew that such words violated the "we" spirit; they would only make the workers feel small and resistant. Instead, he simply reached into a pocket, took out three cigars, and gave one to each, saying, "Boys, have a cigar on me. But I would appreciate it if you would not smoke it during working hours."

Someone once asked Schwab how he came to have such loyal, hard-working employees. "I never criticize anyone," he explained. "The way to develop the best that is in a person is by appreciation and encouragement." He knew how to ask.[14]

—Excerpted from *Ask for the Moon*

6. GIVE IN ORDER TO GET

"They're only puttin' in a nickel, but they want a dollar song."
—Song Title

You give before you get. —Napoleon Hill

Give something to get something.

There is a Chinese legend that nicely illustrates the necessity to give before you may expect to receive:

On a certain street in a Chinese city there was a poor beggar who held out his cup all day begging for rice or whatever the passers-by chose to give him.

One day the beggar saw a great parade coming down his street headed by the Emperor riding in his stately rickshaw and freely handing out gifts to his subjects. The poor beggar was filled with delight.

"Now," thought Woo, "my great opportunity has come. For once I shall receive a worthy gift," and he danced with joy.

When the Emperor reached him, Woo held out his cup with great earnestness, but instead of the expected gift from the Emperor his Majesty asked Woo for a gift.

Poor Woo was greatly disappointed and vexed, so he reached in his cup and with much grumbling handed the Emperor two of the smallest grains of rice he could find. The Emperor passed on.

All that day Woo fumed and grumbled. He denounced the Emperor, he berated Buddha, he was cross to those who spoke to him and few people even stopped to speak to him or drop grains of rice in his cup.

That night when Woo reached his poor hut and poured out his scant supply of rice, he found in his cup two nuggets of gold just the size of the grains of rice he had given to the Emperor.

You have to give to get.

I believe you can get everything in life you want if you will just help enough other people get what they want. —Zig Ziglar

Years ago, near a seldom-used trail in the Amargosa Desert in California, there stood a rundown hut. Nearby was a well, the only source of water for miles around. Attached to the pump was a tin baking powder can with a message inside, written in pencil on a sheet of brown wrapping paper.

This was the message . . .

> This pump is all right as of June 1932. I put a new sucker washer into it and it ought to last five years. But the washer dries out and the pump has got to be primed. Under the white rock I buried a bottle of water, out of the sun and cork end up. There's enough water in it to prime this pump but not if you drink some first. Pour in about 1/4 and let her soak to wet the leather. Then pour in the rest medium fast and pump like hell. You'll get water. The well never has ran dry. Have faith.
>
> When you get watered up, fill the bottle and put it back like you found it for the next feller.
>
> SIGNED: Desert Pete
>
> P.S. Don't go drinking the water first! Prime the pump with it and you'll get all you can hold. And next time you pray, remember that God is like the pump. He has to be primed. I've given my last dime away a dozen times to prime the pump of my prayers, and I've fed my last beans to a stranger while saying Amen. It never failed yet to get me an answer. You got to get your heart fixed to give before you can be given to.[15]   —*The Best of Bits and Pieces*

When you're nice to people, they want to be nice back to you.
—Jack Canfield

Dr. Paddi Lund, a dentist in Brisbane, Australia, has a dental practice with a long waiting list of people clamoring to get in. They have freshly baked bread and rolls and fresh brewed herbal tea available for all of their clients while they wait. Here's how one of his clients responded when he was asked, "Why do you come to this place when you could have gone anywhere for that procedure?"

"I come here because they like me."

"What do you mean?"

"Well, a couple of weeks ago I was supposed to come in here for a visit, and they messed it up for some reason. The laboratory didn't deliver the stuff they needed, so they rang me and apologized profusely, and that night they delivered a bottle of cognac to me with a note saying, 'I'm sorry.' It really blew me away."

Paddi gives a lot to his patients and he asks for a lot back in return.

When I first started my dental practice, I had a number of people ring me up in the evenings for emergency care. Once a week, at least, I'd be up in the middle of the night. Since we've given people our phone numbers, I've never been up in the middle of the night. I've been rung up a few times just for reassurance, but that's it. Isn't that weird? When you give people your phone number, they don't ring. When you don't, they do. I believe that the reason is that when you've got something in your hand, you think, "I could ring if I wanted to, but I can hang on a little longer. It'll be okay. He was nice enough to give his number to me. I don't want to disturb him." **—Paddi Lund, Australian dentist**

Give a gift.

He that bringeth a present findeth the door open.
—Thomas Fuller

Getting inside the housewife's door has always been the number-one problem of door-to-door salesmen. Fuller's major contribution to the art of legal entry came in 1915, when he got Fuller Brush men to give away a vegetable brush.

Fuller Brush salesmen were taught to carry the sample in the sample case, to call it a gift instead of a sample, and to present it inside the house rather than on the doorstep.

A Fuller Brush man was taught how to respond to a housewife who wanted to take the sample without seeing his line. (With a helpless gesture he would indicate the impossibility of opening his sample case out there.)

If the housewife said she was too busy, he should say he would just step in for a minute. If she didn't want the brush he should just say, "I get credit for giving them out."
—American Business

Give compliments or praise.

Praise does wonders for the sense of hearing.
—Source Unknown

Everybody likes a compliment.   —**Abraham Lincoln**

Explain what's in it for them.

Never make your appeal to a man's better nature; he may not have one. Always make your appeal to his self-interest.

—**Lazarus Long**

"Stupid salesman kept mistaking me for
Joan Collins!"

One of the first men to use this rule in an advertisement was Benjamin Franklin. He tells about it in his autobiography, which is required reading for all ambitious salesmen.

Franklin was commissioned by General Braddock, back in April 1755, to secure for him 150 wagons with four horses to each wagon. These the general wanted for what proved to be his ill-fated expedition against Fort Duquesne.

Franklin went to Lancaster, and, on April 26, 1755, published an advertisement. The purpose of the advertisement was to get the farmers interested in supplying the wagons. What did it contain? One single paragraph about what Braddock wanted and six numbered paragraphs about what the farmers would get. Good salesman that he was, Franklin told the farmers how they would benefit from the transaction.

Franklin comments in his autobiography on the "great and sudden effect it produced" and says further, "In three weeks the one hundred and fifty wagons, with two hundred and fifty-nine carrying horses, were on their march for the camp."

Suppose that instead of arousing the interest of the farmers by telling them what they would get out of it, Franklin had told them what Braddock wanted—would he have secured equally good results? We don't have to guess. Braddock had tried it previously in Maryland, on a "we-want-wagons-or-else" basis. The net result, wrote Franklin, was ". . . twenty-five wagons and not all of those in serviceable condition."   **—Percy H. Whiting**

Tell your partner how it benefits him or her.

It always helps to explain to somebody why you're asking and how what you're asking for is going to benefit them.

"Honey, I really would love it if before we go to bed each night, no matter how tired you are, you reach over and just give me a hug or say something sweet to me. That's going to make me feel like no matter what's going on in the day, that I really make a difference to you. And that supports me because you know how much in my life I felt like I was just giving and giving and not getting anything back. That's going to go so far with me and really make me feel special more than anything else you could do. When I feel that way, I am probably going to be a lot less tense during the day." Now he understands what it means to me and why.

"If you compliment me more and that makes me feel more desired, I'm going to want to sleep with you more." So, it's seeing the payoff for the favor.

7. ASK REPEATEDLY

You have to ask, ask, ask, ask, ask, ask, ask, ask, ask, ask, ask, ask, ask, ask, ask, ask, ask, ask, ask, ask, ask, ask, ask, ask, ask, ask, ask, ask, ask, ask, ask, ask, ask, ask, ask, ask, ask, ask, ask, ask, ask, ask, ask, ask, ask, ask, ask, ask, ask, ask, ask, ask, ask, ask, ask, ask, ask, ask, ask, ask, ask, ask, ask, ask, ask, ask, ask, ask, ask, ask, ask, ask, ask, ask, ask, ask, ask, ask, ask, ask, ask, ask, ask, ask, ask, ask, ask, ask, ask, ask, ask, ask, ask, ask!

—Mark Victor Hansen

Just say NEXT!

Translate every NO into a next! A no does not mean stop. It simply means not here, not now, not yet! So what, Keep asking. If someone says, "No," you say "Next!" By latest count there are about five billion people on the planet. That is a lot of people to make a request of. Out there somewhere is a yes worthy to be asked. You just have to find it.

The key to getting everything you want is to never put all your begs in one ask-it!
—Anonymous

Jack asked one of his recent seminar participants to share her experience of getting into the seminar in a letter so we could include it in the book. Here it is. It speaks to the issue of continuing to ask until you get what you are after.

Dear Jack,

After attending your Self-Esteem I Seminar, I felt determined, actually compelled, to attend the advanced seminar. The obstacles of money, child care, and family approval seemed minor compared to the reasons to attend. I am the mother of five, a foster parent, and a recovering codependent. But the ultimate reason I needed to be at the Self-Esteem II was for myself.

At Self-Esteem I, Rebecca had given me a copy of *Chicken Soup for the Soul* with instructions to read it to my children. One story in particular by Rick Gelinas spurred me on my quest to attend SE II.

My first priority was to secure financial assistance. So I hosted a family dinner with my parents and siblings. Enthusiastically at mid-dinner, I announced my intent to attend SE II and stated that in lieu of traditional birthday and Christmas gifts, I would appreciate donations for tuition assistance to the seminar. This was met with frowns, silence, and indifference. We continued to eat. NEXT!

Chicken Soup for the Soul was so encouraging and I noticed that in the back of the book were the addresses of many of the contributors. A lightbulb flashed and I wrote an anonymous chain letter with four positive choices: 1) Tuition Assistance, 2) Encouraging Words, 3) Forward to a friend, 4) All the above. NEXT!

I received $ 50.00 from my parents for Christmas. With that I placed an ad in the classified section of three local papers and the college newspaper. NEXT!

I asked my classmates for donations. NEXT!

I asked for ideas and stayed in touch with the local group sponsoring the seminar to see if there had been any response. NEXT!

The day before the seminar I set my sights on telling my story personally to you, Jack. I wrote a letter and delivered it to where you were staying.

Although it had not been confirmed, I immediately started making preparations for child care for my children and calling my family and friends to let them know I would be at the seminar and how they could contact me in case of an emergency.

My last resort was to show up at the seminar facility and be a participant. I never thought I wasn't going to be at that seminar, and even if my last resort did not work, I was prepared to say NEXT!

At 11 p.m., the night before the seminar, my phone rang. It was Rebecca informing me that you had read my letter and given me the OK to attend SE II. I cried.   —**Laurie Little John,** **St. Louis, MO**

Look forward to the no's.

In the past ten years, more than three thousand persons have said yes to me, and have donated (or made grants) amounting to more than $2,000,000 for our work. Sometimes I'm tempted to take getting a "yes" for granted, but then I remember the early days and I have to smile.

I learned the meaning of getting "yes" and getting "no" when I was twenty-two. It was the year that I sold life insurance door-to-door. Back then we used a sales method, no longer in use, called "debit." As a "debit" salesman, I had a fixed route to walk, like a mailman, and my job was to collect weekly premiums and try to sell the policy holders on some kind of upgrade to their insurance. Mostly, I sold burial insurance and accident insurance. And mostly I sold to poor people, like myself. The premiums ranged from about 50 cents to about $2 per week.

When I started that job, my sales trainer told me (and I totally believed him) that to make a sale I had to collect seven no-sales first. In other words, I could look forward to making one sale for every seven times I was turned down. Wow! I got so excited about this guaranteed sale, that I actually looked forward with great glee to being turned down! I almost cheered every time someone said "no," and I would rush laughing to the next door on the street in order to get the next "no" out of the way just as fast as I could, because I knew in my bones that every "no" was putting me that much closer to a great big sweet old "YES!"

And did I get discouraged when the eighth door and the ninth door yielded yet two more "no's"? OF COURSE NOT!!

Those eighth and ninth "no's" were like money in the bank! Soon after FOURTEEN "no"s there would be TWO great big sweet old "YES'S"!! And if I racked up TWENTY-ONE "no's," I knew I had THREE "yes's" coming! Every "no" was good news!!

By working hard every day with that attitude, within six months of taking that job with the insurance company I won first prize in their national sales contest, winning in competition with more than two thousand other men and women, as the beginner with the most sales.

That formula still works for me. The ratio of seven to one has changed, but the concept is etched in the stars, and it can't fail. To this day, I know if I call on enough people there will always be a YES waiting for me—and I'll come to it in good time. So getting a "no" is still good news!   **—Rick Gelinas**

Ask the same people again and again.

Here's an interesting statistic: 46% of all salespeople ask for business one time. 24% of all salespeople ask for business two times. 14% of all salespeople ask for business three times. 12% of all salespeople ask for business four times. Only 4% of all salespeople ask the same person for their business five times . . . which represents 60% of all business sold . . . so, ask, ask, ask, ask, ask!

Be tenacious, persevere, never give up.

Never, never, never, never give up.   **—Winston Churchill**

If at first you don't succeed, try, try again.

—William E. Hickson

I was volunteering my time on the enrollment team for a seminar I had taken that had really transformed my life. It was my job to call people on a phone list I was given and try to get them to enroll in the seminar. The first eighty-one people I called all said no. The next nine people all said yes. If I had stopped after fifty, which is what I felt like doing, those nine people would never have received the benefits of the seminar, and I never would have learned the power of sticking with it until you get

the result you want. Someone is always out there. If you just
keep asking long enough, you'll find them.   —Janet Carson

*Perseverance is a great element of success. If you only knock
long enough and loud enough at the gate, you are sure to
wake up somebody.*   —Henry Wadsworth Longfellow

Rick Little kept on asking.

At twenty years old, Rick Little became obsessed with his vision of a program for high school students that would teach
them how to get along better with the people in their lives, how
to find and keep a job, how to handle conflict, how to be a
good parent and how to handle money. For over two years Rick
wrote and sent out 155 grant proposals. On his one hundred
and fifty-sixth try, spurred on by the power of his conviction,
he managed to talk himself past several secretaries and secured a lunch date with Dr. Russ Mawby, President of the
Kellogg Foundation.

Two weeks later, Dr. Mawby called him and told him that
the trustees had voted against the $55,000 Rick had re-
quested. Rick felt tears pressing behind his eyes. Then he
heard these words. "However, the trustees *did* vote unanimously to give you $130,000."

What if Rick had given up after the one hundredth try?
What if he had not persevered. Since that time Rick has raised
over one hundred million dollars to fund his dream. The Quest
Living Skills Programs are currently taught in over 30,000
schools in all 50 states and 32 countries. Three million kids
per year are being taught important life skills because one
twenty-year-old refused to take "no" for an answer. Rick Little's life is a testament to the power of commitment to a high
vision, coupled with a willingness to keep on asking until one
manifests the dream.

In the end, the only people who fail are those who do not try.
     —David Viscott

Just one more time?

Never give up, for that is just the place and time that the tide will turn.   —Harriet Beecher Stowe

We have no idea whether this story is true, but the message is powerful. It reportedly took place in 1942. According to the account:

> Rafael Solano was physically exhausted and defeated. As he sat on a boulder in the dry river bed he announced to his companions, "I'm through. There's no use going on any longer. See this pebble. It makes 999,999 I've picked up without finding one diamond. One more pebble makes a million, but what's the use? I quit!"
>
> The exploration crew had spent months prospecting for diamonds in a Venezuelan watercourse. Their efforts focused on finding signs of valuable diamonds. Mentally, physically, and emotionally they were exhausted. Their clothes were tattered and their spirits weak.
>
> "Pick up one more and make it a million," one man said. Solano consented and pulled forth a stone the size of a hen's egg. It was different than the others, and the crew soon realized they had discovered a diamond. It is reported Harry Winston, a New York jewel dealer, paid Rafael Solano $200,000 for that millionth pebble. The stone was named the Liberator and to date is the largest and purest diamond ever found.[16]

8. HOW TO DEAL WITH RESISTANCE

Don't lose your cool!

> My father died unexpectedly between Christmas and New Year's. I called US Air and got eight tickets at the bereavement rate. When we got to the airport we had to stand in line for three hours. When we finally got to the counter, we were told the flight was canceled because they couldn't get an aircraft there.
>
> I remember reading an article that said if you have a confirmed ticket and there was a problem with the flight, you had the right to compel them to buy you another ticket on another airline. But if you didn't ask for it, they didn't have to do it.

The next plane that was available was TWA and it wasn't for three hours, and it was on the other side of the terminal. Those people that don't know Los Angeles airport, it's a mass of shuttles. You've got to get to another shuttle and go about a half mile around the corner. You can't walk it, and when you have eight people and probably twelve pieces of paraphernalia, you've got to actually rent a shuttle to do it. You can't get on a regular shuttle. I had to rent a shuttle just to get over there.

But I was still in the line and I said, "So just because it's canceled what are you going to do about it?" We had a stand-off. The woman said, "It's your responsibility to book another." I said, "Why?" She said, "Because it's canceled." I was very polite but I kept saying, "Why is it my problem?" She kept saying, "Because the equipment is canceled." I said, "Well, fine! Please put in writing the fact that I had confirmed tickets, your equipment couldn't make it, you told me you had no obligation or right to buy me a ticket and have your supervisor sign it," I waited.

She said, "But all these people are waiting in line." I said, "Who cares, there's no other equipment for three hours. What are they going to do?" We had a very polite stand-off.

To make a long story short, they bought us eight tickets on TWA which is not inconsequential, because at the last minute it's like $10,000!

So we shuttle over to TWA and it's a nightmare because they have a little 727 and they have a canceled flight they are trying to squeeze on along with their other passengers. The flight people were pulling their hair out, but we asked them because we had all these little kids, "Would you try to get us seats together?"

They assured us they would try and that they might have to do it after we got on because it was a nightmare. We had eight seats and none of them were together.

So we get on finally, and the first seat that we come to is on a bulkhead. We asked the flight attendant to ask the man that was on the outside aisle if he would relinquish his seat and trade with one of us. He looked at us indignantly and said, "Absolutely not! I reserved this six weeks ago. I'm not going to give it up. I travel a lot and I need to relax."

I started getting livid, and my wife started laughing. I'm looking at her and thinking, "What's wrong with this picture? She sees something I don't."

She bent down, took the car seat, fastened the car seat in the one seat next to the man, put our six-month-old baby in it, looked at the man, handed him a bottle and said, "If the baby cries a little give him this and if he cries a lot try that." She gave him diapers and baby wipes and left. In that minute I realized it wasn't our problem, it was his, and it's how you look at life, and if we realize we don't have problems, other people do. In that instant it changed the whole picture.　　　**—Jay Abraham**

What needs to happen for me to . . .

I missed a plane once and I had an airline ticket that was non-refundable. It was for an airline that didn't even have any more flights that afternoon and I had to be in a city in Canada where I was going to make some speaking engagements for about 350 people. So it was obvious that I had to be there. I went to a different airline with my non-refundable/non-exchangeable ticket. I got myself in a really clear place of coming from *This is going to happen.* I wasn't anticipating failure—I was not assured that it would be successful, but at least where I was coming from *It was going to happen.*

Then I shared from my heart and my experience. Instead of telling the other person what they should do or what they needed to do to help me, I figured they could handle the problem, they could figure out the how of this. What I needed to do was to be clear on where was I coming from and to be able to share that with my heart in a real genuine and compassionate way.

I went up to the counter and I shared what happened, not what I needed to have happen, but what had just happened—that I had missed my plane, this was my ticket, that I was a speaker and I needed to be in this city at this time. I just put my ticket down. Then I just asked her the question, "**What needs to happen for me to be on this plane?**" Then I was totally quiet.

Essentially what happened after that was that she just talked herself into putting me on the plane. Because there was a lot of silence and there was a lot of room and I wasn't adding anything to her. . . I was letting her roam free toward a solution. I wasn't putting any obstacles up or any idea in the way of her coming to her own way of handling it. All I was doing was leaving total open room for her and just being there with her.

Essentially she went through this series of comments: "Well, there's nothing I can do. I hope you understand this is a non-refundable ticket." Then there was silence, and then of course she started talking again. She said, "I really wish I could help you, and it's probably not going to be possible to get you on this flight. Maybe we can get you on a different flight, but it's going to cost you another six hundred dollars."

Then there was a pause. I wouldn't say anything. I would

just be there, and I wasn't angry or upset or anything. I was very calm and very loving and very open. In fact, I would have spoken if it would have been appropriate, but she wasn't done speaking yet. There was so much room, she just kept going. She said, "Gee, I just got an idea, maybe we can do this or that." I just stood there hanging out. By the end of maybe five or ten minutes, she was in this totally enthusiastic state, absolutely thrilled, and she was saying, "You know what I'm going to do, I'm going to make a decision and put you on that plane and we're going to get you there on time and it's not going to cost you any more money, and we'll use this ticket."

She felt thrilled that she could be of service to me. So, if I had jumped in and tried to handle it for her or done anything to give her a way to do it, or been upset or angry or complaining or any of those things—I wouldn't have made it to Canada. All I did was stand filling in the facts that I was okay, that this could happen, that this would in fact happen, and then let it unfold.

—**Marcia Martin**

Don't create resistance.

A powerful request can only be powerful if you're also willing to be declined. You can't ask for things only with wanting to get a yes. Because that cuts off half of the possibilities. If you cut off half the possibilities you're really cutting off half the truth and if you cut off half the truth then you don't have the real thing. You have to include the possibility of being declined. The more willing you are to be declined the more you increase the probability of actually being accepted. I would say getting declined is actually a bonus. Keep track of all the great times you get declined because you can add them all up and say, "Okay, I got that handled." Instead of it being a failure, count it as a success. "Great, I succeeded, I got declined again." That's the good news, that you can get declined. You can send yourself out knowing that you don't have to lose anything, everybody else is just scared, and if I get a decline, I win. That gives me a little bit more courage to do it, perhaps.   —**Marcia Martin**

Ask with authority and be prepared for a no.

When Christian Herter was governor of Massachusetts, he was running hard for a second term in office. One day, after a busy morning chasing votes (and no lunch) he arrived at a church barbecue. It was late afternoon and Herter was famished.

As Herter moved down the serving line, he held out his plate to the woman serving chicken. She put a piece on his plate and turned to the next person in line.

"Excuse me," Governor Herter said, "do you mind if I have another piece of chicken?"

"Sorry," the woman told him. "I'm supposed to give one piece of chicken to each person."

"But I'm starved," the governor said.

"Sorry," the woman said again. "Only one to a customer."

Governor Herter was a modest and unassuming man, but he decided that this time he would throw a little weight around.

"Do you know who I am?" he said. "I am the governor of this state."

"Do you know who I am?" the woman said. "I'm the lady in charge of the chicken. Move along, mister."[17]

A no may be a blessing in disguise.

Years ago in Scotland, the Clark family had a dream. Clark and his wife worked and saved, making plans for their family of nine children to travel the United States. It had taken years, but they had finally saved enough money. They got their passports and made reservations for the family on a new oceanliner.

The entire family was filled with anticipation and excitement about their venture. However, several days before the departure, the youngest son was bitten by a dog. The doctor stitched the leg, but hung a yellow flag on the Clark's front door. Because of the possibility of rabies, the entire family was quarantined for fourteen days.

The family's dream was dashed. They would not be able to make the trip to America as planned. The father, filled with disappointment and anger, stomped to the dock to watch the ship leave—without the Clark family. The father shed bitter tears and cursed his son and God for their misfortune.

Five days later, the tragic news spread throughout Scotland and the world—the mighty *Titanic* had sunk. The unsinkable ship had sunk taking hundreds of lives with it. The Clark family was to have been on that ship, but because their son had been bitten by a dog, they were left behind.

When Mr. Clark heard the news, he hugged his son, and gave thanks to God for saving his family and turning what was believed to have been a tragedy into a blessing. **—Anonymous**

Be gracious in accepting a NO.

Models and actors may have several job interviews every day. Most of the interviews end in rejections. Rather than stomping out with an attitude of "What a wasted effort," we encouraged our models to send thank you notes. We taught them to be grateful for those who had spent time with them and to thank them for the opportunity to "try out" for the job. With each interview came a new potential friend in the business and a new experience that would give the model or actor a better chance the next time. One of my top models, David Schnitzer, sent not only thank you notes, but also flowers, even when he did not get the job. As a result, he was never forgotten—and was always included in future interviews.　　　　　　**—Betty Mazzetti Hatch**

Don't burn your bridges.

There are times when a model or actor waits the better part of a day to be interviewed for a job, and is then treated rudely by the interviewer. Temptation to return the attitude can be very great. The tables can be turned, however, if the job seeker understands that the interviewer may also be exhausted, after a long day of seeing people who are totally wrong for the clothes or part. The following statements have sometimes landed our models the job: "I understand that I have not been selected and I want you to know how much I appreciate your time with me. I really enjoyed talking to you and look forward to a future date, when I might be the right person for you." Or another positive reply might be: "If 'no' is your response to me this time, what might I do to get a 'yes' next time?"

Responses such as these have registered so positively with clients further opportunities to test have been given—the bridge was never burned.　　　　　　**—Betty Mazzetti Hatch**

8

ASK AT HOME

◆

A daughter rushed home to her father. "Dad, Bill asked me to marry him."
The Father replied, "How much money does he have?"
The daughter answered: "You men are all alike. He asked the same thing about you."

◆

Do you want more time? More attention? Undivided attention? More respect? Longer hugs? More kisses? A back rub? A massage? More sex? More intimacy? More romance? More surprises? More money? Less pressure? More fun? More love and support? Less criticism? Help with the dishes? Help with the housework? Help with your homework? Permission to date? An allowance? More privacy? Your parents to stop fighting? Less noise? More peace and quiet? People to put things away after they use them? Help with the bills? More cooperation? A vacation? Someone to baby-sit? Help with the errands? People not to borrow your clothes without asking? Someone to make dinner? Help with the kids? Someone to stop drinking? Someone to open up and tell the truth about their problems? Someone to help you kick a self-destructive habit? Your partner to take birth control measures? Your spouse to see a counselor? To know what's going on? Clearer boundaries? Someone to be less defensive? Help with the rent? The car returned with a full tank of gas?

Ask Your Spouse

If he really loved me, I wouldn't have to ask!

This false belief has created endless pain and suffering for couples. Unless you are married to a psychic mind reader, your partner will not know what you want unless you ask him or her. It is that simple. It does not mean that your partner doesn't love you. It just means that he or she does not have psychic powers.

Just as the genie of the lamp cannot grant Aladdin a wish unless he tells him what he wants, your spouse or lover cannot fulfill your desires if he or she does not know what they are. If you want more romance, attention, affection or help with the dishes, you are going to have to ask for it.

What's love got to do with it? The answer is nothing!

How many times have you heard people say "If you really loved me, I wouldn't have to ask!" Well, it is not true. It is really possible that someone could love you and still not know what you want. The two don't necessarily go together! Go ahead, make requests. Be specific. Give the person the chance to respond. If you want a picnic at the ocean for your birthday, ask for it. If you want a back massage before you go to bed, ask for it. If you want your meal prepared a certain way, ask for it. If you want . . . ask for it!

My Mom sent me button-down shirts three years in a row. If I had just kept accepting them because I didn't want to hurt her feelings, I would have gotten a new button down shirt for the next twenty years of my life. It took three years to get the message across, but it finally worked.   —Jack Canfield

Ask for hugs.

Research indicates we need four hugs a day for survival, eight for maintenance and twelve for growth. If we want to be growing, we need twelve hugs a day. Hugs have a healing effect on the body. Hugs bolster our immune systems. Hugs help us to feel special. They nurture the little child within us. They help us feel close to our family and friends.

Unfortunately, many of us were raised in homes where there was not a lot of hugging, and we may be uncomfortable asking for and giving hugs. We may have even been teased for being "too needy." During a one-year research project, we found out

that 83 percent of the people we polled received less than one hug a day (an average of about four a week). 97 percent of the same people we polled wanted more hugs than they were already getting. Don't ever be ashamed of your natural human need for touching and hugs.

We encouraage you to reach out and ask for the hugs that you need. A simple "May I have a hug?" goes a long way toward getting more hugs. Make it a goal to ask for and get your twelve hugs a day.

Ask for tenderness and intimacy.

You may need to ask your partner to slow down and be more tender. To be gentler and more romantic in his or her conversation, touch or way of being. Dr. Barbara De Angelis teaches people in her relationships seminars to take time for "love snacks"—little five-minute periods of kissing, holding, caressing, sustained eye contact, love talk—whatever it is that makes you feel more loved.

Be willing to ask for what you need in the arena of initimacy, romance and tenderness.

Ask, don't tell!

Make sure that when you are asking for what you want from your spouse, you are really asking! When we get afraid or unconscious, we often revert to old patterns of behavior such as whining, complaining, nagging and "shoulding" on our partner. No one likes to have a pile of shoulds heaped upon them. The natural tendency is to rebel and resist.

Whenever you hear yourself saying "should" to your partner, stop and ask yourself, "What do I really want here?" Then make a clear and succinct request.

Many people in my seminars challenge this idea of it's better to ask than to tell. Here's how I handled one particular situation:

Some macho guy said, "Now, wait a minute, Joe, there's a time when you've got to *tell* people."

I retorted, "There may be, but I'm not totally convinced of that, even though I used to be a drill instructor in the Marine Corps. Are you married?"

"Yes."

"Did you propose to your wife?"

"Yes."

"Then I assume you *told* her 'You're going to marry me, right?'"

The he-man said, "Well, no."

I then asked, "What did you do?"

"I asked her," he replied.

I then explained that if he would stop and reflect he would realize that when there's any *major* thing you really wanted to consummate or close, any kind of important transaction, when the chips are really down, you don't tell—you ask. Most people understood and agreed.

—**Joe Batten**

When you are emotionally upset

When you want your spouse to change his or her behavior because something your spouse is doing is upsetting to you, remember to use the following formula.

When you _____, I think _____, and I feel _____.

My request is that you _____.

When you use this formula for communication, you are owning your feelings. You are not making the other person responsible for your feelings. You are just telling them what you do inside when they do what they do. Then you are making a request. They have the right to honor it or not, but at least they now know what you want and why you want it.

When stated this way, your request will not create defensiveness in the listener. It is easier to hear because there is no blame attached to the communication. Therefore, there is nothing to defend against. That way the listener can put all of

CATHY   BY CATHY GUISEWITE

their attention on whether or not they want to meet your request.

Ask for help around the house.

SALLY FORTH By Greg Howard

Percentage of women who would rather watch a man wash dishes than dance naked: 61 percent. —Details, March 1995

No man was ever shot by his wife while doing the dishes.
—Source Unknown

Women want their husbands and boyfriends to help out with chores around the house: doing the dishes, taking out the garbage, putting the kids to bed, cleaning up and running errands. When they don't get these things, they tend to harbor deep resentments toward their men, especially if the wife also works an eight-hour day on a job. If these resentments are not communicated and turned into clear requests, they can eventually lead to an emotional gulf in the relationship. Romance disappears, intimacy disappears and sex goes out the window.

It is very important to keep all of your expectations and requests clearly communicated so that love and intimacy can flourish.

Ask for acknowledgment and appreciation.

It is okay to ask to be appreciated. One night after spending the better part of a day cooking a wonderful dinner for family and a few friends, Jack's wife Georgia stood up at the end of the meal and said, "I would appreciate a standing ovation for this fabulous meal I spent the day preparing." It was said with humor and with sincerity and it resulted in a standing ovation and lots of praise for a fine meal.

An exercise we recommend for couples is to sit opposite each other and go back and forth sharing things you appreciate about your partner.

He: I appreciate how perseverent you are.
She: I appreciate what a good father you are.
He: I appreciate how hard you work on decorating the house.
She: I appreciate all the back-rubs you give me.
He: I admire how you stand up to your boss at work.
She: I love how you always remember to call me when you're going to be late.

And so on. We recommend you do this exercise at least once a week. It is something you can ask your partner to do with you.

EXERCISES FOR COUPLES

Here are a couple of specific activities that you can do with your spouse or significant other that will increase your comfort in asking for what you want. We guarantee that if you do these activities with 100 percent commitment, they can radically improve the quality of your relationship.

Clarify your expectations.[18]

Many times in relationships we have expectations of our partners that we don't express, but we still want. Drs. Jordan and Margaret Paul have compiled a useful list of these unstated expectations in their book *Do I Have to Give Up Me to Be Loved by You? The Work Book*. We suggest you photocopy the list below and mark those that you expect from your partner on a scale of 1 to 5, 1 being "I hardly ever expect this," and 5 being "I expect this a great deal."

When you and your partner have both marked your lists, exchange your lists and read over what it is that your partner expects while your partner reads your list.

Then discuss each item where you feel your expectations are not being met. Talk about how important the item is to you, and, if appropriate, make specific requests for what you want. Give your partner the space to make a commitment, to say no or to renegotiate the request until you can find a mutually satisfactory solution.

If many of these issues are emotionally charged, it may take you several sessions together to go through the entire list.

My Stated Or Unstated Expectations

____ 1. Never do anything that upsets me.
____ 2. Remember my birthday (or anniversary).
____ 3. Never be late.
____ 4. Call me when you're going to be late.
____ 5. Be turned on to me.
____ 6. Make love to me whenever I want to.
____ 7. Never want to do anything without me.
____ 8. Never walk away when I'm talking.
____ 9. Stop reading when I walk in the room.
___ 10. Watch TV with me.
___ 11. Always want to do what I want.
___ 12. Agree with me.
___ 13. Have the same interests I do.
___ 14. Lose weight or gain weight.
___ 15. Make more money.
___ 16. Spend less money.
___ 17. Keep the house clean.
___ 18. Do the dishes.
___ 19. Eat right.
___ 20. Take your vitamins.
___ 21. Dress the way I want you to.
___ 22. Be affectionate.

____ 23. Be affectionate in public.

____ 24. Put your clothes away.

____ 25. Share the responsibilities at home.

____ 26. Put the toilet seat down after you pee.

____ 27. Put the toilet seat up after you pee.

____ 28. Always swallow my semen.

____ 29. Don't have an orgasm until I do.

____ 30. Wash your genitals before coming to bed.

____ 31. Make me happy.

____ 32. Never take vacations without me.

____ 33. Take care of me.

____ 34. Always have dinner ready.

____ 35. Always look nice.

____ 36. Read my mind.

____ 37. Anticipate my needs.

____ 38. Never let me oversleep.

____ 39. Never be attracted to anyone else.

____ 40. Never make love to anyone else.

____ 41. Make my needs more important than your own.

____ 42. Give in to me.

____ 43. Do things my way.

____ 44. Call me every day.

____ 45. Make up first.

____ 46. Never buy me expensive presents.

____ 47. Give me more money.

____ 48. Solve my problems for me.

____ 49. Do all the things that I don't like to do.

____ 50. Make me feel good about myself.

____ 51. Take care of me whenever I'm sick.

____ 52. Don't have outside interests or hobbies.

____ 53. Always want to be with me.

____ 54. Stop drinking.

____ 55. Stop taking drugs.

____ 56. Come home earlier from work.

____ 57. Spend more time with the kids.

____ 58. Stop watching so much TV.

____ 59. Go to bed the same time I do.

____ 60. Take a shower every day.

___ 61. Never lie to me.

___ 62. Never think of old lovers.

___ 63. Make my unhappiness go away.

___ 64. Stop being friends with old lovers.

___ 65. Stop being friends with people I don't like.

___ 66. Tear up your old love letters.

___ 67. Be excited about the things that excite me.

___ 68. Be interested in my problems.

___ 69. Make everything right for me.

___ 70. Be serious when I want to be serious.

___ 71. Include me in conversations.

___ 72. Have the same beliefs and values I have.

___ 73. Tell me what you think and feel without me asking.

A word of advice

Don't expect your partner to be able or willing to fulfill every one of your needs. No one person can do that. You will need to reach out to other people in your life as well. We often don't do this because we are afraid of rejection. Making demands on our partners teaches less work and less risk than reaching out to others, so we often keep placing too many demands on one person. It's easier, but it won't work. We will need to take risks with others in our life as well.

Different friends and family members contribute different things in our lives. One may be funny, another a trusted counselor. One may be a good financial adviser, someone else a great listener. One may be a great spiritual companion, while another is a great problem solver. Make sure you have many friends and relatives in your network of support.

Justin Stewart once advised Jack's wife, "Don't expect your husband to be intimate with you in the same way as your best girlfriend. It will never happen. Make sure you have a best girlfriend to fulfill that need."

The giving and receiving exercise

The purpose of this activity is to assist you and your partner in expanding your awareness and deepening your commitment in the area of asking for and getting what you want.

Set aside thirty minutes to be together and answer the following questions about giving and receiving in your relationship. Sit facing each other to maintain contact and hold your partner's hands throughout the exercise.

Start with the first incomplete section and go back and forth taking turns answering that question until neither of you have anything further to say. Then move on to the second question and do the same thing. Repeat the process until you have completed all the questions.

1. One of the ways I make it difficult for you to give me what I want is . . .
2. The scary thing about expressing what I want is . . .
3. Something I want and have difficulty asking for is . . .
4. What I would like more of is . . .
5. I feel loved and appreciated by you when you . . .
6. I feel invisible and unappreciated when you . . .
7. Sometimes I withhold expressions of appreciation when . . .
8. The good news about allowing you to feel invisible and unappreciated is . . .
9. By causing you to wonder if I really love you, I . . .
10. If I were more willing to let you know how much you really matter to me, I'd, . . . and you'd . . .
11. What I love and appreciate about you is . . .

Here are some typical answers from past seminar participants:

1. One of the ways I make it difficult for you to give me what I want is . . .
   I pretend I don't need anything.
   I rarely ask you for it.
   I make vague hints and innuendos instead of asking directly.
   I overschedule myself so I am never available to receive.
2. The scary thing about expressing what I want is . . .
   I imagine you will get angry at me.
   You seem so irritated when I talk about my needs.

I'm afraid you'll reject me.
I feel hurt when you don't say yes.
3. Something I want and have difficulty asking for is . . .
For you to come home from work sooner.
For you to control your spending and shopping.
For you to take a shower before we make love.
For you to see a counselor about your excessive drinking.

And so on . . .

Getting more of what you want

Women are afraid to ask for what they want because they are afraid at a deep subconscious level that they will get replaced by someone less demanding and more compliant and men don't even acknowledge that they want or need anything because, if they do, it implies that they are not a real man. So we have two people sitting around wanting all these things from each other, probably capable of giving each other many of them, but not talking about it. Then they both feel depressed, both feel resentful, both feel deprived, they cheat on each other and you have a divorce. It all could be prevented by straight talk and clear asking.
                                            —Barbara De Angelis

The I Want Lists[19]

This next activitiy will help you clarify what you want from your partner and make it easier for you to ask for it. As a result, it will help you to put more romance, pleasure and joy back into your relationship. Set aside at least a half hour to do this exercise.

This activity has five steps to it.

1. The first step is to identify what your partner is already doing that pleases you. Complete the following sentence in as many ways as you can by listing behaviors, words and symbols your partner is currently using that make you feel cared about and loved.

I feel loved and cared about when you . . .

For example, I feel loved and cared about when you . . .

- Call me from work just to chat.
- Kiss me before you leave the house.
- Tell me you love me.
- Want to make love to me.
- Pray with me and for me.
- Go for a long walk with me.
- Check with me first before making plans.
- Massage my back.
- Sit close to me when we're watching TV.
- Compliment me on the way I look.

2. Now recall the earliest days of your relationship—when you were first courting and falling in love with each other—the "romantic stage." Are there any caring behaviors that your partner used to do for you that he or she no longer does? Complete the sentence below by listing the ways your partner made you feel loved and cared about in the past.

   I used to feel loved and cared about when you . . .

   For example, I used to feel loved and cared about when you . . .

   - Wrote me letters.
   - Whispered sexy things in my ear.
   - Made love to me more than once a day.
   - Held my hand as we walked.
   - Cooked a special meal for me.
   - Necked with me in the car.
   - Bought me surprise presents.

3. Now think about some caring and loving behaviors that you have always wanted but have never asked for. These may come from your fantasized vision of a perfect mate or from some prior experience. Complete the following sentence by listing all the things you would like your partner to do.

I would like you to . . .

Examples might include

- Massage my shoulders while we watch TV.
- Bring me breakfast in bed.
- Go backpacking with me three times each summer.
- Read a novel to me in bed while we're on vacation.
- Sleep in the nude.
- Take a shower with me.
- Massage me for thirty minutes without stopping.
- Go out to brunch with me once a month.
- Learn to play golf with me.

4. Go back over each list and indicate the relative importance of each behavior by rank ordering them. Put the number 1 next to the behavior you would like most, number 2 next to the next most important and so on.

5. Exchange lists. Starting tomorrow, do at least two of the behaviors each day for the next two months, starting with the ones that are the easiest for you to do. If there are certain items that are just not possible for you to do—for whatever reason—don't make a big issue out of them. Simply don't do them.

If more items occur to you later, you can add them to your lists. When your partner does a caring behavior for you, acknowledge it with an appreciative comment.

Keep your lists where you will see them every day, e.g., on the refrigerator, in your daily planning book, on the bathroom mirror, under the glass on your desk or on a bulletin board. One person we know programmed his computer, so his partner's "I Want List" is the first thing to come up on his screen whenever he turns his computer on.

Remember: These caring behaviors are gifts, not obligations. Do them regardless of how you feel about your partner, and regardless of the number of caring behaviors your partner gives you. This is an opportunity to give nurturance, joy and pleasure to each other, not to keep score!

Asking the most important people in my life to love me in very specific ways is one of the most significant things I've ever asked for. Here's a list of "The Ten Ways I'd Most Like You To Love Me" that I made for the man in my life.

1. Surprise me with something unexpected at least twice a month.
2. Call me up and leave me a few loving messages during the week.
3. Bring me flowers a couple of times a month.
4. Write down positive feelings about our relationship. This will help us to connect more.
5. Take undivided time to completely listen to me a few times a week.
6. Plan exciting dates ahead. For example, if you know *Phantom of the Opera* is coming to town, get tickets several months in advance and tell me so that we can look forward to going together.
7. Plan a surprise trip. Tell me we're going somewhere for the weekend but don't tell me anything about it. (Not even tell me where we're going to go.)
8. One of the best ways you can love me is to ask for what you want from me. Tell me, in detail, as I am doing by making this list.
9. Tell me what you appreciate about me on a regular basis, verbally and in writing.
10. Support me in reaching my dreams. Take time to share yours with me so that we can support each other in building our dreams together.

—**Diane Loomans, Author of** *Full Esteem Ahead*

The Fun List

1. Make a list of fun and exciting activities you would like to do with your partner. These should include face-to-face experiences and any body contact that is physically pleasurable. Examples include tennis, dancing, wrestling, showering together, sex, massage, tickling, jumping rope, bicycling, body paints, hot tubbing, playing with squirt guns, drawing with crayons together.
2. Share your lists and later compile a third list that combines all of your suggestions.
3. Every week pick one activity from the list and do it.

(Note: You may experience some resistance to taking part in such exuberant, childlike activities—especially if you have a conflicted relationship. It is important that you do this exercise nonetheless.)

Ask for feedback on how to improve the quality of the relationship.

The question is this: "On a scale of 1 to 10, what's been the quality of our relationship these past two weeks or month (or whatever period you're doing)?" Anything that gets less than a 10 has a follow-up question, which is: "What would it take to make it a 10?" These two questions will provide you with some of the most valuable feedback that you'll ever get because most people never know what it is that they're doing and how they could improve. They just get qualitative feedback like "I'm not happy with you," or "You're a jerk," or "I hate you."

Ask for clarification.

Sometimes when we communicate with our partners, we attribute meanings to their communication that are not always accurate. We make assumptions about the intent or meaning of their communication which may not be true. Whenever you find yourself talking about emotionally charged issues, check out the other person's meaning by using this very simple question: *"Do you mean . . . ?*

For example, let's say your partner says to you, "I'd like to go away for the weekend without you." Thinking this means your partner doesn't love you, you are starting to feel hurt. But then you remember to ask, "Do you mean . . . ?"

So you ask, "Do you mean you don't love me anymore?"

"No. I love you very much."

"Do you mean that you don't enjoy being with me anymore?"

"No, that's not what I mean at all. I love being with you."

"Do you mean that you just need to get away and chill out

with no demands at all on you so you can recover from writing that grant proposal?"

"Yes, that's exactly what I mean. I just want to sleep and vegetate for a few days and I don't think I can do that with you or the kids around."

"Okay, I get it. Thanks for letting me explore that with you."

You keep on asking "Do you mean . . . ?" until you get a yes. Remember the old adage, "When in doubt, check it out." Check out your assumptions by asking!

ASK YOUR KIDS

Ask your children clarifying questions.

Some parents complain that their children never mow the lawn, clean their rooms or take out the garbage. Many of these parents have never taken their children aside, looked them in the eye and said clearly and firmly—but without threat or resentment—what they want done.

> I think that telling is the most futile thing there is. It compresses, represses and depresses. Asking empowers, enhances and expands.
> —**Joe Batten**

Ask, don't tell.

> We need to treat children with much more respect. We need to listen to them and take them seriously. Instead of always telling them what happened, what caused it to happen, how they should feel about it and what they should do about it, we should ask them the following clarifying questions:
>
> What did you do?
> What happened?
> How do you feel about it?
> What were you trying to accomplish?
> If you didn't get the results you wanted, what did you learn from it?
> How can you use that information in the future?

This will teach them how to think about the consequences of their behavior and how to do better in the future. It will also keep them open and communicating instead of closed down and withdrawn.

Education comes from the Latin word *educare*—which means "to draw forth." Most of us do too much stuffing things in and not enough drawing things forth. We need to ask more questions with a real interest. Instead of saying, "Well, that's what you get," say, "Oh, that's interesting. What happened? Let's talk about that. How do you feel about it?" Or, "What did you learn from it?" Instead of trying to scold or rescue, we need to help kids explore more.
                                                              —Jane Nelsen

Make sure the message of love gets through.

I once received a call from a frantic single mother who was caught in a real power struggle with her fourteen-year-old daughter. She had found a six-pack of beer in her daughter's closet, so when her daughter came home, she said, "Okay, Maria, what is this?"

"It looks like a six-pack of beer to me, Mom."

"Don't get smart with me, young lady. You tell me about this."

"Well, I don't know what you're talking about."

"I found this six-pack in your closet young lady. You'd better explain."

Maria thinks real fast and says, "Oh yeah, I was hiding that for a friend."

"You expect me to believe that?"

Maria gets mad and stomps off to her bedroom and slams the door.

When the mother called me, I asked her, "Why were you so concerned with finding a six-pack of beer in her closet?"

"Because I don't want her to get into trouble."

"I understand that, but why is it you don't want her to get into trouble?" By this time I could tell she was really sorry she had called.

She answered, "Well, because I don't want her to ruin her life."

"I understand that, but why is it that you don't want her to ruin her life?"

Finally she got it, "Well, because I love her."

Then I asked her, "Do you think she got that message?"

"The answer is 'Of course not!' "

I then asked her, "What do you think would happen if you started with that message?" If she were to start with, "Honey, I love you so much that I got really scared when I found this six-pack of beer in your closet. Could we talk about this? Because I'm real afraid you could get into trouble. Could we talk about it?" In this approach you start by being vulnerable and telling your deeper truth instead of conducting an inquisition that inevitably leads to denial. Starting from the position of love and vulnerability evokes closeness and trust so that the child can then open up and work together with you on some kind of solution.

—Jane Nelsen

Kids are the very best natural born salespeople there are. They can convince a reluctant parent to buy the newest candy-coated cereal and feel as if they will be doing the best thing for the child. That is why these two popular techniques—tie-down asking and alternate of choice asking, used primarily in selling, work so well with children. You are speaking their language.

When she was about six years old, my daughter, and I were walking over to her best friend Amanda's house. She was feeling particularly tired that day, and so she presented me with an opportunity I couldn't refuse.

"Daddy, you like to be nice to me, don't you?"

"Yes, Elisabeth, of course I do."

"Then, Daddy, if you're really, really nice to me . . . I'll let you carry me all the way to Amanda's house."

One of the best uses of tie-down asking I have ever heard.

—Mark Victor Hansen

Use tie-downs.

Tie-down asking consists of constructing your question so that the answer is a consistent yes. The following phrases are attached to the question to create a momentum that helps your child come into agreement.

1. "Aren't they?"
2. "Aren't you?"
3. "Can't you?"
4. "Couldn't it?"
5. "Doesn't it?"
6. "Don't you agree?"
7. "Don't we?"

8. "Shouldn't it?"
9. "Wouldn't it?"
10. "Haven't they?"
11. "Hasn't he?"
12. "Hasn't she?"
13. "Isn't it?"
14. "Isn't that right?"
15. "Didn't it?"
16. "Wasn't it?"
17. "Won't they?"
18. "Won't you?"

"Have you done your homework?"

"Not yet, Mom."

"Sit down for a minute; I'd like to discuss this. You would like to do well on your test Friday, wouldn't you?"

"Sure."

"Having more knowledge about your subject would help, wouldn't it?"

"Yeah."

"So if you were to spend the time now on your homework, you might have some extra time later to bone up a little, wouldn't you?"

"I guess."

"So doing your homework now, before it gets any later looks like a good idea, don't you agree?"

"Okay . . . okay . . . okay."

Use alternate of choice asking.

This technique helps your child build a sense of good self-esteem because he or she retains the power of choice. Do you want (or would you prefer) to *set the table now* or *after this program*? to *wear your red pajamas* or *green pajamas*? to *eat cereal* or *eggs*? *Cheerios* or *cornflakes*?

This is especially effective to direct the child's attention away from an object or circumstance that you want to say no to. For instance, back in the cereal section of the store again . . .

"Mom, Mom, we want Barbie cereal!"

"We can't get that one today, do you want to buy Wheaties or granola?"

"Barbie!"

Calmly, but firmly, repeat the choices.

"Wheaties or granola?"

Eventually their desire to make a choice will prevail and everyone comes out of the grocery store feeling like a winner.

ASK AT SCHOOL

◆

Children enter school as question marks and leave as periods.
—Neil Postman

◆

Do you need more attention? Clarification? A question answered? Private tutoring? Someone to listen? Someone to care? Help with your homework? Directions to a certain building on campus? A scholarship? A student loan? A roommate? Lunch money? A ride home? To be excused from PE? To go to the bathroom? To know what you missed while you were sick? Help writing a paper? Instructions on the use of the computer? Help filling out college application forms? Help from the librarian? Help resolving a conflict? An extension on a paper? A date for the prom? Coaching? Someone to join your band? A teacher's aid? More supplies? Parent volunteers? Transportation for the field trip? People to join the fund-raising committee?

Ask your child's teacher to care.

Here's a wonderful letter written by Ron Barnes to his daughter's teacher:

Dear Teacher:

I am entrusting my child to your care for this school year. I do this willingly, but with concern and a degree of parental trepidation.

You see, my child has a priceless possession—her spirit. My role has been to nurture and protect it. I want you to be sure to do this as well. Therefore, let me offer a few suggestions that may help you to understand and appreciate her, and be the kind of supportive guide she needs as the two of you begin this adventure together.

First of all, I ask that, above all, you cherish and preserve her spirit. She may not be the brightest child in your class, but the lift of her spirit will be as radiant as any. It glows when praise and encouragement are offered; it withers when disparagement and humiliation prevail.

Her spirit will either carry her forward into a life where she will apply her energy with purpose, caring, and a goal for achievement, or into a future where she will settle for routine and mediocrity. I want her to run toward challenges, not away from them. I want her to test her strength against the harsh realities of life, imbued with an inner courage that tells her she can overcome whatever obstacles she encounters. Please help her spirit grow.

Her self-esteem is emerging. She is attaining a sense of self as she begins to grasp who she is and what she can do. But her developing self is fragile, her steps are tentative and she will need your hand. Encourage her as she gropes her way forward, crawling when she should run, and passive when you know she should lead. She is young, after all, so inconsistency is her standard behavior.

Discover her skills, boost her abilities and cheer her accomplishments while quietly identifying her limitations. Then help her improve, circumvent or overcome whatever it is that impedes or blocks her progress. She knows better than you how to overcome them. Please be her caring assistant.

My child is coming to you eager to learn. Do not, I beseech you, disappoint her. Make her studies stimulating and enjoyable. So far, in her young life, it has been mostly fun. Her educational experiences have been as natural as breathing. Please continue this pattern. Place her learning as a higher priority than your teaching, and make her and her classmates the focus of your class.

Finally, help her discover the wonder and excitement of self-knowledge so that at the end of the year, she has a better understanding of what she can and cannot ask herself to do. I want her to leave your class more confident in her abilities to succeed, more competent as a learner and person, and better prepared to take the next step in the educational ladder.

You see, this is the year you will become one of the most important persons in her life. She will decide to emulate your values and standards or reject them. She will respect and re-member you for the rest of her life, or she will dismiss you and feel disheartened for what you refused to give her. I sincerely want you to be the subject of her admiration—it will be up to you.

Oh yes, and when your year together is completed, give her a hug and thank her for being part of your life, as I hope to thank you for being part of hers. With love and hope, Her father[20]

Ask for another teacher.

Let's say you believe your child's teacher is destroying your child's self-esteem or is not giving your child the individual-ized attention he or she needs. How do you go about asking for and getting what you want? We asked former school superin-tendent John Prieskorn how to be effective in asking for and getting what you want from a school or school district. He of-fered the following advice:

The first step is to sit down with yourself and clarify what it is you are after. What outcome are you looking for? Are you look-ing for information? What do you want to find out? What do you want to know? Think of two or three good questions that you can ask them to elicit that information.

Do you want them to take some specific action? Do you want them to do something different? What do you want to have happen? What is your specific request? Think in terms of what you want, not what you don't want. If possible, think of several possible solutions to your problem or concern.

The second thing is to make sure that you are as relaxed and calm as possible. Know ahead of time that you might get some kind of negative response or some kind of sidestepping the is-sue. As much as you can, stay in a neutral place, a neutral state of mind. It is helpful to rehearse in your mind how you will respond in a neutral and calm way when and if they don't re-spond the way you want them to.

If you've done your homework and you've prepared yourself well and you've done everything you can to focus on the outcome that you want and you have an idea of how to create it, how you're going to get that, then at least you've set yourself up for a possible success if it's at all available.

And you have to realize that what you want may not always be available in that school due to laws, policies, budget restrictions, and so forth. Or they may just be unable or unwilling to give you what you want due to the dysfunctionality of the system.

If that doesn't work, then methodically start going up the ranks step by step. What's frustrating to administrators is when people come to the superintendent's office before talking to the teacher or the principal. Because they're all going to be told to go back to the original person anyway.

If you go to the teacher first and then you go to the vice principal in charge of this, if you've gone through two or three steps at the right level, you've done your homework, you've planned well, and you've prepared yourself with the right questions and the right state of mind, and you still haven't gotten any success, then go to the district level.

Find out who the appropriate person is, whoever the supervisor of that principal is, for instance, and keep asking. Pretty soon you're going to get someone's attention. People at the bottom don't like that kind of moving through the ranks, and once you start, it usually provides a response of a different kind.

One more thing to understand is that there is no guarantee that you'll get what you want. I once took over a district in the Santa Rosa Valley that was totally unresponsive to the community. Eighty-two percent of the community had answered in a survey that the school district stunk because it didn't respond to the clients' needs and questions.

That's when you have to escalate your asking to the political level. You organize politically and call for the hiring of a new school superintendent or you elect a new school board. You might even run for school board. Before I was hired, they had fired the last superintendent within three months of his starting. The whole system was in an uproar. Six hundred parents had signed a petition and the parents were carrying placards.

And then, of course, there is always the option of moving to a community with a more responsive school system or placing your child in a private school more to your liking.

Let me add one more thing that I have found to be very effective. Let's say you feel your child has been placed in the wrong class. There's a personality conflict between your child and the teacher, and you believe another teacher would work better with your child. You would like to have your child transferred to another teacher's class. You would be better off not starting with your upset or a demand. It is more effective to start with the question "What would it take to get a child moved from one class to another in this school (or district)?"

The reason this question is more effective is that you are starting by eliciting their criteria rather than confronting them with your demand. If you start with your demand, you create a defensiveness on the other side. If you start out with asking them their criteria or their procedure, then you're much more likely to find ways to fit your need into their way of doing things. Then it becomes much more difficult for them to say, "No."

—John Prieskorn

Ask for special attention.

If you feel you need special attention for yourself or for your child, ask for it. You can request extra time, counseling, tutoring, special classes, whatever it is that you need. There are often special teachers, extra funds, and so on, available for meeting your requests.

Sometimes it is as simple as asking a teacher after class to clarify or explain a concept. Most teachers like to teach; that is why they are there. Take the risk to ask. You might just learn something.

Ask for an extension.

Sometimes family pressures, travel, medical emergencies and natural disasters such as earthquakes and flooding make it difficult for you to finish an assignment on time. By all means, ask for an extension. Remember to be specific in your request. Tell the teacher how long you'd like and why.

Ask teachers for help in achieving your goals.

When I reached my final semester in college, I realized that I was very close to becoming a Phi Beta Kappa. After explaining this to my father, who had not gone to college, he began to brag to his friends. He was so thrilled that he said I could do anything I wanted after college, if I got him that key! I visited each of my

teachers and told them my goal of becoming a Phi Beta Kappa graduate. I'm sure that sharing my story and my goal with my father and my teachers made a difference. I made the grade and I gave my father the key I was awarded. He wore it as a tie clasp until he died.
                                            —Betty Mazzetti Hatch

Ask to have your grade or results reviewed.

When Jack's wife took her oral examination for her California marriage, family and child counselor license, she received notice that she had failed. Since she felt she had answered all of the questions adequately, she called the state board and asked if there was an appeal process. Georgia wrote a letter outlining her reasons for believing she had passed the examination. Upon review, she was granted her license. This saved her countless hours of having to prepare for the exam again six months later.

You, too, can ask a teacher or professor to reconsider a grade, test score or examination result. Just be prepared to make a case. Remember that, except in mathematics, most grades are very subjective anyway. In one study conducted by the National Council of Teachers of English, the same essay was given to one hundred teachers, who were asked to grade it. That same paper received everything from an A to an F!

You may get your grade raised. And even if you don't, you'll learn more about your teacher's criteria for a high grade.

Ask for a scholarship.

Each year large amounts of scholarship money go unclaimed because (1) people don't know the funds exist and (2) people don't apply for them. The money is there but people don't ask.

College scholarship committees and loan officers have told us that they are always willing to entertain requests for money. They may not always grant the requests, but they advise people to come in and talk about their needs. There are often many ways to get funds outside of the normally considered ones.

One of Jack's college roommates actually got an increase in his academic scholarship from Harvard so that he could buy a motorcycle. He convinced the scholarship committee that he needed it to adequately de-stress himself after the pressures of class and football practice so that he could study better at night. We don't know if you could pull that one off in today's financially restricted academic institutions, but who knows unless you ask?

Get a copy of *The Scholarship Book*.[21] It contains information on all of the scholarships that are available, what the requirements are and how to apply for them.

Ask for the real reason.

While we were writing this book, Mark and Patty Hansen were invited to come to their daughter's school to discuss the fact that she had missed so many days due to several extended family vacations. The day before the meeting, Mark was interviewing Dave Yoho, Jr., and Dave made the following useful suggestions that we share with you here:

You need to say to the principal, "I want to thank you for asking us to come in. I really appreciate you showing this much interest in Elisabeth. I know you are very disappointed. You know, you could have been upset and not said anything to us, so we are glad that you called this meeting." I would keep that part brief. Then let the principal say whatever her concerns and upsets are. Just hear her out until she is finished.

Then say, "Okay, I think I understand all that. I'm unclear on a couple of things. Do you mind if I ask you a few questions?" What's she going to say, "No"? Then ask, "How has this affected her schooling?" Her answer will probably be, "Well, she's a straight A student; I guess it probably hasn't." Then I would say, "How has this affected her relationship with the other children?" If she says it has, ask, "How's that? Can you give me an example of which kids and how that happens?"

Now, if she hasn't given you a good answer, sit back in your chair and say, "Look, I came here today out of a sense of cooperation," (Keep your arms open when you do this.) "and out of respect to you, but I guess, I sense that there is another reason that you are upset, because maybe my thinking is faulty, but I just don't see how this has affected Elisabeth in an adverse way. I guess from my way of thinking this travel has really broadened her culturally and made her a better person. So it seems to me that there might be something else bothering you. Like maybe she's not keeping your rules and the problem might be that you're more upset about her not being here as much as you would like her to be." Now, it's pretty risky to drop that on her but that could very well be what it is. Then you can deal with the real issue. —Dave Yoho, Jr.

A superintendent asks the entire district to cooperate.

I was a classroom teacher, then a principal, and then a superintendent. I was superintendent in San Lorenzo Valley in Santa Cruz for eleven years.

Asking wasn't always easy, but I decided it was necessary if I was going to get anything done. I was committed to creating a successful school district out of one that had been a miserable failure. I knew that I needed to get a lot of cooperation from all the employees, from the school board and from the community. If I didn't have cooperation and support from those people, it wouldn't have happened. The district was so messed up, it was in chaos. I made a commitment to myself as well as to the board when I took that job, that I wouldn't take it unless I was making a significant change for the better while I was there. Through that commitment, I needed to get their cooperation and support. That comes only from asking. You can't get it without asking.

My approach initially was to have a series of meetings with each board member individually, so that I understood what this human being needed and wanted as part of their commitment to serving on the board. When I got that collectively, I made some generalizations and helped them come together. Basically, I did the same with every faction. My approach was to meet with representatives from each of the groups—the teachers group, the parents group, the classified employees group, and the management group—to find out what was bugging them, what their needs were, and what they thought was most useful if this school district was going to work. Then I began to put all those responses together into a package and look for the similarity.

First, I asked them:

What problems and concerns do you have?
What's bugging you, what's eating you?
What kind of things have been getting in the way in the past?
What do you think has contributed to the failure of this school system?

After I got all that, I began asking questions like:

So what would it take to fix it?
What do you think is missing?
What's lacking?
What would it take to cause this school district to be a success?

The initial response that I uniformly got from all the groups was "Well, if somebody else would change, then . . ." For six months I got nothing but their frustration with others. My decision to go beyond that was to go back with each of those same representatives a second time and say, "Okay, I understood what you said about what's wrong and what somebody else needs to do. I'd also like to know specifically, what can you—

you yourself, you personally, and your organization—do, to contribute to the turnaround? Assuming that everyone else is going to make their contribution to improve it as well, what can you contribute to the change?"

Then I began getting some different responses. Then I began getting some personal commitment. I don't know how else I could have gotten it without accepting and allowing all of their anger and frustration and all of their lack of trust to come out the first time. I think if I would have denied and rejected, that they would have rejected me, my questions, and the whole process. I had to go through the negative stuff to get to the positive. They all contributed positive stuff later.

That whole process took about a year. We had a lot of good information in the first six months, but we didn't start getting cooperation until the end of the first year. I wouldn't count it as a real success that we could tangibly measure until about two or three years later, but by the end of the first year everybody realized and accepted the fact that we had made the turnaround.
—**John Prieskorn**

ASK AT WORK

◆

If you follow your bliss, doors will open for you that wouldn't have opened for anyone else.
—Joseph Campbell

◆

Do you need time off? A vacation? A promotion? A raise? Your own office? More instruction? More appreciation? More recognition? More support? Better equipment? Someone to listen to your idea? Someone to help you solve a problem? Less backbiting? More cooperation? More understanding? Less stress? More room? More acknowledgment and appreciation? More recognition? A promotion? A transfer? Someone to trade shifts with you? Someone to quit harassing you? An assistant? To be included in the decision making? An advance on your salary or commission? Permission to attend a seminar, a training or a conference? A leave of absence? An explanation? A change of policy? A temporary to help get a job done? A bigger budget? Budgetary control? An extension? A flexible schedule? More commitment from your employees? More creative ideas?

Ask for a chance.

My father operated a fruit and vegetable market and sold produce from the back of a truck in the alleys of Holyoke, Massachusetts. One day, when I was nine, my dad asked me to throw out a case of strawberries that had gone bad. There were twenty-four quart baskets of strawberries in the case. I asked if I could have them, since they were to be thrown out. He said no, that he wouldn't give them to me even though they had been destined for the garbage can, since they hadn't been given to him. But he did offer to sell them to me on credit and on "spec."

"Spec," from the word speculation, meant that if I didn't sell them, I wouldn't owe him for them. I agreed to do that, and we quickly negotiated a price. I remember that the price was foolishly low, even for those days—maybe a nickel a quart. Then he doubled it, he explained, to cover his risk. This was my first lesson in the cost of credit and investor returns.

I sorted out the berries, put the good ones in clean baskets, and salvaged eight quarts. Then I put them in my wagon and dragged my wagon through the alleys behind the tenement blocks near our store. (Yes, I wanted very much to be my father's son in that regard; and no, you don't bring a wagon load of strawberries safely up and down long, steep flights of stairs. You leave all but one basket with the lady on the first floor. It's also a good way to get her to buy some.) In less than an hour I had sold out and was back for more. There were no more berries to sell that day, but my father did "extend" me some aging sweet corn and potatoes, also on spec. I sold those in about an hour, too.

After that, whenever I did an especially good job at cleaning out the storeroom, or sweeping the floor, or polishing the apples, I was rewarded with a wagon load of goods that I could go sell in the tenements. The money I made, I got to keep, after I paid my father a negotiated price for his goods. Being allowed by my father to negotiate prices with him made me feel like his equal in a sense, though I was only nine years old, and that boosted my self-esteem enormously! My mom was always nearby to help us sort out differences of opinion about the value of his semi-rotten potatoes, and what his fair return should be for selling on spec, and she would never, it seems to me, side with either her son or her husband out of love or sympathy. She just insisted that we both do the right thing by one another. And, largely because of her, we always did.   —**Rick Gelinas**

It doesn't matter how old or how young you are. You can always ask for more and get it. Whether you are a salesperson, a manager, a secretary, a receptionist, a clerk, an assembly line worker in the plant, a forklift operator, a postal employee or a small business owner, if you increase the amount and quality of your requests, you can increase your productivity, your bottom line and the quality of your work life.

Ask for a job . . . and more!

In the early 1980s Jack started the Foundation for Self-Esteem for the purpose of doing educational and charitable work in the fields of education, welfare and corrections. He wanted to train teachers, social workers and prison workers to deliver self-esteem and self-empowerment trainings to students, welfare recipients and prisoners. In addition, he sponsored a self-esteem conference for eight hundred educators in southern California.

As a result of attending one of those conferences, Larry Price decided to make a career change. He wanted to make a larger difference in the community. He decided he could do that through the Foundation for Self-Esteem. Here's his story of how he made that dream come true.

I had just finished working for the 1984 Los Angeles Olympic Committee and I wanted to find another position where I could be of service to the community. I began asking around and I discovered Jack Canfield's Foundation for Self-Esteem. I asked Norm Fry about the foundation because he knew Jack Canfield and he said as far as he knew there was no one running the foundation, so I called Jack and asked if we could get together and discuss his nonprofit foundation.

We met for lunch and I said, "I want to come to work for your foundation."

Jack replied, "I'm not hiring anybody. All the foundation does at this point is put on an annual self-esteem conference for teachers, and we have just enough money left over after each conference to advertise the next one."

I said, "That doesn't matter. I still want to come work for you. I want to run your foundation."

"You're not listening. I'm not in a position to pay you anything. There is no money for your salary."

"You're not listening to me. I don't care about the money. I want to run your foundation and I'll figure out where to get the money."

"Well then, okay. How can I lose with an offer like that?"

My wife, Linda, knowing that I was about to embark on a new path that was very important to me, volunteered to go back to work until the foundation was up and running and able to pay me.

Now I had two new challenges. I had never run a foundation before and I had to raise enough money to pay my own salary. I asked everyone I knew who was even remotely involved with nonprofits, "How do you do this?" They either gave me advice or referred me to other people. I also took a seminar from a woman who raised funds for the county of L.A. and who really knew what she was doing. I asked her if she would tell me how to raise funds for a nonprofit.

She said, "There is a request for proposals that has been issued by the county office of education that you should respond to."

I asked, "How do I do that?" She sent me to another person at the county office of education, who then got me on the proposal list.

Once I had done that, I went to a pre-bid conference where I met the people who wrote the video specifications for the proposal request. I approached them and asked them if they would team up with me. They thought it was a good match. Then I went to one other potential bidder—Dolores Ratcliffe—and asked her to join us. Two months and a lot of writing later, our proposal was selected. The amount of the grant was $579,000. I had created my salary and a major project for the foundation all in four months and all by asking for what I wanted and needed.   **—Larry Price**

Just start asking.

Marilyn Kriegel told us the following story about her son Otis. He and his girlfriend had returned to San Francisco from college for the summer break. They both wanted to get a job for the summer. The difference in their approaches demonstrates the power of asking. The girl began to prepare her résumé. She spent the next two days at the typewriter, getting ready to ask. Otis simply got on the phone and started calling people to find out if they had any job openings. Two days later she had a half written resume. Otis had six serious job possibilities, one of which turned into a summer job.

For more information on how to go about finding jobs and

careers, we highly recommend *What Color Is Your Parachute — 1995* by Richard N. Bolles (Berkeley, CA: 10 Speed Press, 1995). We met Richard Bolles at a recent convention of the American Booksellers Association and discovered that he is someone who really cares about you and wants to make a difference in your life. Let this wonderful big-hearted man contribute to your life through this wonderful book.

Ask for encouragement.

Encouragement is the oxygen of the soul.   —Anonymous

In 1980 I became aware that I wanted to quit my very successful career in real estate so that I could sing, dance and write — with the ultimate goal of producing and performing in a musical on Broadway. I was clear that this is what I wanted to do, but I recognized that something important was missing — and that something was support! Every time I told somebody what my dream was, they would say, "You're crazy."

So I made up a blue ribbon with gold letters that said, "Who I am makes a difference." I started to walk around and tell people how great they were and ask them what their dreams were. I said, "I will encourage you to go for your dream, and I would also like you to encourage me to go for mine. You see, I want to perform in a Broadway musical on March 31, 2002, and every time you see me, I want you to give me a thumbs-up and say "Keep on going, Helice."   —Helice Bridges

Ask for someone to mentor you.

Boy: Teach me what you know, Jim.
Reverend Jim: That would take hours, Terry. Ah, what the heck! We've all got a little Obi-Wan Kenobi in us.   —Taxi

Here is the basic rule for winning success. Let's mark it in the mind and remember it. The rule is: Success depends on the support of other people. The only hurdle between you and what you want to be is the support of other people.
—David Joseph Schwartz

Samuel A. Cypert, editorial advisor to the Napoleon Hill Foundation, suggests that you might approach someone to be your mentor by saying something like this:

"I really admire the way you do things. You're successful at what you do, and I think you are an exceptional role model. I would like to spend some time with you and have the benefit of your experience. Would you mind helping me?"

It has been our experience that most people, when approached this positively, will respond by spending time with you. You can ask local people to spend time in person with you. You can ask people who live at a distance to spend time on the phone with you.

When Jack quit his job and decided to create his own training and development company, he called Lou Tice, the founder and president of the Pacific Institute, told him he admired his work and said, "If you ever come to Los Angeles to do a speech or a workshop, I would like the opportunity to pick you up at the airport and act as your chauffeur in exchange for the privilege of picking your brain during the time we are driving around. Is that something you would be willing to do?"

Lou was gracious enough to say yes, and Jack spent half a day driving Lou around Los Angeles. He was able to ask him all the questions he wanted about how to be successful in the seminar and training business, and Lou answered all of his questions with great advice and practical, usable information. Jack figures he received over $5,000 worth of valuable consulting in exchange for four hours of driving—and all because he asked.

The thing that we have learned over the years is that some of the busiest and most successful people in the world are available if you can figure out a way that is easy for them. Lou would have had to take a cab anyway. Jack saved Lou some money and gave him an opportunity to do what he loves best— teach what he knows to others.

Mentoring can also be done in groups.

For the last several years Mark has conducted mentoring sessions in groups for chiropractors. He will meet with ten people in a hotel room and work intensely with them on how to increase their practices. His current promise is to teach them how to triple their income while doubling their time off. He now charges for this service, but it all started with a group of chiropractors wanting to spend more time with Mark and his seeing the value of doing it in a group. It was more time effective for Mark and it was more valuable for the chiropractors because they learned from one another as well as Mark.

Why not form a group and invite the people you want to learn from to come and teach you?

> *Come to the edge, He said.*
> *They said, We are afraid.*
> *Come to the edge, He said.*
> *They came.*
> *He pushed them . . . and they flew.*
> —Guillaume Apollinaire

We believe that we all need someone in our lives at times to coach us to greater and greater levels of excellence in our chosen areas of pursuit. To get better, we often need a teacher or a coach. This may be someone to coach you in athletics, the arts, financially or professionally. Perhaps you would like a personal trainer at the gym, a music teacher, a voice coach, a dance instructor or a golf pro. You can hire a writing coach, a drama coach or a speech coach. Why not also seek out a financial planner, a holistic health consultant and a career coach? You can find someone who will challenge you to excel in any area of your life that you want.

We've asked for advice and coaching from racquetball pros, tennis instructors, dive coaches, race car drivers, guitar players, jugglers, professional speakers, actors, self-made millionaires, best-selling authors, infomercial producers, meditation teachers, yoga instructors, ministers, prayer consultants, bankers, audiovisual specialists, literary agents, publicists, midwives and artists.

"How do you do that?"

"Can you show me what you just did?"

"Can you give me a few pointers that would help me to improve my . . . ?"

"Do you have any advice for someone who is . . . ?"

"Do you ever take on students?"

"Would you be willing to . . . ?"

"Do you know anyone who . . . ?"

You'll be amazed at how many people will say yes. If they say no, so what. Just ask somebody else.

Join or create a master mind group.

Probably the one book that has had the most profound effect on both of our careers is Napoleon Hill's *Think and Grow Rich*. This book has been credited with changing the lives of many of our most successful entrepreneurs, people such as Wally Amos, founder of Famous Amos Cookies, and Thomas Monaghan, founder of Domino's Pizza. One of the most important techniques Hill shares is how to create and utilize a mastermind alliance.

A mastermind alliance is two or more people who come together to work in a spirit of perfect harmony toward the achievement of a common objective. The two of us have several mastermind alliances which meet to forward our careers and our goals. These groups include Murray Fischer, an incredible writer and editor; Martin Rutte, a corporate consultant; Doug Kruschke, an organizational development specialist; John Assaraff, the owner of RE/MAX of Indiana and an incredible entrepreneur; Peter Vegso and Gary Seidller, our publishers at Health Communications; and Bernie Dohrmann, founder of Income Builders International; as well as the two of us.

Jack once belonged to a mastermind alliance that included a

doctor, a consultant, a photographer and Barbara De Angelis, one of the world's most successful authors and a relationships expert. They would meet every Tuesday morning from 6:30 A.M. to 8:30 A.M. and then leave for work. That requires a lot of commitment to get up at 5:00 in the morning for a mastermind meeting, but everyone in that group has gone on to unprecedented levels of success both professionally and financially.

What we recommend is that you make a list of four to six people you would like to have in your mastermind alliance. Pick people that you believe can contribute to you and to whom you will make a commitment to contribute back. Call up each person on your list and invite them to join you in a mastermind alliance. Explain that you would like to meet at least twice a month for two hours at a time. Explain that the purpose of the meeting will be to provide mutual support and accountability in the achievement of your goals—both personally and professionally.

Some of the things you can do in these meetings are ask for advice, feedback, resources and coaching. You can role-play difficult presentations. You can critique one another's business plans, strategies and ideas. You can brainstorm new possibilities, share contacts and save problems. Most importantly, you stretch one another into thinking bigger and hold one another accountable for achieving goals that are set to be accomplished before the next meeting.

Mark was in New York making a presentation to nine thousand people for the New York Chiropractic Society. Tony Robbins was the other speaker on the program. Mark said to Tony, "Jack and I are as smart and talented as you. How come you're making 50 million dollars a year and we're only making a million each?"

Tony asked, "How much money do each of the people in your mastermind alliance make?"

Mark replied, "About a million or so. Why?"

"That's your problem," Tony said. "Everyone in my group makes about a hundred million a year. You need to surround yourself with people that are already manifesting at the level you want to reach. They will stretch you into a bigger game."

So we too are constantly stretching our limits of what is possible. We too are constantly reaching out to more and more people that share a common goal of making a difference in the lives of others while also doing well financially. We are constantly asking individuals, organizations and the universe to support us in creating a more fulfilling reality.

Now, a million or a hundred million may be way beyond where you are now, but the point here is for you to find a way to hang out with people who are further along than you are. They will stretch your self-concept, your mind and your behavior. They will expand your image of what is possible.

You don't have to be rich.

A woman with two children living on welfare in a housing project in Chicago's Cabrini Green district decided she wanted out of the projects and out of the ghetto. She knew she couldn't do it alone. She needed a skill she could sell. In order to become a typist, she would need to return to school and get some training. How could she pull this off with two kids to watch all day?

She solved the problem by asking the other mothers in the project to join her in forming a mastermind alliance. The first thing they did was create a cooperative child care program—a fancy term for "I'll take your kids on Tuesdays, Thursdays and Saturdays if you'll take mine on Monday, Wednesdays and Fridays." Having freed up three days a week, she took typing and business skills classes at a nearby community college. Two years later she and several others landed secretarial jobs and moved themselves and their children out of the projects.

Ask for more money.

> Literally, I feel the most outrageous request I ever made was when I asked for a thousand dollars for a speaking fee. I was so nervous I couldn't believe it. —**Jane Bluestein**

When Jack first started out as an educational consultant, he was charging $300 a day. He later found out that a friend of his was making $800 a day for the same services. He was shocked. "How do you get $800 a day?" He asked in disbelief.

"It's simple," he said. "I ask for it."

"Wow, I didn't know schools paid that kind of money for seminars and trainings." Inwardly Jack was thinking "I am as good as he is. I'm just as smart, funny and inspirational in my seminars."

So he decided to ask for $800 the next time somebody wanted to hire him. In less than a week, he was given the opportunity to ask. When the person on the other end of the phone asked him what his fee was, he literally choked. He couldn't get the words out. "Eigh-eigh-eigh—six hundred dollars!" He finally blurted out, thinking he would probably scream at him something like "You've got to be kidding!"

What he did say was "No sweat!"

"No sweat?" Had he heard correctly? "What would have been sweat?" he asked.

"Oh, we had $1,200 in the budget for the speaker," he responded.

Unbelievable! Jack had left $600 on the table that could have been his if he had simply asked for it.

Ask for a raise.

Research shows that it pays to ask for a raise. *USA Today* published the results of a survey of heads of households conducted by the Lutheran Brotherhood in which they found that of those people who had asked for a raise in their current job, 45 percent of the women and 59 percent of the men had received one. So, your chances are 50/50 that you'll get the raise simply by asking for it. Remember, once again, the worst that can happen is that they will say no. So what! You don't really lose anything, do you?

Ask your boss, employees, clients and suppliers for feedback.

Ask all the people you do business with—your boss, your employees, your suppliers and your clients—the same question we covered in Chapter Eight:

> *On a scale of 1 to 10, what has been the quality of our relationship this past month?*

If you get anything less than a 10, follow it up with

> *What would it take to make it a 10?*

You'll receive such valuable information if you will do this.

How can we help?

The headquarters staff of Kwik Kopy, the world's largest printing franchise company, with approximately $350 million in annual revenues, created a team of "sweat hogs" who spend their days on the phone calling every franchise owner at least once a month, asking, "Are you all right? Do you need anything? Give me one thing to do for you."

Responses are immediately entered into the computer for follow-up, and at the end of the call, franchisees are asked to rate the call on a scale of 1 to 10 with 10 being the top score. The current company-side rating stands at 9.057.

Ask for a promotion.

Once you are clear about your career plans, tell your boss or manager what your aspirations are and ask what you would have to do to qualify for a promotion: "Mr. Smith, I'd like to become a systems analyst instead of a programmer. If I take the appropriate courses at USC, can I be considered for a promotion?"

Ask for a loan.

You can ask an employer, ex-employer or credit union to loan you money to get you through difficult times.

My house was about to go into foreclosure and I did not want to compromise the title to the house. I crossed the fear line and asked an ex-boss, who had recently let me go, for a ninety-day $6,500 loan. He gave me the money in cash the next day! He gave it to me without hesitation.   **—Pam Herrington**

You can also ask a bank for a loan. We asked former bank president Somers White to share his insights on how to get approval for a bank loan.

What do you tell a banker?

If you want a commercial loan there are five things the lender wants to know in the first ninety seconds:

1. How many dollars do you want?
2. How long do you want the money?
3. What are you going to do with the money?
4. How are you going to repay the loan?
5. If something goes wrong, what is the alternate method of repayment?

When you tell the banker how much is needed, *ask for a little extra* because most people underestimate and once you have the loan it is very difficult to come back and get more money.

In getting a commercial loan, there are only three purposes for which a loan is made: to buy or carry an asset, to decrease a liability or pay an expense, and to buy out capital.

Bankers talk about the *seven c's* of credit: character, capital, capacity, cash flow, conditions, currentness of the information and collateral.

Character is the most important. What will the borrower do if he or she gets in trouble? His integrity is more important than any legal document or loophole.

Cash flow is the next most important because over 90 percent of the time, business loans are repaid from cash flow.

What to ask when you are rejected.

When a banker turns you down, the banker feels a little guilty. Make this work for you by asking these simple questions so you learn how to turn a "no" into a "yes" when you go to the next bank.

Question 1: Mr. or Ms. Banker, as I understand it, you are turning me down for a loan. (Shut up. He who speaks first, loses.)

Question 2: Mr. or Ms. Banker, what would you do if you were in my position? (Shut up. He who speaks first, loses.)

Question 3: Well, then it sounds like I should go to another bank.

Question 4: Which bank?

Question 5: Why?

Question 6: Who should I ask for?

Question 7: Why?

Question 8: What should I tell him or her?

"We were wondering if we could extend
the maximum limit on our
charge account?"

A good boss delegates.

An admiral and a commander were having a heated discussion about lovemaking. The admiral claimed it was 80 percent work and 20 percent pleasure. The commander said the admiral was nuts; it was 10 percent work and 90 percent pleasure. They were at loggerheads on the issue and wanted an impartial opinion. They saw the chief petty officer and called him in on it. They explained the dispute and asked his opinion.

The chief said, "Sirs, with all due respect, you're both wrong." They wanted to know how an admiral and a commander could be wrong about anything. He said, "Well, if there were any work to it, you'd both have me doing it for you."

— *Speaker's Library of Business Stories*
by Joe Griffith

Ask for better tools and equipment.

If you feel you need better tools or newer equipment to perform your job better, ask. Make a clear case for what you believe your need is, how much it will cost, where it could be purchased, how it will increase your job performance, safety, etc. and what you're willing to do to help get the new equipment or tools.

Many years ago there was a huge oil refinery fire. Flames shot hundreds of feet into the air. The sky was thick with grimy, black smoke. The heat was intense—so intense that firefighters had to park their trucks a block away and wait for the heat to die down before they could begin to fight the fire. However, it was about to rage out of control.

Then all of a sudden, from several blocks away came a fire truck, racing down the street with its brakes screeching. It hit the curb in front of the fire. The firefighters jumped out and began to battle the blaze. All the firefighters who were a block away saw this, and they jumped into their trucks, drove down the block and began to fight the fire, too. As a result of that cooperative effort, they were just barely able to bring the fire under control.

The people who saw the teamwork thought, "My goodness, the man who drove that lead fire truck—what an act of bravery!" They decided to give him a special award to recognize him for bravery in leading the charge.

At the ceremony the mayor said, "Captain, we want to honor you for your fantastic act of bravery. You prevented the loss of property—perhaps even the loss of life. If there is one special thing you could have—just about anything—what would it be?"

Without hesitation the captain replied. "Your Honor, a new set of brakes would be dandy!"   **—Mike Wickett**

Ask for excellence.

Former Secretary of State Henry Kissinger asked an assistant to prepare an analysis. The assistant worked day and night on the report. An hour after he gave it to Kissinger, he got it back. There was a note attached that said to redo it.

The assistant stayed up all night redoing the report. Again Kissinger asked him to redo it.

After redoing the report three times, the assistant asked to see Kissinger. He told him, "I've done the best I can do."

Kissinger said, "In that case, I'll read it now."

—Speaker's Library of Business Stories
by Joe Griffith

Explain the consequences clearly.

Everybody but Sam had signed up for a new company pension plan that called for a small employee contribution. The company was paying all the rest.

Unfortunately, 100 percent employee participation was needed; otherwise the plan was off.

Sam's boss and his fellow workers pleaded and cajoled, but to no avail. Sam said the plan would never pay off.

Finally the company president called Sam into his office. "Sam," he said, "here's a copy of the new pension plan and here's a pen. I want you to sign the papers. I'm sorry, but if you don't sign, you're fired. As of right now."

Sam signed the papers immediately.

"Now," said the president, "would you mind telling me why you couldn't have signed earlier?"

"Well, sir," replied Sam, "nobody explained it to me quite so clearly before."[22]   *—The Best of Bits and Pieces*

Ask diplomatically.

When the Civil War ended, some people were clamoring for the capture and hanging of Jefferson Davis, head of the Confederacy.

President Abraham Lincoln, eager to heal the nation's wounds as soon as possible, felt there were good reasons to resist these demands, but it was not politic for him to come out and say it.

Finally, General Sherman met with Lincoln and asked whether the President wanted him to capture Davis or let him escape.

"Let me tell you what I think of taking Jeff Davis," Lincoln replied. "Out in Sangamon County there was an old temperance lecturer who was very strict in the doctrine and practice of total abstinence. One day, after a long ride in the hot sun, he stopped at the house of a friend, who proposed making him a lemonade. As it was being mixed the friend asked if he wouldn't like a drop of something stronger to brace his nerves after the exhausting heat and exercise.

"No," said the lecturer, "I wouldn't think of it. I'm opposed to it on principle, but if you could manage to put in a drop unbeknownst to me, I guess it wouldn't hurt me much."

"Now, General," Lincoln said, "I am bound to oppose the escape of Jeff Davis, but if you could manage to let him slip out, unbeknownst like, I guess it wouldn't hurt me much."[23]

—The Best of Bits and Pieces

Make outrageous requests.

Great things are only possible with outrageous requests.

—Thea Alexander

I'll tell you what's outrageous. We had a consulting assignment with what I considered to be, not financially but corporate emotionally, an unstable client. The consulting fee was $68,000. I asked for the whole sixty-eight grand in front and got it. I simply told them that's how we got paid.   —Dave Yoho, Jr.

Do the impossible in one day.

When I took a course on telemarketing fundraising—the Cash Workshop—led by Bill Reidler at the Global Relationship Center in Austin, Texas, there was a woman who shared that she felt she was at a plateau in her career as a fund-raiser. She wanted to have more impact and make more money, and she didn't see how she could do that because she was maxed out in the number of fund-raising events she could do in a year. Bill said, "Well, since you know so much about putting together these events, why don't you conduct a seminar on it? I'll help you design it and we can offer the first one right here in Dallas one month from now."

While we were on our lunch break, the staff copied lists of all kinds of nonprofits in the local area for us to call and enroll people in her as-yet-undesigned seminar. When we came back from lunch, they said, "Go to it, start asking." We called everyone on the lists they provided, plus people we knew as well.

They also provided us with a phone script that they had created while we were at lunch which gave us specific questions and details on how to ask. They said, "Be relentless, and don't give up." For example: If someone said, "I can't come," we'd ask, "Is there someone else in your organization you could send?" If they said, "A thousand dollars is a lot of money for a seminar," we would counter with "Well, if you want to increase your effectiveness and bring in more money, it's guaranteed to bring in more money than you're going to spend. There is a money back guarantee." The other thing we did was to stress the scarcity. "This seminar is only going to be offered once in Austin and there are only fifty spots available. If you don't sign up now, you're going to lose out."

In three or four hours we enrolled almost forty people in the seminar. I got three of those people myself. The energy in the room was incredible. Every time somebody got an enrollment, they would beep a bicycle horn. I learned a lot about the power of asking that day. We went from an idea to $40,000 worth of enrollments in less than six hours. I learned that anything is possible if you go for it. —**Larry Price**

ASKING IN SALES

May I make a suggestion?

I learned a very valuable phrase years ago—"May I make a suggestion?" When you are going to ask somebody to do something, first say, "May I make a suggestion." You are now going to tell them to do it instead of asking them to do it. For example, if I were making a call on an executive, chances are that when I'm brought into the executive's office the executive is going to sit behind the desk and I'm going sit in one of those two chairs on the far side of the desk. I don't mind sitting there at first, but if I have to show this person something, trying to show the person across the desk puts me at a very terrible disadvantage. It will also not allow me to have an open conversation with this guy, especially when I ask him some questions.

So, I don't look at him; I look at his desk and I say, "Gee, I had a couple of things to show you; I don't see the room here and I want to save you as much time as possible. I know you've got a busy day; so do I." I then look over at the other chair and I say, "May I make a suggestion?" When he says, "Yes!" I say, "Move over here and I'll save you a lot of time showing you this." Then I just turn my chair to face the other chair.

They get up from behind the desk and walk over to the other chair and you show it to them. Now you've got them on the same side of the desk as you.

That's something that most people just wouldn't have the guts to do. The funny thing about it is people will do almost anything you ask them to do if they think it's in their best interest.   —Dave Yoho, Jr.

Ask for an appointment.

The big businessman had died and gone to—well, not to heaven. He had hardly settled down for a nice long smoke when a hearty hand slapped him on the back, and into his ear boomed the voice of a persistent salesman who had pestered him on earth. "Well, Mr. Smith," chortled the salesman, "I'm here for the appointment."

"What appointment?"

"Why, don't you remember?" the salesman went on. "Every time I entered your office on earth you told me you'd see me here!"   —Source Unknown

We recently heard of a successful New York salesman who, though his clients were big businessmen, rarely had difficulty in getting an appointment. This astounding record he explained by the fact that he always asked for an appointment at an odd time. That is, instead of suggesting eleven o'clock, for instance, he would specify 10:50. Of course the busy executive would have another engagement at eleven, but probably no engagement at such an odd hour. The executive also somehow got the idea that this salesman's time was valuable and that he would be interested in making the interview as concise as possible.

—Manager's Magazine

Persevere to get an appointment.

When Aristotle Onassis was in his twenties, he lived in Argentina. He worked at night as an operator for the telephone company, which left his days free to do better things. Wanting to make more money, he became interested in the possibility of importing and selling oriental tobacco to the local cigarette manufacturers. At that time, Argentina was importing large quantities of Cuban and Brazilian leaf but only a handful of oriental brands. Over time he was able to persuade his father to send him some samples of the best leaf that was grown in the Peloponnese.

When the shipment finally arrived, Onassis made the rounds of Buenos Aires cigarette manufacturers. He got nowhere fast. He left samples in the hopes that one of the buyers would call him back, but no one ever did. Unable to get an appointment with anyone who could make a decision, young Onassis targeted Juan Gaona, the managing director of one of the country's biggest cigarette manufacturers. Each day he would stand outside Gaona's office and look silently and hopefully at him. Every other day he would stand outside Gaona's home as he would return from work. Fourteen days later Gaona succumbed. He asked his secretary to find out who this guy was and why he was haunting him.

When Gaona asked him in, Onassis explained all he wanted was to sell first-class oriental tobacco to his firm. Amused and mildly relieved, Gaona sent him to the firm's buying office, where Onassis finally achieved his goal—serious examination of his leaf samples.

Since the quality really was excellent, Gaona's buyers promptly ordered $10,000 worth of the tobacco leaf. Onassis charged his father the standard trade commission of 5 percent. Onassis often said that the $500 he received was the foundation of his fortune.[24]

Gunther Kleinfeld, a New York businessman, wanted to get a meeting with Aristotle Onassis while he was in New York. Unable to get an appointment, he used Onassis's own technique on him. He knew Onassis was staying in a penthouse apartment suite, so he went to the apartment building and rode up and down in the single elevator all day long, knowing that at some point Onassis would have to join him in the elevator to get in or out of the building. Later that day, he sold Onassis a deal as they descended from the top to the bottom floor.

Ask to come along for the ride.

Sid Friedman, who specializes in selling life insurance in Philadelphia, gets appointments with his busy prospective clients by offering to purchase a ticket and accompany them on their next plane flight. He rides along with them, establishes rapport, elicits their financial planning and insurance needs and sells a lot of insurance.

Our whole show is based on asking.

Each episode of "America's Funniest Home Videos" takes an average of forty clips. Our ratio is one hundred to one so we need four thousand submissions to make one episode of the show.

Very often we will offer an Assignment to America and ask our 27 million viewers to send in tapes that pertain to specific themes, such as Baby's first haircut, funny ways to crack an egg or eating spaghetti and we will say nothing more than that. We will get thousands of videos—an incredible collection of interpretation of what that could be, from a toothless senior citizen scooping up the last string of spaghetti to a baby eating his first bowl of spaghetti.

The request has to be specific because people have a tendency to take direction. If we tell them to send a specific theme, they send it in. If you leave it open, they judge for themselves too harshly. I cannot tell you how many people who have won our grand prize were people who have hoarded their own videos. They held onto them for two years thinking that their video wasn't worthy. People don't often believe that they have anything viable to contribute, and of course, in almost every case everyone does.   —Lloyd Weintraub,
Executive Vice President,
Vin Di Bona Productions

He asked for clarification and built a career.

Many television interviewers just ask a question because that was the question they had written down, and very often they don't listen to the answer. I learned early on that if I listened to the answer, and didn't quite understand what was being said, I had to assume that I wasn't alone, that other people might also not quite understand what someone had said. I think it came out of an interview with the economist John Kenneth Galbraith. We were talking about the economy in the early seventies and I didn't quite understand one of his concepts and I said, "Look, I'm the man from Mars and I just landed on Earth and I haven't the foggiest idea of what's going on. Explain it to me as if I were the man from Mars." Since then I have always used that "Man from Mars" approach on difficult situations and difficult concepts . . .

I am the least sports-oriented person in the world, but people liked how I interviewed so I got to do a half-hour documentary with a place kicker with the L.A. Rams. At the time they were using a kicker who kicked soccer style. His name was Frank Corral. I knew nothing about sports. To tell you how much I knew nothing about sports, I'd never ever been to a professional football game, and I was given a documentary to do on this guy. So I said, "Frank, let's start from ground zero. How do you kick the ball?" That's where we started from, and from that I got a series called "Road to Moscow." I went out and interviewed eighty-seven Olympic athletes and was always very successful because I asked them, "Show us how you do it and what you do," and I wasn't afraid to ask questions about what I didn't understand.

Most other people don't know any more than I do, but they are afraid to ask because they think they'll look stupid: I was not afraid to say, "You know what, I don't understand."

—**Vin Di Bona, Producer,**
America's Funniest Home Videos

Ask for referrals.

No matter what your business or profession is, ask for referrals from your current customers and clients. It has the potential of doubling or even tripling your business. Patti Lund, a dentist in Brisbane, Australia, has taken his practice from five days a week to three days a week, while doubling his income and creating an amazing environment to work in.

We used to ask everyone for referrals. Now I only do it with selected people—about 20 percent of my clients. We have A-1 clients, A-2 clients, etc. For example, Lee is an A-1 person so I said, "Lee, it's really nice to have you here today, and, as you know, we only take people by referral, and it was real nice of Carol to refer you. You probably read the little bargain we have on the back of our brochure. Is it okay if I just go through it with you again?

"We only take people by referral and it's important that people refer people to us because, unless we get referrals, we are not going to be here when you want us. So . . . I want you to refer one person of comparable quality to yourself." You'd think the response I would get would be "Go take a short walk off a long pier," but it isn't. The most common response is "Oh, does that mean I can only refer one person?"   —Paddi Lund

Ask a simple question.

Since last year, my average sale has increased to $640,000. How does a six-feet two-inch, black, former professional player sell homes to a predominantly affluent, Jewish clientele? Basically, it's very simple. When people come to an open house, I assume this person is looking for something. They may not be looking for what you have in that particular home but I get beyond that by asking one simple question: "How do you like the house?" That little simple question just opens up an area of conversation because it doesn't really matter what the answer is. If they like the house, then you talk to them about that house. If they don't like the house, you ask them, "What are you looking for?"

—Bruce "Bear Man" Smith

Ask a sophisticated question.

Years ago Dr. Blaine Lee, who works with Steven Covey, came up to me at the end of one of my presentations and said, "I waited until all the other people left the room because I wanted to speak with you alone for a moment. I really enjoyed your presentation and many of the things you did were right on target and very valuable for me, and I think you could be a whole lot better. Would you like to know how?"

How do you say no to that one? I ended up hiring him three times to fly into La Jolla and Arizona to help with strategic planning and developing my skills. As a matter of fact, I even flew into Utah one time to meet with him on his turf and to get some coaching on my speaking techniques. **—Jim Cathcart**

Ask for a standing ovation.

Most of the high spots in our lives come about through encouragement. I don't care how great, how famous, how successful a man may be, he hungers for applause. **—Anonymous**

Recently I was being introduced to give a keynote address and the people were still shuffling in and I realized that I didn't want to be introduced that way. I would prefer to have 100 percent attention from the audience. I like to feel really honored, so I asked everybody to give me a standing ovation.

I stood up in the front and said, "In a moment what I'd like to do is ask for a standing ovation for two reasons. One is because I deserve it and the second is because, if you give me a standing ovation, you, too, will know that you can ask for anything you want for yourself." **—Helice Bridges**

ASK THE WORLD

◆

The world is full of genies
waiting to grant your wishes.
—Percy Ross

◆

Our good friend Dr. Lou Tartaglia sent us the following story
about one of his encounters with Mother Teresa:

"Mother, I need help. I need a doctor to help me. I need a
psychiatrist," said Brother Angelo to Mother Teresa, with frustration in his voice.

"God will provide," said Mother, patting him on the
shoulder.

We were the last few people in the chapel at the Mother
House of the Missionaries of Charity. Mass had ended and
Brother Angelo was telling Mother about the terrible night he
had with a very ill drug addict. "I need a psychiatrist who
knows about recovery and spirituality. I can't do this alone,"
he said.

"God will provide," said Mother, patting him on the
shoulder.

Since I was a psychiatrist with a subspecialty in addiction
medicine, I figured that must be my cue. We talked for a while,
and when Mother Teresa realized what I did, she said, "See,
Brother, God has provided."

I smiled and asked what I could do.

"Teach him everything you know about addictions," said
Mother. "Go do something beautiful for Jesus."

Angelo and I started talking. We discussed the case he'd had last night. We made arrangements for me to appear on behalf of Mother Teresa at the Calcutta Chamber to discuss spirituality and addiction treatment.

Finally Father Scolozzi asked me if I would like to sit down. He wanted to take notes as I outlined how they could organize a rehab.

Mother had other ideas. She came up to me and looked me in the eye and shook her index finger in the air in front of my chest. "Don't sit around talking. Why don't you work as you are talking? Grab a broom, Doctor. Now go over to the rehab," she said, "and while you talk you could be sweeping it out."

I looked at her in disbelief. She not only wanted me to teach addiction treatment but she wanted me to sweep up at the same time.

"It would be a sin to only talk and not work. After you're finished sweeping, you can paint the place, too." She waited for me to say "Yes, Mother." It was impossible to resist the request. It just seemed like the right thing to do when she suggested it.

"Good," said Mother Teresa. "Now run off you two, and go do something beautiful for Jesus."

We swept, we painted, we worked. I taught and then continued to work for her and the Universal Fraternity of the Word, an order she and Brother Angelo founded.

Eight years later and I still am doing things for her. I find her requests always seem so reasonable. Mother once told me that she was a pencil in the hand of God, ministering to the least of His brothers one by one. I don't think she ever asks for anything for herself, only for Christ disguised in the disfigured body of the people she ministers to. Who can refuse a request made for Jesus? I certainly can't.[25]

—Brother Louis A. Tartaglia, M.D., U.F.W.

Mother Teresa asks everybody she meets.

Mother Teresa asked us to help her start her first drug and alcohol rehabilitation center. She's a master at it and what I found is these great people have a deep commitment to a purpose. The most important question I have ever been asked was "If you lived your life from the end forward, what would you want the inscription to say on the headstone of your grave?" I believe these great people have worked backward and they have established a tremendous purpose for living. A purpose for service, and because of that commitment to that sincere purpose to help others, they have not been hesitant to ask.

I think any great salesman who's committed to a quality product, a quality service, will have no hesitation because they believe in their product. They believe in their service. They know it can be of immense benefit to someone else.

—Donna Nelson

Ron Chapman asked for $20 and got $244,240.

On March 31, 1988, Ron Chapman went on the air at 6:00 A.M. as usual. As the most prominent disc jockey in Dallas, he spends four hours each morning giving cheer and encouragement to his loyal listeners as they head out to face another day. For twenty years they've depended on him to keep them laughing when their life is no fun, to make them feel good about themselves when they're insecure, and to help those stalled in the rush hour traffic to dare to dream. In return they've been faithful. They turned up when he gave out bananas from the drive-through window of a bank, they filled the Cotton Bowl to be extras for the movie *Semi-Tough*, and they came out by the thousands at the crack of dawn to hear the Dallas Wind Symphony play at a Labor Day Sunrise Party he sponsored.

Ron Chapman's fans don't dare miss a morning of KVIL for fear they'll miss the chance of a lifetime. They never know what he'll come up with next: a new car a year for life, a weekend trip to London, or a camel race in Egypt.

March 31 was different. Ron asked something of his listeners. "Send me twenty dollars. That's all I want." No promises. No explanations. Nothing in return. He knew some of them would do it, but even he was amazed when the next morning four thousand checks arrived in the mail, and another five thousand came in on Monday. He went on the air Monday afternoon and said, "That's enough! Don't send anymore. We don't even know what we're going to do with all this money." In spite of this announcement, people kept sending money. Some slipped checks under the door at night or begged the janitor to take their money after hours. There was a stampede to give away twenty dollars for no reason at all.

No worthy cause—no feeding of orphans, no relief for earthquake victims—but in their hearts, the donors all knew that if Ron Chapman asked for the money, they wanted to be part of whatever he had up his sleeve. They didn't want to miss out. They listened each morning as Ron counted up the money and totaled the 12,156 checks amounting to more than $240,000, almost a quarter of a million! Not bad for three days' work! "It was like deadline time at the IRS," Ron Chapman said with excitement.

Newspapers picked up the story and some asked, "Is this legal?" One listener called the Federal Communications Commission in Washington and talked to the supervisor of investigations in the mass media division. After hearing the simplicity of the request he replied, "As long as they don't make any promises or say they'll spend the money one way and then spend it on something else, there doesn't seem to be anything fraudulent about that. There's nothing wrong with saying, 'Send us your money.'"

In fact, after he thought about it for a while, the investigator added, "That's unbelievable. I may have to move to Dallas!"

Newspapers and radio stations from all over the country began to call and ask questions. "Where did you get the idea? How did you dare to ask for money for no good cause?"

Ron explained that he had been at a staff meeting with the new owners of the radio station and had told them how successful his contests and promotions had been in the past. "We get a better response to those than anyone in the business. I even believe if KVIL were to go on the air and say, 'Send us twenty dollars,' people would do it.'" The group laughed at this possibility and that was all Ron needed to hear. That challenged him to try it. "I'll show them," he said to himself.

He spent no time planning what to do with the money and spent no money on the promotion. He just made the request and the checks poured in. "I thought maybe I'd mail them back their checks with two dollars interest and a T-shirt," he said, "but that was before I saw the response. We can have fun on the air for weeks deciding what to do with the money." And they did have fun, taking in suggestions ranging from building a museum for Lawrence Welk in South Dakota to sending a Dallas group of cheerleaders to a contest in Australia.

Headlines all over the country captioned "KVIL DJ gets big bucks after appeal to listeners." "DJ leaves listeners red-faced, in the red."

Star sent a photographer who had Chapman lie on the floor covered with checks with his head peering out from the piles of money. *People* published his picture holding handfuls of checks and with more heaped up on the desk before him. Their headline stated, "Ask and Ye Shall Receive, Believes Dallas Deejay Ron Chapman—Which Is How He Made $244, 240."

They went on to say, without so much as hinting at salvation, suicide, or the last days, that "Ron Chapman, a deejay at Dallas radio station KVIL, triggered a flood of donations from his audiophilic flock. On March 31, as a whimsical test of his medium's power, he made a simple on-air request: Go to your checkbooks, quoth he. Write a check payable to KVIL. Fun and Games. Make it in the amount of $20 and mail it to this address. That's all he said. He never stated why he wanted the money or what he'd do with it. "I thought I might get three or four hundred checks," says Chapman, 51, who'd planned to return the money to each donor with a bag of sponsor goodies. But it quickly became obvious that many goodies would be needed. Four thousand checks came in the next day's mail; 5,000 arrived the day after. Recently KVIL announced that a total of 12,212 checks—worth $244,240—had been received. And according to the FCC, since no promises were made, there's no fraud. But KVIL won't keep the loot. Instead, it will be donated to charities and civic projects. "We've done some crazy stunts," says Chapman, "but this is the biggest."

Interviewers asked, "Do people want their money back? Is anyone angry?"

"Nobody is angry," Chapman said. "The only anger we have had has been from people who could not send their check to us once we put the deadline on it. That's when they were angry. They were angry because they could no longer send us their money for a reason they did not know."

As the ratings of KVIL were climbing by the minute, competitors stood by in amazement. How could a promotion that cost nothing produce so much publicity?

"If it was planned as a promotion, it shows signs of genius," said the station manager of a rival station. "I ask myself, would I send somebody twenty dollars just because they asked for it?" It's unfathomable. In all my years of broadcasting I've never seen anything like it.

Newspapers and magazines as different as the *Baptist Journal* and *USA Today* wrote lead articles about the incident. Tom Brokaw on NBC and Peter Jennings on ABC interviewed Ron Chapman on their news programs, and "Entertainment Tonight" made him a special feature. *Newsweek* did a column on him, and papers in Australia, New Zealand, Great Britain, and Germany told the tale of the disc jockey who tuned in to $240,000 for no reason, no strings attached.[26]   —Florence Littauer

He asked for cards and he got his life.

In the fall of 1988 Craig Shergold discovered he had a brain tumor. It was lodged in a very dangerous spot: near the top of the brain stem, which controls breathing, heart rate and blood pressure.

His mom, Marion, pleaded for her son's life. "Lord, Craig's not ready for you. I won't let you take him, because it's not his time yet."

It seems her prayers went unanswered. After hours of surgery, the surgeon reported that he could not remove all of the tumor because of its dangerous location. Two weeks later came the dreaded news: the pathology report indicated a malignant teratoma, an aggressive cancer of the brain. After his recovery from surgery, Craig would receive further treatment, but his death seemed all but inevitable.

Craig received so many get-well cards from family, friends and soccer-team members that his doctor joked, "You ought to go for the *Guinness Book of World Records.*"

Craig's medical condition had worsened, however. His legs and left arm became weaker, his speech slow and deliberate, his vision blurred. For all his pain, though, Craig never lost his sense of humor. He even joked about the baldness caused by the chemotherapy. "Knock, Knock," he would say. "Who's there?" a visitor would respond. "Ad-air," Craig answered. "Ad-air who?" "Ad-air once, but now I'm bald!" came the punch line.

"Mum," he said, "I'll think about the cards. Every time I do, it makes me feel better." In September, in an attempt to build Craig's morale, the Shergolds told the press he would try to establish a Guinness record for most cards received.

The outpouring led to more publicity—which generated thousands more cards. He received cards from Margaret Thatcher, Prince Charles, George Bush, Ronald Reagan, Mikhail Gorbachev and two of Craig's idols: Michael Jackson and Sylvester Stallone.

Craig started having real hope of beating the record for the most cards collected—1,000,265—held by another English boy. This gave him a sense of purpose, made his condition something more than a cruel twist of fate. In fact, so many cards were pouring in that Craig received his own "selection box" at the central post office in London—making him the first person in British history to be designated like a city for mail processing.

On November 17, 1989, the big night arrived. Craig, although shaky, was allowed to go to the local soccer club for the ceremony. As three hundred people gathered around, the local post office manager presented Craig with card No. 1,000,266— the record breaker. As Craig said thank you, everyone began singing "For He's a Jolly Good Fellow."

Some thirty-eight hundred miles away, in Charlottesville, Virginia, John Kluge was a billionaire who made his fortune in the communications business. Kluge's friends told him about Craig and all his get-well cards. They urged Kluge to send a card too. As Kluge considered mailing a card, an inexplicable feeling came over him. Amid all the attention focused on the card campaign, he couldn't help wondering: Had every medical possibility been explored? Was there some treatment he could arrange for the boy?

While Kluge had donated millions to worthy causes, he had never given money to an individual. He didn't want to start a precedent. And he didn't want to raise false hopes for Craig's family. Still, he couldn't shake the idea that there might be some hope for Craig.

Kluge phoned a close friend, Dr. Neal Kassell, professor of neurosurgery at the University of Virginia Health Sciences Center. "Neal," he asked, "could you contact the Shergold family? I have a feeling something important might have been overlooked. I'll pay the expenses."

Unable to reach the Shergolds by phone, Kassel air-expressed a letter on August 7. Days passed, and the Shergolds did not answer. His letter, of course, had disappeared into the millions of others.

Since breaking the record, the number of cards had skyrocketed to over 26 million. Craig had been in and out of the hospital regularly. September 20, Craig's physician, Dr. Diana Tait, asked Marion and Ernie to come to her office. The news was not good. "The latest scans show Craig's tumor is growing again," Tait said. The outlook was bleak. The Shergolds were devastated. This time they avoided telling Craig the news.

The next morning, to get her mind off the situation, Marion decided to open some of Craig's get-well cards. From the stacks of envelopes, Marion plucked the air-express packet that contained Kasell's letter. As she read it, her hands began to tremble. "I can't believe this!" she cried.

Marion called Kassel immediately and told him of the discouraging prognosis. Kassel said he could promise nothing, but added that his medical center had recently purchased a "gamma knife," a new instrument that could fire high energy radiation beams directly into brain tumors, "a possible treatment for Craig," he said.

When Ernie returned home from work, Marion handed him the letter. "I think God may have given us a miracle," she said.

The surgery, on March 1, had taken more than five hours. Kassell did not need the gamma knife. Exhilarated, Kassell left the operating room and went to tell Craig's parents the good news. Marion leaped up and kissed him.

In the intensive-care unit Marion leaned over Craig's bedside and whispered, "Craig, the cancer is gone. All gone."

Craig's eyes flickered open, and he smiled.

Craig's recovery was remarkable. His speech became faster and clearer immediately. He could now pronounce words. Two days after surgery, when Kassell walked into Craig's room, Craig said, "Doc, you're supercalifragilisticexpialidocious"— and broke out laughing.

Lab tests found no trace of malignant cells in the tumor tissue. No one would ever know for certain what had eliminated them. The important thing was that Craig's tumor was benign.

A few weeks later, John Kluge came to the hospital to meet the Shergolds. When the businessman entered the room, Marion grasped his hand and thanked him. "You are our guardian angel," she said.

Kluge handed Craig a two-headed quarter. "This way," he said, grinning, "you'll never lose."

Then Craig presented a gift to Kluge: a mounted photograph of himself in a triumphant *Rocky* pose taken by his mother several months earlier. In it, Craig wore boxing trunks and gloves; an American flag hung in the background. The inscription read: "Thank you for helping me win the biggest fight of all."[27]

—**John Pekkanen**

They asked for a solution.

Life has meaning only in the struggle. Triumph or defeat is in the hands of the Gods . . . So let us celebrate the struggle!"

—**Swahili Warrior Song**

The movie *Lorenzo's Oil* chronicles the extraordinary true story of Augusto and Michaela Odone after they receive the sobering news that their five-year-old son, Lorenzo, has a rare terminal disease. Despite the prognosis the Odones set out to save their child, colliding with doctors, scientists and support groups who tried to discourage the couple in their quest for a cure. Their relentless struggle tests the strength of their marriage, the depth of their beliefs and the boundaries of the medical community.

Augusto Odone asks his wife and himself to do their own research. He doesn't believe that Lorenzo should suffer from their own ignorance of ALD—adrenoleukodystrophy—an inborn hereditary disease. At one point in the drama, when Augusto explains his theory of the disease to his wife and his sister-in-law, he draws a diagram of a kitchen sink to represent Lorenzo's biosynthesis system. Michaela makes a joke about being married to a plumber and Augusto merely replies that she "married a simple man who asks simple questions." Those simple questions lead to a very important discovery of fatty-acid manipulation.

Through their research the Odones were introduced to the ALD Conference, a support group for families with children affected by the disease. The directors of the foundation, how-ever, were interested in offering a means of support to the par-ents and families, not in searching for a cure for the children. When the Odones invited the directors for dinner one evening to ask that the ALD Conference circulate a newsletter to the other parents about Lorenzo's progress, they were denied be-cause the organization preferred to take their answers from a medical advisory board rather than from an individual's suc-cess story. The following is part of the conversation during that dinner:

Augusto: As parents, we should challenge these guys, push them. Unless someone is willing to ask questions, to provoke, how will there be progress?

President: Are you going to teach the doctors? Back where Loretta and I come from, we call that arrogance.

Augusto: Arrogance, right! Do you know where the word arrogance is derived from? It's from the Latin word *arrogare*, which means to claim for oneself. And I claim the right to fight for my kid's life, and no doctor, no researcher and no bloody foundation has the right to stop me from asking questions which might help me save him and you have no right to stop me from sharing infor-mation!

The Odones began asking on an international level, and through their conviction were able to organize the first international ALD symposium to accelerate the exchange of information among the researchers working on this disease.

The Odones were right to ask and they were right to share their information. Lorenzo is now a teenager on his way to recovery. Lorenzo's Oil has stopped the progression of ALD in Lorenzo and others with this disease (and has staved off the disease in hundreds of others), who hope to recover lost function with the help of the Odone's new endeavor—The Myelin Project.*

Ask for peace.

In 1983, Samantha Smith, a fifth grader from Manchester, Maine, wrote the newly elected Yuri Andropov of the Soviet Union congratulating him "on your new job" and asking him, "Why do you want to conquer the whole world, or at least our country?" She shared her fears of a world at war and wanted to know if Andropov was going to vote to have a war or not.

Andropov answered her letter, writing, "Samantha, we are endeavoring and doing everything so that there will be no war between our two countries, so that there will be no war at all on earth. . . . We want peace. We have a lot to do: grow grain, build, invent, write books and make space flights. We want peace for ourselves and for all people on the planet, for our own kids and for you, Samantha." In the letter he invited her to visit the Soviet Union during the coming summer. She accepted the invitation and spent two weeks in July touring the Soviet Union on a peace mission.

One little girl who was brave enough to ask the tough ques-

---

*The Myelin Project is Lorenzo's "Chapter Two," a unique nonprofit partnership of top neurologists, dedicated researchers and informed laypeople whose single aim is to accelerate the pace of remyelination research, repair damaged nerves and restore motion, sensation and vision. This research will not only benefit Lorenzo and other children like him, but also patients with multiple sclerosis. If you would like to learn more about the Myelin Project or show your support for this worthwhile organization please call (202) 452-8994. Or you can write to them at The Myelin Project, 1747 Pennsylvania Avenue, N.W., Suite 950, Washington, DC 20006, Attn: Pamela Graff.

230 HE LADDIN ACTOR

tions of a world leader made a world of difference to the millions of people who read about and were inspired by her experiences.

Ask for friendship.

A friend is a gift you give yourself. —Robert Louis Stevenson

One day, Turgenev, the Russian writer, met a beggar who asked him for alms. "I felt in all my pockets," he says, "but there was nothing there. The beggar waited, and his outstretched hand twitched and trembled slightly. Embarrassed and confused, I seized his dirty hand and pressed it. 'Do not be angry with me, brother,' I said, 'I have nothing with me.' The beggar raised his bloodshot eyes and smiled, 'You called me brother,' he said, 'that was indeed a gift.' " —*The Best of Bits and Pieces*

Ask for something spectacular.

A few years ago, I was just about to graduate from college with an art degree. A few of my family members suggested that I should take this "phenomenal three-day seminar about life" that they had recently attended which had produced incredible results in their own lives. They were under the impression that it might give me the appropriate attitude adjustment I needed to make it out in the real world, so I went.

One of the most strongly emphasized concepts in the seminar was to figure out what the heck you really did want from life and to go out and not only *get* it, but *ask* for help. Prior to this seminar, I cannot recall ever asking for something without either feeling guilty for asking in the first place or feeling that by merely asking others for help, I was a weak person.

The second day at the seminar, we were all given a "homework" assignment to complete during our lunch break. After we looked at each other half-curious, half-angry that we had to work during our only break, the seminar leader explained the assignment in one short sentence. He said, "At lunch, I want you to ask for something *spectacular*."

I ended up at lunch with about a dozen other attendees. Everyone was laughing and either asking another attendee to dance through the aisles at the restaurant, asking the chef if they could borrow his hat and wear it while they ate, or some-thing else that was fairly amusing. When the waiter came to take my order, I ordered the special and said that I would also like to have a large chocolate birthday cake (*my* idea of spectac-ular). He immediately asked if it was my birthday, to which I politely replied, "No, but I'd still like the cake, and I'd like it for free." Well, by the end of the meal, we were all pitching in for the bill, and unfortunately there was no sign of a free cake, so we headed back because we had a commitment to be on time for the start of the seminar.

Back at the seminar, the leader asked for people to stand up and relate the outcome of their lunch homework. One of the men, at our table at the restaurant Bob, stood up. He said, "At lunch, most of us were just fooling around and asking strangers to dance around the restaurant with us, or asking people if they would trade clothes but Aimée over here had a very specific wish. She asked the waiter for a large chocolate birthday cake—for *free*." At this point, the whole seminar burst out laughing in relation to the "free" part. However, when he was talking, I felt like the only one who didn't really "complete" my homework, or in other words, get what I wanted. He continued to tell the story as I sank further into my chair.

"Well, I was the last one to leave the restaurant and I wanted Aimée to know that as I was leaving, our waiter came out with a huge platter with thirteen individual pieces of chocolate birth-day cake with candles on each one for our whole table." At that moment, everyone in the room started to applaud, Bob started to hug me and I started *asking* for a lot more help.

—**Aimée Hoover**

If you can't, you must.
   If you must, you can.
—**Tony Robbins**

All things are difficult before they are easy.   —**Thomas Fuller**

Ask for books.

After completing David Oldfield's training—The Journey—I asked for some workbooks so my friend Kamalu and the other co-workers who did the training with me could share it with the adolescents we worked with in the emergency youth shelter at Maui Youth and Family services. The next thing I remember is that they were handing me a large box with six thousand dollar's worth of workbooks. They gave them to the agency for free. Over the next two years we were able to share this transformative process with hundreds of teens!   —Lynda Wright

Ask for a better interest rate.

When I saw on the news that credit-card companies sometimes lower their interest rates at the cardholder's request, I wrote a brief, to-the-point letter to two companies. I stated that their interest rates were too high, and that I would no longer use the card unless I was offered a lower rate. I also said that I would like to continue doing business with each company. I didn't hear from one of the companies, whose card I have canceled. But AT&T lowered my interest rate from 15 to 9 percent.

—Barbara from Florida, *Positive Living* magazine

Ask for money.

I was doing great in sales. So in the summer of 1982 my wife and I decided it was the perfect time to buy a piece of land on which to build our dream home. The project was $240,000 and we hired a general contractor to start work.

The foundations were poured in November with the finish date planned for February 1993. Two weeks later the company I worked for went bankrupt. I had no job, my wife wasn't working, and we had a three-month-old son and a three-year-old daughter to care for. I didn't have a clue what I was going to do.

One day, sitting in my basement, an idea literally exploded in my head. I called it Achievers Canada. The concept was to build a seminar program featuring top speakers who would come into Calgary on a monthly basis. I would earn money by selling yearly memberships to business people. It was unique!

My builder called and said, "I need $125,000 immediately to get your new home under construction."

I approached my bank manager and convinced him through a mixture of high energy, raw enthusiasm, and a vague game plan to give me a $125,000 mortgage. During the process he asked about the speakers. I showed him a ten minute video of my mentor Jim Rohn. He asked me if I had any more of his material, so I loaned him a six cassette album called "The Challenge to Succeed." The next day he called and said he was putting the mortgage together and to meet him on Friday to sign the papers. I told the builder to get his crew ready and hugged my wife, Fran—we were on our way.

On Friday I marched confidently into the bank and asked for Colin the Bank Manager. The receptionist said two words, "He's quit!"

In total shock I said, "When?"

She said, "Yesterday."

Later that evening I called Colin at home and arranged to meet him. My first words were "Couldn't you have waited two more days—you know how important this mortgage is to me—what happened?"

He said, "You know those Jim Rohn tapes you gave me. Well, I listened to them all. In fact I took eleven pages of notes. I've been in the bank for fifteen years and I hate it—Jim Rohn's message inspired me to leave, so I quit!"

The next day I called on the new bank manager to see if I could salvage the mortgage. I didn't know the woman at all. The conversation was brief. She said, "I don't know how this mortgage was arranged, but there's no way I can agree to this—you don't have a track record in business."

In desperation I laid out the plans of the home to show her my dilemma. She looked at them closely and said, "I could never afford a home like this." That was the end of the deal. What now?

Another mentor reminded me that there's always a way if you want it badly enough. He said, "Keep asking." So I did. A month later an old friend who I used to play soccer with appeared out of nowhere. He just happened to be the new regional manager at another bank. This time he bought my story, didn't hear any Jim Rohn cassettes, and I got my mortgage.

We proudly moved into our brand new home a few months later.

The Bible says, "Ask and you shall receive." Now I know it works!   **Les Hewitt,**
Founder, Achievers Canada Seminars Inc.

Ask an entire nation.

Terry Fox was an outstanding Canadian athlete, ready to go into pro sports when he started having problems with his right leg. When the medical doctors examined him, they found out he had cancer ravaging his leg. When the doctor came back into the consulting room, he said, "Terry, I'm sorry to tell you this, but you've got cancer shooting through your right leg. We're going to have to amputate it today. And since you're over twenty-one, you've got to sign off on your own leg."

Terry bit the bullet, signed off and toughed it out. While he was convalescing in the hospital, he flashed on one little thoughtful affirmation his high school coach had given him, and that was "Terry, you can do anything if you want to do it with your whole heart."

He decided what he wanted to do was to run from one end of Canada to the other, raise $100,000 and give it to cancer research, so no other young person would suffer the pain, anguish, torment, and travail that he'd gone through.

And he got out of the wheelchair, got fitted for a prosthesis, and started hobbling around. He got his strength and courage up.

Terry wanted to call his run Terry Fox's Marathon of Hope. He announced it to his parents and they said, "Look, boy, it's a noble idea, but just now, we've got enough money and we want for you to go back to college and make a real contribution, and drop all this silliness and nonsense."

On the way to school Terry stopped at the Cancer Society and announced his intent. They said, "We think you're right, it's a noble idea, but just now we've got to procrastinate. Come back and see us some other time."

He talked his college roommate into dropping out of school. They flew to the east coast of Canada. Terry dropped his crutch in the great Atlantic and that day started running through Canada.

When he broke into English-speaking Canada, he was instantly a front-page media sensation. You saw that the blood was trickling down his prosthesis, he had a grimace across his face, but he kept on trucking.

He got to meet the Prime Minister, who wasn't reading his vita that day and said, "Forgive me, but who are you?" and Terry said, "My name is Terry Fox and I'm doing the Marathon of Hope. My goal is to raise a hundred grand—as of yesterday, we got that. I thought with your help, Mr. Prime Minister, we'd go a million dollars."

That's the first time you started seeing him in the U.S. on TV. "Real People" came up and filmed him. And as they skated him across hockey rinks, they collected buckets of money in the grandstands.

He kept on trucking valiantly and vigorously at thirty-one miles a day—more than a Boston marathon daily. By the time he got to Thunder Bay, Ontario, he had deep respiratory problems.

In the next town the medical doctor said, "Terry, you've got to cease and desist." He said, "Doc, you don't know who you're talking to. In the beginning my parents told me to buzz off. Provincial government had told me I'm cluttering the highways, I've got to cease and desist. The cancer society would not assist me. I decided to raise a hundred grand. I did that. I extended it to a million; three days ago we got a million. When I leave your office, I'm collecting one dollar from every living Canadian, 24.1 million dollars."

Doc said, "Look, kid, I wish you could do it, but the truth is, you've got cancer ravaging up through your chest. Top end, you're probably only going to live another six or eight hours. You've got an Air Force jet, 'cause the whole country's behind you. You've gotten us to drop language barriers and provincial nonsense. You've become the nation's hero. You should be put on a pedestal. We're going to fly you back to BC and we've taken the liberty to call your parents. They'll be there when we get there."

Many of you remember watching the evening news as they rolled him into the emergency room. A nineteen-year-old journalist, hot for a story, came lobbing on top of Terry in bed with a microphone and TV cameras going into the ER, and said, "Terry, what are you going to do next?"

Looking into the eye of media, he was a pro until the end. He said, "Are you going to finish my run? Are you going to finish my run? Are you going to finish my run?"

As you know, he died a short time after that. By December 24 that year, millions of individuals had gone out, and they had raised $24.1 million (or $1 for every living Canadian). That was Terry Fox's vision.

Some of you will say, "Well, what can I do? I'm only one person, I'm so weak and helpless. There's nothing I can do."

But God, in all His wisdom, said just build a better you. The good news is, as good as you are, you can be even better, if you really want to with your whole head and heart.

—**Mark Victor Hansen**

Ask for a wife.

I was a single parent with the custody of two kids for almost twelve years. I did all the conventional dating things that single people do. I went to the singles bars, which was a total disaster. I went to singles events in which I found a combination of some nice people and some lovable losers and then some walking

wounded and an awful lot of predators. It never produced anyone I wanted to spend any time with, and I began to realize
that if I were going to meet somebody, it would probably be in
the context of my work. Yet I couldn't date anybody who was
one of my students at the university where I was teaching; I
didn't feel that was ethical. So where was I going to meet somebody? Then I thought, "Well, gosh. I speak to thousands of people every year." One particular year I counted about forty-five-
thousand people.

I began to fantasize that maybe this person would be in one
of my audiences somewhere. So every time I would get up to
give a speech I would look out in the audience and think maybe
the magic woman for me is here in this audience. That went on
for a while, and then I thought, "Well, they can't read minds so
I better start asking, I better tell the universe what I want."

I wrote a new introduction which included the following: "Dr.
McCarty is a single parent with full custody of his kids." Then I
began to add to it. As I began my speech or workshop, I would
tell a story about loneliness or a story about the breakup of a
relationship and what that does to your self-esteem, and that as
you put yourself together, you begin to look around the world
for someone to be with and what that process is like, and what
that does to your self-esteem.

That was my way of asking the universe. By saying, "Hey,
I'm here and available," but trying to do it in a non-predatory
way that would be professionally appropriate. Immediately
more people would come up and talk to me and the people that
would come up and talk to me were female.

Two or three times I would show a full-color slide of each
child. I said something about being single and that they were
very good kids and that a woman would really have to go far
to find such a wonderful family. My nephew who is a lawyer in
Los Angeles came to one workshop. He stood there with me and
he later told me (because he is a compulsive counter) that at the
end of my speech there were over eighty people patiently waiting in line to talk to me or hug me. He said at least forty of them
were women who indicated that they were available, and that
he had never seen such a successful dating service.

All this worked, because I actually met Meladee, my wife, at
a conference. As I was leaving the house to go to the conference,
my son Ethan, who was only eleven at the time, said, "Daddy,
can I introduce you at the conference?"

I said, "Are you serious? You're going to get up in front of
eleven hundred people? Teachers, counselors, superintendents
and all that kind of stuff?" He said, "Sure."

So I said, "Get in the car." He gets in the car and he begins
interviewing me, asking me what introducers say. I give him

what the categories are and he starts asking me questions around those categories. While we are setting things up he writes his intro and gets up on stage. He gave the most brilliant introduction of me I have ever had in my life. And at the end he sweeps his arms the way Ed McMahon used to do, and says, "Heeeerrrreee's *Daddy!*"

Well, people were screaming with laughter and delight, and in that audience was a woman who fell in love with Ethan. She was taken by him completely, and as I was leading the small group in some activities, she chose to be his partner. The two of them made the most beautiful connection. At the end of the conference he came up and said, "Daddy, I want to introduce you to my new friend." That was Meladee and five years later I married her. **—Hanoch McCarty**

Ask for massive participation.

A group of fifty of us were participating in a personal growth seminar in which we were challenged to feed a thousand homeless people at a downtown mission. We were to provide a hot meal with entertainment and give away clothing. We were directed to do this within twenty-four hours and not spend a dime of our own money. We did it; we fed eleven hundred people.

I got on the phone and called Western Bagels and I said, "We'd like to get one thousand bagels from you." They said, "It takes two weeks to get an acquisition."

I said, "We don't have two weeks, we've got to have it tomorrow."

The guy sensed the urgency, the seriousness and commitment in my voice, and he said, "You've got it." We did this over and over. We got Von's to donate bread, cold cuts and all kinds of things. In twenty-four hours we did it all. It permanently changed my belief about what is possible. **—Michael Jeffreys**

Ask a stranger.

We awaken in others the same attitude of mind we hold toward them. **—Elbert Hubbard**

I sat quietly, relaxing and breathing in the rays of the sun on a park bench two hundred feet above the Pacific Ocean. Sitting on a bench only fifty feet away was an older woman. She was frail and bent over from the weight of her shoulders. She had a large, witchlike beak nose, but despite her appearance, something about this woman drew me to her.

I walked over to where she was seated and sat down beside her, keeping my focus on the ocean. For a very long time I didn't say anything, and then, without thinking, I spontaneously turned to this old woman and quietly asked, "If we never saw each other again, what would you really like me to know about who you really are?"

There was no answer—silence lingered in the air for what seemed an hour. Suddenly, tears rolled down her cheeks. "No one has ever cared that much about me," she sobbed.

I placed my hand lightly on her shoulder to comfort her and said, "I care."

"Ever since I was a little girl," she whimpered, "I have always wanted to be a ballerina, but my mother told me I was too clumsy. I was never given the chance to learn how to dance. But I have a secret. I've never told anyone this before. You see, ever since I've been four years old, I've been practicing my dance. I used to hide in my closet and practice so my mother wouldn't see me." "Isabel, show me your dance," I urged.

Isabel looked at me in surprise. "You want to see *me* dance?"

"Absolutely," I insisted.

That was when I saw the miracle. Isabel's face seemed to shed years of pain. Her face softened, she sat up proud, head erect, shoulders back. She stood up, turned and faced me. It was as if the world stood still for her. This was the stage that she had been waiting for all of her life. I could see it in her face. She wanted to dance for me.

Isabel stood before me, took a deep breath and relaxed. Only moments before, her brown eyes were sunk deep into her skull; now they were bright and alive. Elegantly she pointed her toe forward while gracefully stretching out her hand. The move was masterful. She took my breath away. I was witnessing a miracle before my eyes. One minute, she was an ugly, old, miserable woman; the next, she was Cinderella wearing a glass slipper.

Her dance took a lifetime to learn and only a moment to do. But she had fulfilled her life's dream. She had danced!

Isabel began to laugh and cry almost at the same time. In my presence, she had become human again. We continued to speak about math and science and all the things that Isabel loved. I listened and hung on her every word. "You are a very great dancer, Isabel. I am proud to have met you." And I really meant it.

I never saw Isabel after that. I still remember smiling and waving good-bye to her. Since that day, I have taken the time to stop and acknowledge people everywhere. I have asked them what their dreams are. I have rooted them on. Each time I do this, I witness a miracle. **—Helice Bridges**

Always ask for a discount.

I needed a new travel bag and so I went into Bloomingdales in Virginia. I walked into the luggage department and a woman saw me and walked right to me and said, "Welcome to our luggage department, how may I help you?" She helped me find the piece of luggage I wanted and it was around $300.

I have a fairly standard script that I use when I'm buying something in a retail store because most people will drop the price. The question I ask is "When will this go on sale?"

She looked at me and said, "Boy, isn't that a shame. This *was* on sale and the sale was over yesterday."

I said, "Really? What was the sale?"

"Twenty-five percent off."

Well I did some very quick arithmetic and I knew we were talking about $75. I looked her in the eye and said, "I must tell you, now that you've told me, that I cannot in good conscience pay you $300 for a bag that I could have had yesterday for $225. I can't do that. You have to help me get this for $225."

She said, "Well, the sale is off."

I said, "Look, if they were selling it for $225 yesterday, they'll sell it for $225 today. Why don't you just go find someone that has the authority to do that and tell them that either I thought it was finished today or I was sick, just tell them whatever you want."

So she went away and came back five minutes later. She said, "Look, thank you for your patience. I still haven't found the person I'm looking for. I found one person, but I want to find someone who will give us the answer we want." She then comes back five minutes later, and says, "Good news! I got it for you." **—Dave Yoho, Jr.**

Ask the world to write your book.

I wrote a book called *Secrets of Successful Speakers*. When the publisher received the final manuscript, I was delighted that I was finally done with the project. But the publisher had other ideas: "Just flush it out another 100 pages." With a long sigh I picked a few books off my bookshelf on speaking and one of them was called *Executive Speeches*. In the first paragraph the author announced, "I went to thirty of the top executives in the country who give speeches and much of what follows is their expertise." I thought, "What an idiot I've been!" I have a database with thousand of speakers. I talk to these speakers all the time, why not just ask a bunch of them for a few quotes each? That will flush out the book and it will have actual quotes from other people. "What a great idea." Well, the book flushed out all right. About 250 pages of great new material!

In the next book, *What to Say When You're Dying on the Platform*, I had only 40 rotten things that happen to you as a professional speaker when I sold it. But, when I got done I had over 130! Mainly because when I asked people they'd say, "Well, you know, when so and so got sick in the middle of my speech . . ." and I would think, "Oh, yeah, what do you do when that happens?" So I was able to add thousands of solutions.

Ask, ask, ask by fax, fax, fax!

Because of my business, I already have a fax set up with 500 fax numbers that I can access in a flick of a button. So that's what I did. I also have a huge E-mail database and I E-mailed a bunch of people around the world. The advantage of using E-mail, by the way, is when people write back to you as E-mail, you don't have to retype it. As a writer this is a super time-saver and much more accurate; I can just download the text.

If they didn't respond to faxes and E-mail I actually call them. I find you get a lot more information when you call. People are much more willing to talk to you. In total, I'd say I sent out 500 to 600 inquiries to different people.   —Lilly Walters

Tell everyone what you want to do and someone will want to help you do it.   —W. Clement Stone

While making reservations for a trip, I happened to comment to my travel agent that I felt I was spending too much time running my business rather than out doing the work I love. I love training. I love consulting. What I really need, I suggested, is someone like a business manager who would just run the office and let me do what I do best. To my amazement, he said he knew someone who just left his company and has some money he was looking to invest in a worthwhile project. So he hooked me up with this guy. After attending one of my presentations, he said he was impressed and might be interested in getting involved after he's had a chance to study the situation for a couple of months.

I said, "That's terrific, but I don't have a couple of months. If I don't come up with some cash by next week, I'm going to be out of business." He literally took out his checkbook, and sat there and wrote $18,000 worth of checks to cover my bills. Truly, a gift from the universe.

The key to getting what I want and need, I believe, is being true to myself and to my real purpose. As long as what I am doing is consistent with my purpose, then, as my experience proves, I will be supported.　　　**—Frank Siccone**

On the lighter side

Dear United States Army:

My husband asked me to write a recommendation that he supports his family. He cannot read, so don't tell him. Just take him. He ain't no good to me. He ain't done nothing but raise hell and drink lemon essence since I married him eight years ago, and I got to feed seven kids of his. Maybe you can get him to carry a gun. He's good on squirrels and eating. Take him and welcome. I need the grub and his bed for the kids. Don't tell him this but just take him.　　　**—Hand-delivered by an Arkansas man to his draft board in 1943**

Ask a book.

It never fails to amaze us how few people consult a book when they need information. According to one recent study only one in seven adults in America will ever go into a bookstore to buy a book after they graduate high school. They may purchase a novel for entertainment from the supermarket, discount store or airport newsstand, but not a how-to-do-it book or a book that would advance their professional career, improve their marriage or make them a better parent. This is really a sad statistic when you consider how much information has been written down that can truly help people in all walks of life.

If you were to read one book a week in your chosen field, in ten years you will have read over five hundred books. That will put you in the top 1 percent of your field.　　　**—Jim Rohn**

Ask a biography.

In high school I was the only support of my mother. I read every biography I could find, hearing the voices in the library books. I was reading Amelia Earhart's biography the day I suddenly realized my friends were leaving for college, leaving me behind. No college for me—instead I had taken on two more jobs.

But Amelia whispered to me, "Some of us have great runways already built for us. If you have one, take off! But if you don't have one, realize it is your responsibility to grab a shovel! Build one for yourself, and for all those who will follow you."

I determined that day not to be uneducated. I enjoy reading at least six biographies a week, tucking them all over my home, office and car. I often tell Amelia, "Thank you, dear friend of the mind, I heard you. I grabbed the shovel!"

> —**Dottie Walters, author, speaker, magazine publisher, consultant, International Speakers Bureau Owner**

Ask a librarian.

Most library cards are free. The ones that are not are usually very inexpensive—usually less than the cost of one book. Get one and use it.

To find an academic library contact the Association of College and Research Libraries, American Library Association, 50 Huron Street, Chicago, IL 60611, (312) 944-6780. At no cost to you, this organization will help you find college and research libraries that specialize in the subject you are interested in.

Unlike the stereotypical librarian portrayed in movies, most librarians are very friendly people. They enjoy helping people. That is what they are there for. So when you get to a library, ask the reference librarian for help. By enlisting his or her help, you can save a lot of time.

If the library doesn't have the book you want, ask them if they can get it for you. Most people give up, if they don't find what they are looking for. Libraries will often purchase a book if they are convinced it will be used. Libraries also lend one another books on "interlibrary loan." Ask if they can do this for you.

For some information you can call your local library's reference department on the phone. At no charge, the library will usually try to find any fact you need. For example, you could ask, "What's the flying time from Los Angeles to Singapore?" Or "When was the clock invented?" Answering such questions by mail or phone is a public service most every library provides.

Here are a few other useful all-purpose resources that you may wish to consult:

The New York Times Index is an index to articles published in the *New York Times*. You simply look up key words, such as a subject or a person's name, and the index provides a brief summary of all the pertinent articles published, including the date of publication and the page. You can find this index in almost every library.

The Readers' Guide to Periodical Literature (H.W. Wilson Company) indexes articles published in about 240 popular magazines, such as *Time, Newsweek, Ms., Sports Illustrated* and *Popular Science*. Also available in almost every library.

The Business Periodicals Index is an index to articles published in nearly 350 periodicals oriented toward business. Almost all libraries have it.

Subject Guide to Books in Print (R.R. Bowker Company) lists by subject all new and old books—both hardbound and paperback—that are currently in print by subject. All libraries and bookstores will have a copy.

ASK YOURSELF

◆

*Others have seen what is and asked why. I have seen what
could be and asked why not.*
—**Robert F. Kennedy**

*Always the beautiful answer
who asks a more beautiful question.*
—**e. e. cummings**

◆

Ask good questions.

A friend once asked Isidor I. Rabi, a Nobel Prize winner in
physics, how he became a scientist.

Rabi replied that every day after school his mother would
talk to him about his school day. She wasn't so much interested
in what he had learned that day, but she always inquired, "Did
you ask a good question today?"

"Asking good questions," Rabi said, "made me become a
scientist."
                                    —*The Best of Bits and Pieces*

Jacob was on his hands and knees searching for something
underneath a street lamp, and a man approached and asked
Jacob what he was looking for.

"My key," Jacob answered.

"Would you like me to help you look for it?"

"Yes, I would love your help." So Harry then joined Jacob in
the search for the lost key.

After a fruitless half hour of searching, Harry said, "Your key
doesn't seem to be here. Are you sure you lost it here under the
street lamp?"

"Oh, no," replied Jacob. "I lost it in my house, but there's more light out here." —*The Best of Bits and Pieces*

B.C. BY JOHNNY HART

By permission of Johnny Hart and Creators Syndicate, Inc.

How often do you spend your time looking for the answers to your questions outside of yourself, when you could be asking yourself these same questions. Perhaps the better answer lies deep within your unconscious mind. You can access wisdom, guidance and love by asking your unconscious the right questions.

QUESTIONS THAT CAN CHANGE YOUR LIFE

We asked over one hundred people, "What question were you asked by another or did you ask yourself that literally changed your life?" Here are some of the responses. We think they would make great questions to ask yourself. Don't just ask these questions once. Ask them over and over. Live with the question for weeks at a time. Write them down and revisit them often. Meditate upon them.

Just as these universal questions have radically changed the lives of others, they can deepen and transform your life as well. Here are the questions and some of the stories that grew out of them.

What am I pretending not to know?

That was the question Bill McGrane asked me in 1979. "What are you pretending not to know?" Up until then I had made excuses for the way things were in my life. The question taught me to assume responsibility for the choices in my life.

—**Dave Yoho, Jr.**

What is your purpose?

"What's your purpose in living? What would you do if you knew you couldn't fail?" Off of that I started looking at whether my goals were worthy of me, instead of whether I was worthy of my goals, and I honestly believe that what I am about is a more peaceful, harmonious, and just planet.   —**Brian Klemmer**

Aren't you the one?

I began a tiny advertising business on foot, pushing my two small children ahead of me down country roads. My husband took me to hear Bill Gove speak at the Shrine Auditorium. There were no women on the platform in those days. As I listened, I suddenly thought, "Aren't you the woman who should speak as Bill does?"

My heart answered, "I am the one!" I have now spoken all over the world. Listen to the message in your heart. Respond to the call.

—Dottie Walters, coauthor with daughter Lilly Walters,
Speak and Grow Rich

If you could be anything at all . . .

Years ago a gentleman asked me, "If you could be anything at all in your life, what would you be and how would you do it? "
I said, "I would decide that every single day I could do anything I wanted. I would make up every day my own self." And that's what I've been doing ever since.   **—Helice Bridges**

Am I willing to do whatever it takes to get what I want?

Ask yourself the question "Am I willing to do whatever it takes to get what I want?" "If not, why not?" Is there something else that needs to be taken into consideration? Some other part of my life that demands equal attention? If so, factor that in, and then ask the question again. "How much am I willing to commit? Do I think that will be enough to produce the result?"

What else can I do?

What else can you do before the day is out that would forward your progress towards the goal? It has to do with action, like what kind of physical thing could you do to move yourself towards the goal. I do a little set of rituals in the morning. When I get up, there is a set of things that I ask myself. The first one has a heart, and I ask, "Does this path have heart? Is what I'm doing today having heart?" The second question is "Am I following my higher calling?"
"Am I showing up?"
"What is my level of participation? Is my life balanced? Am I diving deep enough or am I just staying on the surface?"

—Tim Piering

How would the person I'd like to be do the things I'm about to do?

The question "How would the person I'd like to be do the things I'm about to do?" has got to be one of the most stimulating questions I've ever heard. It forces you to focus on the nobler side of yourself, focus on the part of you that you really admire and would like to see living more fully in you.

Start asking yourself, "How would that good part of me, how would that talented part of me, the intelligent part, the giving part of me do the things I'm about to do?" This will shift your perspective, but that shift will accomplish everything because you will start to be a little bit more considerate, a little bit more thorough, and a little bit more thoughtful before doing something.

A guy named Tim Seward came up to me after a speech and asked me for some input. He was working for a company called Tidy Car, an auto detailing company. I told him about that question and he went home and applied that thinking and did very well in his business.

When it came time for their international sales convention, I was MC that evening at the banquet. Denis Waitley had given a speech and I turned the microphone over to the President and he said, "Ladies and Gentlemen, in a few minutes I'm going to give away that white Corvette in the corner. That Corvette is going to go to the person who won our International Sales Contest. This year the contest was very tight all the way up to position number two, but number one led the contest with three hundred more points than number two. Number two lead number three by one point, three led four by two points, so that gives you some idea of the spread. This year the winner of that white Corvette, the International Sales Leader, from Bay City, Michigan, is Tim Seward."

The place went nuts. Tim was lifted onto their shoulders and they brought him to the front of the room and sat him down by the Corvette. After the hubbub died down a bit, I got through the crowd and gave him a big hug and asked, "How'd you do it?"

He said, "You know, I was just nineteen years old when I started this thing—I didn't have any business experience so I went home and I asked myself, 'How would the international figure, the person I'd like to be, do the things I'm going to do?' " He continued, "I straightened up my uniform, I got my files better organized, I followed through better with each client, I did a better job on each car, I planned my days a little bit more thoroughly, and just using that daily question caused me to upgrade everything. The upgrade compounded day after day throughout the year and now I'm International Sales Leader."

I said, "That's phenomenal."

He said, "It gets better. I was sitting at home thinking, 'How would the International Sales Leader go to the International Convention in New Orleans?' I figured he'd go first class, one way."

I said, "Wait a minute, you didn't know you'd won and you bought a first-class one-way ticket to New Orleans?"

He said, "Do I need a ride home?"

I said, "No, you certainly don't; you won the Corvette."

—**Jim Cathcart**

What do you want to be an expert on?

Earl Nightingale said something that was a major turning point for me and he said it on the radio in 1972, when I was working as a clerk for the Little Rock Housing Authority. I was listening to "Our Changing World", just sort of out of the corner of my mind because he was in the next room on the radio. I was sitting there at my desk, just doodling because I was bored and had no work to do and he said, "If you will spend an extra hour every day and study, in five years or less you will be a national expert." So the question that popped into my mind was "If I could do that in an hour a day extra and I'm a government clerk with eight hours a day of free time, I could change the world by Thursday. So what would I like to do?" And I didn't know! That's a very disturbing question. When you know you could become a national expert in the next five years and you don't know what you want to be an expert on, there's reason to stay awake. So I did. For weeks on end I sat there and thought about that. Finally it occurred to me that what I wanted to do most of all was help people grow. I wanted to do what Nightingale was doing. And as you know, I've been doing that now for eighteen years full time.

—**Jim Cathcart**

When are you going to know you've won?

One day I was working out at the fitness club at the Ritz Carlton in Atlanta and across the room from me there was this guy who was one of these "pumping iron" types. I was on my Stairmaster just doing my daily fitness routine and he was over there just really sweating over some serious exercise and I could tell he was into body building and quite an achiever type. He said, "How long are you going to be on that Stairmaster?" I said, "Oh, thirty minutes or so." He said, "I went two hours." Then he continued to pump weights and then he started telling me how much weight he could lift and how he'd accomplished various things and how fast he could run, how big his car was, how big his house was, what kind of deal he got, what kind of sales he'd made lately. And I said, "Excuse me! When are you going to know you've won?" He said, "What do you mean?" I said, "It's obvious your whole life is a competition with other people. When are you going to realize you've already won?" He said, "I don't even understand the question." Then he started telling me about another business deal he was working on. The guy didn't have a clue! But I would imagine, later, if he stopped to think about what he had been asked, that question would reach to the core of what was going on with him. Because it was real clear he wasn't very happy inside otherwise he wouldn't be comparing himself with everyone else.   —Jim Cathcart

"Who am I and where am I going?"

Henry Martin: © 1971 by Saturday Review/World

Ask yourself St. Peter's questions.

The world's foremost researchers on death and dying say that what they hear universally from people who have died, gone to the other side and returned to tell of their experiences is that they were asked these salient questions:

1. How did you expand your ability to love while you were alive?
2. What wisdom did you learn from your life's experience?

ASK YOUR UNCONSCIOUS

The primary success that I have found is asking questions of myself. I was going through some serious personal problems about twelve years ago and I began out of frustration because nothing else was working for me. I had read something about building a relationship with my inner self, my inner mind. I knew nothing about that and thought it was a little kooky at first, but since nothing else was working, I decided to start trying. As I began getting some success from that, I decided to quit drinking after twenty-five years. Using this process of asking my inner self, I was able to stop drinking by myself—alone and unsupported, without outside resources. That was a very big success that rooted me in the process.

I've come to the conclusion that it is my job—the conscious mind—to ask the questions. The inner self or my inner mind then provides answers. The third step is for me to put the answers into action in the outside world. And then I can go back and do another reflective process with my inner self and mind.

When I began the process eleven or twelve years ago, I didn't know what I was doing and it was a little slow at first, but what I discovered after a little bit of practice, with better clarity of my questions, was that I began getting many more useful and helpful responses.

When I first started, all of my questions regarded solving problems I was having, but I have evolved to asking about what I want to do in the world, where I'm going with my life. About a year and a half ago I began asking questions on my spiritual life. As I got closer and closer to age sixty, I began to do some serious reflecting on my life. "Who am I and why am I here?" I began asking.

"What would it take for me to be successful *and* develop a worthwhile spiritual journey for myself and the rest of my life?"

With each answer I get, I refine my question, then I get more and more specificity in the responses. I've dubbed this process "mental coaching."

I coach myself, and I also use these questions to coach others.

I've discovered it is by far most effective when those questions are neutral and non-judgmental. When I do not pretend that I already know the answer, or imply the answer in my question.

One of the responses that I got in that process of developing a spiritual journey was to come to the conclusion that I needed to do something of a more giving nature. Cooperating with the universe and how it operates rather than working as an independent entity. The kinds of questions I began asking then were something like this:

"What can I be doing in my spiritual journey that will contribute to others, that will contribute to the universe, or the world?"

I just keep getting more specific with the question, so that if for instance it says, "spiritual journey," I then ask: "Okay, so then, what can I do to carry that out?"

The response I got was to prepare something that is worthwhile or valuable to others. To write a book that will help others on their spiritual path.

In a sense I'm having a dialogue with myself and I'm just asking for greater and greater specificity and then I just wait for the answer. If the next answer is not totally clear, then I ask another clarifying question. It's like peeling the layers of an onion. I just keep going deeper and deeper. I am establishing a greater level of cooperation between my conscious and my unconscious mind.

People ask me how I get the answers. Sometimes I hear them as words or sentences. Sometimes I get images. Other times I get emotional feelings, that may or may not have other images with them. If I stay with those, because often I'm not sure how to interpret those kinesthetic responses, if I stay with them, I eventually do get an image—sometimes with words, sometimes without. Sometimes those images are rather metaphorical. So I say, "Help me understand what that means." That way I get further information on what the intention is. What's the deeper intention from that? I can get at the intention sometimes from directly asking, "What is the intention of that?" Or, "What did you intend by that?" Or, "What is the meaning of that?"

—John Prieskorn

Sitting for ideas

Dr. Elmer Gates's own life proved that his methods of brain and body building could develop a healthy body and increase the efficiency of the mind. Napoleon Hill recalls how, armed with a letter of introduction from Andrew Carnegie, he went to visit Dr. Gates at his Chevy Chase laboratory. When Napoleon Hill arrived, Dr. Gates's secretary told him, "I'm sorry, but . . . I'm not permitted to disturb Dr. Gates at this time."

"How long do you think it will be before I can see him?" Napoleon Hill asked.

"I don't know, but it might take as long as three hours," she responded.

"Do you mind telling me why you are unable to disturb him?"

She hesitated and then responded, "He is sitting for ideas."

Napoleon Hill smiled. "What does that mean—sitting for ideas?"

She returned the smile and said, "Maybe we'd better let Dr. Gates explain. I really don't know how long it will take, but you're welcome to wait. If you prefer to come again, I'll see if I can make a definite appointment for you."

Mr. Hill decided to wait. It was a valuable decision. What he learned was well worth waiting for. This is how Napoleon Hill tells what happened:

When Dr. Gates finally came into the room and his secretary introduced us, I jokingly told him what his secretary had said. After he read the letter of introduction from Andrew Carnegie, he responded pleasantly, "Would you be interested in seeing where I sit for ideas and how I go about it?"

He led me to a small, soundproof room. The only furniture in the room consisted of a plain table and a chair. On the table were pads of paper, several pencils, and a push button to turn the lights off and on.

In our interview Dr. Gates explained that when he was unable to obtain an answer to a problem, he went into the room, closed the door, sat down, turned off the lights, and engaged in deep concentration. He applied the success principle of controlled attention, asking his subconscious mind to give him an answer to his specific problem, whatever it might be. On some occasions ideas didn't seem to come through. At other times they would immediately flow into his mind. And in some instances it would take as long as two hours before they made an appearance. As soon as ideas began to crystallize, he would turn on the lights and begin to write.

Dr. Elmer Gates refined and perfected more than two hundred patents which other inventors had undertaken but which had fallen just short of success. He was able to add the missing ingredients—the something more. His method was to begin by examining the application for the patent and its drawings until he found its weakness, the something more that was lacking. He would bring a copy of the patent application and drawings into the room. While sitting for ideas, he would concentrate on finding the solution to a specific problem.

When Napoleon Hill asked Dr. Gates to explain the source of his results while sitting for ideas, he gave the following explanation: "The sources of all ideas are:

1. Knowledge stored in the subconscious mind and acquired through individual experience. observation, and education.
2. Knowledge accumulated by others through the same media, which may be communicated by telepathy.
3. The great universal storehouse of Infinite Intelligence, wherein is stored all knowledge and all facts, and which may be contacted through the subconscious section of the mind.

"When I sit for ideas, I may tune into one or all of these sources. If other sources of ideas are available, I do not know what they are."

Dr. Elmer Gates found the time to concentrate and think in his search for something more. He knew specifically what he was looking for. And he followed through with positive action!

—W. Clement Stone[28]

ASK A HIGHER POWER

◆

Let your request be known unto God.
—Philippians 4:6

When a man has done all he can do, still there is a mighty,
mysterious agency over which he needs influence to secure
success. The only way he can reach it is by prayer.
—Russell H. Conwell

◆

Mother Teresa of Calcutta had a dream. She told her superiors, "I have three pennies and a dream from God to build an orphanage."

"Mother Teresa," her superiors chided gently, "you cannot build an orphanage with three pennies. With three pennies, you can't do anything!"

"I know," she said, smiling, "but with God and three pennies I can do anything!"

We are headed towards a point in time in history where the spiritual energy is so powerful. All people need to do is turn toward the energy and ask. In The Bible it says, "Ask and you shall receive." God is waiting and all you need to do is ask even a little bit for help, and it will be there. A lot of people either don't ask or turn their backs.
—Tim Piering

Ask for help.

My wife Fran had cancer. After surgery she lay at home in bed full of fear, her whole body shaking uncontrollably as she thought about dying and leaving her family. She prayed earnestly for help. The response came quickly. She said it was like God laid a warm blanket over the bed and covered her from head to toe and said, "Don't worry: it's going to be okay." She said the experience was not of this world. "My body stopped shaking and I knew I was going to live." She has never looked back. Now life has new meaning and purpose. That was nine years ago.

—Les Hewitt, Founder of Achievers Canada Seminars Inc.

So I tell you, whatever you ask for in prayer, believe that you have received it, and it will be yours.   —Mark

It was in algebra class in high school where I really learned to pray fervently. Our teacher would always have these pop quizzes. As soon as he announced a pop quiz, I would start to pray. I invariably got 100 percent right on the quizzes.

—Mary Hulnick, Co-director, University of Santa Monica

When I pray, coincidences happen, and when I don't, they don't.   —William Temple

In 1976, when I was a counselor in a backpacking camp in northern California's Trinity Alps, I learned a major lesson about "asking." My friend Marilyn and I were leading ten teenage boys and girls through the wilderness for two weeks. On the seventh night, we were camped in rugged mountains in unfamiliar territory. We had not seen anyone else for days. As we slept, a freak summer blizzard unleashed two feet of snow on us. We huddled together through the night to stay warm. As the sun rose, the storm was still so intense that we could barely see two feet in front of us. All the trails had disappeared. We could not see any of the surrounding mountains to read our maps. We had little food because we were due to hike to a "food drop" that day.

I was scared. No, I was quietly terrified. I felt responsible for everyone's safety. If the blizzard continued, our already wet clothes and sleeping bags would no longer keep us warm. We would either suffer from hypothermia and lose some toes and fingers or freeze to death. I remembered the nearby location of a mountain peak we had seen the day before. I left Marilyn with the kids and struggled through the ferocious blizzard which had dumped over three feet of snow by now. Breathless and frozen, I finally arrived on the peak but could not see far enough to get my bearings. I pictured those frightened kids relying upon me.

My terror intensified. Finally, in desperation, I fell to my knees and prayed. I begged God to please lift the storm just enough for me to see the path down the mountain. In that moment, I fully believed that the clouds would magically disappear. After a few minutes, nothing had happened. I began sobbing as I pictured the newspaper headlines detailing our deaths. I pleaded with God, but still nothing happened. Finally, I decided to return to the others and plan a new strategy. As I was walking down from the peak, I found my feet involuntarily moving in another direction. It was strange. I felt like I was being led, for no apparent reason, to the back side of the mountain. As I came around a corner, I looked below me and saw the faintest evidence of the trail. I shouted with glee and rushed back to the others with the life-saving news.   **—Peter Rengel**[29]

Ask for guidance.

I shall always remember the night I was called to make a hospital call on John Wayne, the veteran film actor. He was to be operated on in the morning for what was feared to be cancer. I prayed for divine guidance all the way to the hospital. Should I come right out and ask my friend Duke Wayne if he was prepared to meet God? I was strongly led to reject that approach. Should I ask, "Are you saved and forgiven and if you die tonight will you go to heaven?" The answer came clearly: "No, that is not what you are to say."

Then I heard the "still small voice" that I identify as the Holy Spirit of the living Christ. It said to me, "Simply bring Jesus

Christ into the mind of John Wayne. He will accept or reject Christ. That is what it's all about."

When I arrived at the hospital, I found the famous actor lying on the bed clad only in his shorts. We talked, we related, and then I asked, "Duke, may I pray for you?"

His response came immediately, "You bet, Bob, I need all the help I can get." I recall seeing his eyes close tightly, his rugged face taut with tension, as I prayed.

Without planning or plotting or contriving to manipulate, I heard the following words come from my mouth, "Lord, John Wayne knows about you. He has heard about you all his life. He admires you. He respects you. And deep down he knows that you can and want to forgive him of all of his sins. Deep down in his mind he accepts you and believes in you and loves you, now."

At that point I opened my eyes to see the face of John Wayne as possibly no other person ever say it—peaceful as an Easter sunrise, all tension was gone. There was absolutely no evidence of embarrassment, spiritual uneasiness, or psychological discomfort. Beyond a doubt, I spoke the right words, and he followed them without resistance and with sincere acceptance.

—**Robert H. Schuller**[30]

Asking for a healing.

Let your request be made known unto God.   —Philippians

There was this woman who had cancer and had a tumor that was so big and infected that it hung in a harness on her breast. She would not go to a hospital. She lived in this place that was just a hovel and trash up to the ceiling. She wouldn't let anyone in, but finally she let me in. I befriended her and helped her get her food and supplies. She was extremely sick. She had to go to the hospital on an emergency for a blood transfusion because she was being poisoned by the blood.

So I sat there looking at this picture of Christ, and I said, "God, what can we do about Kathryn? What can we do about her to help her?"

As I'm looking at this picture, the message I get back is "What do you want to do?" All of a sudden the responsibility of another human's life, but also their spiritual life, came upon me.

I thought, "I'm not worthy of this kind of responsibility." It's one thing to ask God to please help, but then the question was "What do you want to do?"

I thought, in a flash, people go through things on earth to learn lessons, and maybe she shouldn't get out of learning a lesson. This might be for her best spiritual good, so maybe she needs this sickness. Another part of me wanted to heal everybody and make everything right.

I had this monstrous realization. I said basically, "In my heart of hearts, if I had my way, I would like to see her healed." Within two weeks, she started going to the hospital and within two months she had gotten some radiation treatment and the cancer was removed and her breast was back to normal. The doctors at the clinic said it was a miracle that she was alive, and it was a miracle this tumor was gone. So that was in response to a particular prayer about another human being that was really in suffering.   —**Tim Piering**

Ask an angel.

In her best-selling book *Embraced by the Light*, Betty J. Eadie states that during her near-death experience in 1973, she saw angels rushing to answer prayers. They were filled with much love and joy by their work. These prayers appeared to be beacons of light, illumination of small penlights, and sparks shooting up from the earth.

"I was distinctly told that all prayers of desire are heard and answered," she continues.

"I understood that once our prayers of desire have been released, we need to let go of them and trust in the power of God to answer them. He knows our needs at all times and is simply waiting for an invitation to help us. He has all power to answer prayers, but he is bound by his own law and by our wills. We must invite his will to become our own. We must trust him. Once we have asked with sincere desire, doubting nothing, we will receive."   —**Sandra Rogers**[31]

Pray for money.

I was walking along in the morning sunshine on a sidewalk in Country Club Plaza in Kansas City. I had a new wallet I had just purchased from a store. As I took it out of the shopping bag, I opened it and looked at it. I had it in my open palms and asked God to bless the wallet so that any money that came to and from it would bless others. At that *very* moment, a station

wagon slowly pulled up alongside me and, without a word, two men threw hundreds of pennies all over me. These were indeed "Pennies from heaven"!
—**Catherine Castle**

Decide to do at least one good action a day.

Decide to do at least one good action a day,
If not several, or innumerable ones.
Talk to God every morning and ask Him,
"What good can I do today?"
He will answer you and guide you, for He is in you.
And you will have given Him life by asking Him.
He cannot manifest Himself without being asked.
God speaks to you through your soul which is the
true guide of your life.
Ask God, talk to God, dialogue with God and you
will be the source of many miracles.
You will produce them all around you.
Do at least one good action a day until the very
end of your life.
Just think what a huge amount of good that
will represent!
And if all 4—7 billion people on Earth do one good
action a day WHAT A PLANET IT WILL BE!
—**Dr. Robert Muller, Chancellor Emeritus, University of Peace, Costa Rica, Former Undersecretary General of the United Nations**[32]

How to pray

One night while baby-sitting, a grandfather passed his grand-daughter's room and overheard her repeating the alphabet in an oddly reverent fashion. "What on earth are you up to?" he asked.

"I'm saying my prayers," explained the little girl. "But I can't think of exactly the right words tonight, so I'm just saying all the letters. God will put them together for me, because he knows what I'm thinking."   —*The Best of Bits and Pieces*

Pray for something and then let it go.

Andrew Glazewsky, when giving a talk at Attingham, mentioned the laws of manifestation and made an interesting statement: "If you keep on praying for a thing, you put into operation the reverse laws." I did not understand what he had meant. He said, "It's quite simple. If you keep praying for a thing, it shows you have not got the faith. You need ask only once and then go ahead in faith." **—David Spangler**

Heaven ne'er helps the men who will not act. —Sophocles

After prayer comes action.

Pray to God, but row for the shore. **—Russian Proverb**

A good and faithful man fell upon financially hard times. Every time he turned around, it seemed another demand was placed upon him until finally, as the saying goes, he was "so poor he couldn't pay attention." One night in his distress, he dropped to his knees, lifted his eyes toward heaven, and prayed, "Dear God, I am destitute. Please let me win the lottery—soon!" The next week, he was optimistic his condition would change. After three months, his faith began to waver, and by the end of a year, he became angry that he had not yet won a single dime.

"Are you there, God?" he pleaded. "I believed you would help me, yet an entire year has passed without you answering my prayers."

Suddenly, a dark cloud appeared in the sky, lightning flashed, and a voice boomed from the heavens: "I hear you . . . I hear you. In fact, I've heard your every prayer, but give me a break. The least you could do is buy a lottery ticket."

Give prayers of thanks.

Our thanks to God should always precede our requests.
—Source Unknown

A single grateful thought toward heaven is the most perfect prayer. **—G. E. Lessing**

WHAT ARE YOU WAITING FOR? GO FOR IT!

◆

The great aim of education is not knowledge but action.
—Herbert Spencer

We should be taught not to wait for inspiration to start a thing. Action always generates inspiration. Inspiration seldom generates action.
—Frank Tibolt

◆

There is no perfect time.

Don't wait. The time will never be just right. —Napoleon Hill

Remember, there is no perfect time for anything. There is only now. We encourage you with all of our hearts to begin your journey to greater levels of fulfillment and productivity now.

Don't wait until everything is just right. It will never be perfect. There will always be challenges, obstacles and less than perfect conditions. So what. Get started now. With each step you take, you will grow stronger and stronger, more and more skilled, more and more self-confident and more and more successful.

Everything you want is out there waiting for you to ask. Everything you want also wants you. But you have to take action to get it.

Dreaming about a thing in order to do it properly is right; but dreaming about it when we should be doing it is wrong.
                                                        —Oswald Chambers

The time for dreaming is over. It is time to get up and start asking for what you want. Start slowly and build up; jump right in and start with bold and outrageous requests. Either way is fine. Do what feels right for you. Just get started.

He who would learn to fly one day must first learn to stand and walk and run and climb and dance; one cannot fly into flying.   —Friedrich Nietzsche

The only way to start is to start.   —Source Unknown

A journey of a thousand miles begins with one step.
                                                        —Confucius

The first step is the hardest.   —Source Unknown

What saves a man is to take a step. Then another step.
                                                —Antoine de Saint-Exupéry

Whatever you can do, or dream you can, begin it. Boldness has genius, power and magic in it.   —Goethe

Nobody can do it for you.　　　　　　　　—Ralph Cordiner

No one will do it for you.　　　　　　　　　—Ben Stein

You have to make it happen.　　　　　　　　—Joe Greene

The man who removes a mountain begins by carrying away small stones.　　　　　　　　　　　　—William Faulkner

We hope you have enjoyed this journey through the world of asking. Hopefully, you now have more awareness about the importance of asking clearly, directly and repeatedly for what you want in life.

Every person you meet and every experience you encounter is a potential genie in your life. All you have to do is be open.

Open your mind to see the opportunity.

Open your heart to hear what you want.

Open your mouth to ask for it.

Open your arms to embrace the gifts you will receive.

And the day came when the risk to remain tight in a bud was more painful than the risk it took to blossom.　　　—Anaïs Nin

Thank you for sharing these pages with us. Our final wish for you is that you ask, ask, ask until all your dreams come true!

15

WE HAVE A REQUEST

◆

We have a request! We want you to write and tell us how this book has affected your life. Share your success stories with us. Let us know what you have done differently as a result of reading this book. What have you asked for and received? What new secrets have you learned about successful asking? What tips do you have that we can pass on to future readers? Do you have a favorite story, quote or insight about asking or risk taking that you would like to share with us? Please send it to us.

We are eager to hear from you. Thanks for participating in our lives!

Please write to us at the following address:

Jack Canfield and Mark Victor Hansen
The Canfield Training Group
P.O. Box 30880
Santa Barbara, CA 93130
FAX: (805) 563-2945

Who Is Jack Canfield?

◆

Jack Canfield is one of America's leading experts in the development of human potential and personal effectiveness. He is both a dynamic and entertaining speaker and a highly sought-after trainer with a wonderful ability to inform and inspire audiences toward increased levels of self-esteem and peak performance.

He is the author and narrator of several best-selling audio and videocassette programs, including *Self-Esteem and Peak Performance, How to Build High Self-Esteem* and *Self-Esteem in the Classroom.* He is regularly seen on television shows such as "Good Morning America," "20/20," and the "NBC Nightly News." He has published eight books including the best-sellers *Chicken Soup for the Soul, A 2nd Helping of Chicken Soup for the Soul, The Chicken Soup for the Soul Cookbook* and *Dare to Win* (all with Mark Victor Hansen).

Jack addresses over one hundred groups each year. His clients include professional associations, school districts, government agencies, churches, sales organizations and corporations. His corporate clients have included the American Management Association, AT&T, Campbell Soup, Clairol, Domino's Pizza, General Electric, ITT Hartford Insurance, Johnson & Johnson, NCR, New England Telephone, Re/Max, Scott Paper, Sunkist, Supercuts, TRW and Virgin Records. Jack is also on the faculties of two schools for entrepreneurs—Income Builders International and the Street Smart Business School.

Jack conducts an annual eight-day Training of Trainers program in the areas of self-esteem and peak performance. It attracts educators, counselors, parenting trainers, corporate trainers, professional speakers, ministers and others interested in developing their speaking and seminar leading skills.

To contact Jack for further information about his books, tapes and trainings, or to schedule him for a presentation, please write to:

The Canfield Training Group
P. O. Box 30880
Santa Barbara, CA 93130
Call toll free 1 (800) 237-8336 or fax (805) 563-2945

Who Is Mark Victor Hansen?

◆

Mark Victor Hansen has been called a human activator—a man who ignites individuals to recognize their full potential. During his twenty-plus years as a professional speaker, he has shared his expertise in sales excellence and strategies, and personal empowerment and development, with over 1 million people in thirty-two countries. In over four thousand presentations, he has inspired hundreds of thousands of people to create a more powerful and purposeful future for themselves while stimulating the sale of millions of dollars' worth of goods and services.

A *New York Times* best-selling author, Mark has written several books, including *Future Diary, How to Achieve Total Prosperity* and *The Miracle of Tithing*. With his best friend, Jack Canfield, Mark has written *Chicken Soup for the Soul, A 2nd Helping of Chicken Soup for the Soul* and *Dare to Win*.

Mark believes strongly in the teaching power of audio and video cassettes. He has produced a complete library of programs that have enabled his audience members to utilize their innate abilities within their business and personal lives. His message has made him a popular radio and television personality, and he starred in his own PBS special, entitled "Build a Better You."

Mark presents an annual Hawaiian retreat, Wake Up in Hawaii, designed for leaders, entrepreneurs and achievers who want to break through spiritual, mental, physical and financial blocks and unlock their highest potential. Because Mark is a strong believer in family values, this retreat includes a children's program that parallels the adult program.

Mark has dedicated his life to making a profound and positive difference in people's lives. He is a big man with a big heart and a big spirit—an inspiration to all who seek to better themselves.

For more information on Mark Victor Hansen's seminars, books and tapes, or to schedule him for a presentation to your company or organization, contact:

M.V. Hansen and Associates, Inc.
P.O. Box 7665
Newport Beach, CA 92658-7665
1 (800) 433-2314 or in CA 1 (714) 759-9304

Bibliography

◆

The person who can read and doesn't has no advantage over the person who can't read.
—Source Unknown

Aladdin by Don Ferguson. Stamford: Longmeadow Press, 1992.

The Art of Self-Discovery by Nathaniel Branden. New York: Bantam, 1994.

Ask For The Moon—And Get It! by Percy Ross with Dick Samson. New York: G.P. Putnam's Sons, 1987.

Ask Your Angels by Alma Daniel, Timothy Wyllie and Andrew Ramer. New York: Ballantine Books, 1992.

Awaken the Giant Within by Anthony Robbins. New York: Summit Books, 1991.

The Best of Bits & Pieces by Arthur G. Lenehan. Fairfield: The Economics Press, 1994.

Beware the Naked Man Who Offers You His Shirt by Harvey Mackay. New York: William Morrow and Company, 1990.

Changing the Game: The New Way to Sell by Larry Wilson with Hersch Wilson. New York: Simon and Schuster, 1987.

Chicken Soup for the Soul: 101 Stories to Open the Heart and Rekindle the Spirit by Jack Canfield and Mark Victor Hansen. Deerfield Beach: Health Communications, Inc., 1993.

Close to Home by John McPherson. Kansas City: Universal Press Syndicate, 1994.

Dangerously Close to Home by John McPherson. Kansas City: Universal Press Syndicate, 1995.

Dare to Dream by Florence Littauer. Dallas: Word Publishing, 1991.

Dare to Win by Jack Canfield and Mark Victor Hansen. NY: Berkley, 1994.

Do It! by Peter McWilliams. Santa Monica: Prelude Press, 1994.

Feel the Fear and Do It Anyway by Susan Jeffers, Ph.D. Orlando: Harcourt Brace Jovanovich Publishers, 1987.

Find It Fast by Robert I. Berkman. New York: Harper Collins Publishers, 1994.

The Five Great Rules of Selling by Percy H. Whiting. New York: Dale Carnegie & Associates, 1974.

Fresh Packet of Sower's Seeds by Brian Cavanaugh, T.O.R. New York: Paulist Press, 1994.

The Geranium on the Window Sill Just Died But Teacher You Went Right On by Albert Cullum. Columbus: Fearon Teacher Aids, 1971.

Getting Unstuck by Dr. Sidney B. Simon. New York: Warner Books, 1988.

High School Isn't Pretty by John McPherson. Kansas City: Universal Press Syndicate, 1993.

How to Locate Anyone Anywhere by Ted L. Gunderson with Roger McGovern. New York: Penguin Books USA, 1989.

How to Win Friends and Influence People by Dale Carnegie. New York: Simon & Schuster, 1981.

If You Could Hear What I Cannot Say by Nathaniel Branden. New York: Bantam, 1986.

It's Yours for the Asking by John H. Stoke. Philadelphia: Dorrance & Company, 1943.

The Laws of Manifestation by David Spangler. Scotland: Findhorn Publications, 1975.

The Leader in You by Dale Carnegie & Associates, Inc. New York: Simon & Schuster, 1993.

Lessons from the Light by Sandra Rogers. New York: Warner Books, 1995.

Life 101 by Peter McWilliams. Santa Monica: Prelude Press, 1994.

The Little, Brown Book of Anecdotes by Clifton Fadiman. Boston: Little, Brown and Company, 1985.

Living Life in Love by Peter Rengel. Larkspur: Imagine Publications, 1994.

Mars and Venus in the Bedroom by John Gray, Ph.D. New York: Harper Collins Publisher, 1995.

Million Dollar Habits by Robert J. Ringer. New York: Ballantine Books, 1990.

More Sower's Seeds by Brian Cavanaugh, T.O.R. New York: Paulist Press, 1992.

A 2nd Helping of Chicken Soup for the Soul: 101 More Stories to Open the Heart and Rekindle the Spirit by Jack Canfield and Mark Victor Hansen. Deerfield Beach: Health Communications, Inc., 1995.

Seize the Day by Danny Cox and John Hoover. Hawthorne: Career Press, 1994.

Self-Esteem: The New Reformation by Robert H. Schuller. Waco: Word Books, 1982.

The Seven Spiritual Laws of Success by Deepak Chopra. San Rafael: Amber-Allen Publishing, 1994.

Sharkproof by Harvey Mackay. New York: Harper Collins Publishers, 1993.

The Sower's Seeds by Brian Cavanaugh, T.O.R. New York: Paulist Press, 1990.

Speaker's Library of Business Stories, Anecdotes and Humor by Joe Griffith. New Jersey: Prentice Hall, 1990.

Speaker's Sourcebook II by Glenn Van Ekeren. New Jersey: Prentice Hall, 1994.

Success Through a Positive Mental Attitude by Napoleon Hill and W. Clement Stone. New Jersey: Prentice Hall, Inc., 1960.

Swim with the Sharks Without Being Eaten Alive by Harvey Mackay. New York: Ballantine Books, 1988.

Unlimited Power by Anthony Robbins. New York: Simon and Schuster, 1986.

The Wish Factory by Jana Lynn Shellman. Fort Wayne: Threadbare Publishing Company, 1995.

The Six Pillars of Self-Esteem by Nathaniel Branden. New York: Bantam Books, 1994.

Notes

◆

[1]From *The Geranium on the Window Sill Just Died But Teacher You Went Right On* by Albert Callum. (Harlin Quist, Inc., 1971.)

[2]Gallup poll quoted in Robert H. Schuller's book *Self-Esteem: The New Reformation* (Waco, TX: Word Books, 1982). Also see *Shortchanging Girls, Shortchanging America,* a study released by the American Association of University Women in 1991, and *Toward a State of Esteem: The Final Report of the California Task Force to Promote Self-Esteem and Personal and Social Responsibility,* which is available for $4.50 from the Bureau of Publications, California State Department of Education, P.O. Box 271, Sacramento, California 95812-0271.

[3]From *Priming the Preacher's Pump* by Dr. David A. Maclennan. Out of print.

[4]Thomas Moriarty, "Crime, Commitment and the Responsive Bystander: Two Field Experiments," *Journal of Personality and Social Psychology.* We first found this study reported in *The Pryor Report,* February 1992.

[5]From *Mars and Venus in the Bedroom* by John Gray. (New York: HarperCollins, 1996. Pages. 184–185.)

[6]For more information on how to do this process and how it builds self-esteem and motivates us to new actions, see the following books by Dr. Nathaniel Branden: *The Six Pillars of Self-Esteem* (New York: Bantam, 1994), *If You Could Hear What I Cannot Say* (New York: Bantam, 1986) and *The Art of Self Discovery* (New York: Bantam, 1994).

[7]We wish to acknowledge Jim Newman, author of *Release Your Brakes,* for first introducing us to the concept of comfort zones.

[8]We wish to acknowledge Larry Wilson for his system "Thanks for the Twenty-Five Dollars," from *Changing the Game: The New Way to Sell.* (New York: Simon & Schuster, 1987).

[9]We wish to acknowledge Jack Wolf for first teaching us this wonderful little technique.

[10]From *Ask for the Moon and Get It* by Percy Ross with Dick Samson. (New York: G. P. Putnam's Sons, 1987. Pages 48–49.)

[11]From *The Best of Bits and Pieces.* (Fairfield, New Jersey: Economics Press, 1994).

[12]From *The Little Brown Book of Anecdotes* by Clifton Fadiman. (Little, 1991.)

[13]From *The Best of Bits and Pieces.* (Fairfield, New Jersey: Economics Press, 1994.)

[14]Excerpted from *Ask for the Moon—And Get It!* by Percy Ross and Dick Samson. (New York: G. P. Putnam's Sons, 1987.)

[15]From *The Best of Bits and Pieces.* (Fairfield, New Jersey: Economics Press, 1994.)

[16]From *Speakers Sourcebook II* by Glen Van Ekeren. (Englewood Cliffs, New Jersey: Prentice Hall, 1994, Pages 281–82.)

[17]From *The Best of Bits and Pieces.* (Fairfield, New Jersey: Economics Press, 1994.)

[18]This exercise is used by permission of Margaret Paul, coauthor of *Do I Have to Give Up Me to Be Loved By You?* For more information on her work and workshops, you can call (310) 390-5993.

[19]Jack and his wife Georgia learned this activity from Harville Hendricks when they attended his Getting the Love You Want workshop in Los Angeles, California. We strongly recommend you read his book *Getting the Love You Want* (New York: Harper Perennial, 1990) if you are in a committed relationship, or *Keeping the Love You Find* (New York: Pocket Books, 1993) if you are single and looking for a relationship. We also strongly recommend his workshops. For a schedule and more information, write The Institute for Relationship Therapy, 1255 Fifth Avenue, Suite C-2, New York, NY 10029 or call (800) 729-1121.

[20]This letter originally appeared in *The Joyful Child Journal*, Vol. 5, No. 4. It is used here by permission of Karen Springs Stevens, editor. For more information on the journal, write P.O. Box 566, Buffalo, NY 14213, or call (716) 831-0574.

[21]*The Scholarship Book* by Daniel J. Cassidy. (Englewood Cliffs, New Jersey: Prentice Hall, 1993).

[22]From *The Best of Bits and Pieces.* (Fairfield, NJ: Economics Press, 1994).

[23]Ibid.

[24]Based on information in *Aristotle Onassis* by Nicholas Fraser, Philip Jacobson, Mark Ottaway and Lewis Chester. (New York: Ballantine Books, 1977. Pages 36–37.)

[25]From private correspondence received from Dr. Louis A. Tartaglia on May 12, 1995.

[26]From *Dare to Dream* by Florence Littauer (Dallas: Word Publishing, 1991).

[27]Condensed from "The Boy and the Billionaire," which originally appeared in the October 1991 issue of *Readers Digest*, pp. 71–76.

[28]From *Success Through a Positive Mental Attitude* by Napoleon Hill and W. Clement Stone. (Englewood Cliffs, NJ: Prentice Hall, 1960.)

[29]From *Living Life in Love* by Peter Rengel. (Larkspur, CA: Imagine Publishing, 1994.)

[30]From *Self-Esteem: The New Reformation* by Robert H. Schuller. (Waco, Texas: Word Books, 1982, pp. 158–159).

[31]*Lessons from Twilight* by Sandra Rogers. (New York: Warner Books, 1995.)

[32]From *Decide to . . . A Booklet of Exhortations* by Dr. Robert Muller. The book is available through the United Nations Bookstore.